Raja Nal and the Goddess

SUSAN SNOW WADLEY

Raja Nal and the Goddess

The North Indian Epic *Dhola* in Performance

INDIANA UNIVERSITY PRESS

Bloomington and Indianapolis

Publication of this book is made possible in part with the assistance of a Challenge Grant from the National Endowment for the Humanities, a federal agency that supports research, education, and public programming in the humanities.

This book is a publication of

Indiana University Press
601 North Morton Street
Bloomington, IN 47404-3797 USA

http://iupress.indiana.edu

Telephone orders 800-842-6796
Fax orders 812-855-7931
Orders by e-mail iuporder.indiana.edu

The paper used in this publication meets the minimum requirements of American National Standard for Information Sciences—Permanence of Paper for Printed Library Materials, ANSI Z39.48-1984.

Manufactured in the United States of America

Library of Congress Cataloging-in-Publication Data

Wadley, Susan Snow, date
Raja Nal and the Goddess : the north Indian epic Dhola in performance / Susan Snow Wadley.
p. cm.
In English; includes translated passages from the Hindi original.
Includes bibliographical references and index.
ISBN 0-253-34478-6 (cloth : alk. paper)—ISBN 0-253-21724-5 (pbk. : alk. paper)
1. Dhola. 2. Nala (Hindu mythology) in literature. 3. Folk literature, Hindi—History and criticism.
4. Epic poetry, Hindi—History and criticism. I. Title.
GR305.W23 2004
398.2′0954′02—dc22

2004009434

1 2 3 4 5 09 08 07 06 05 04

Different parts of the Ocean [of stories] contained different sorts of stories, and . . . because the stories were held here in fluid form, they retained the ability to change, to become new versions of themselves, to join up with other stories and to become yet other stories; so that unlike a library of books, the Ocean of the Streams of Story was much more than a storeroom of yarns. It was not dead but alive.

—Salman Rushdie, *Haroun and the Sea of Stories*

Contents

List of Illustrations ix

Preface xi

Note on Transliteration xv

Part One: *Dhola*

1. Introducing *Dhola* 3
2. The Story of *Dhola* 9
3. *Dhola* as Performed: Two Singers 65

Part Two: *Dhola* Interpreted

4. The Goddess and the Bhakti Traditions of Braj 95
5. Motini, Dumenti, and Other Royal Women 120
6. Oil Pressers, Acrobats, and Other Castes 142
7. Who Is Raja Nal? 171

Appendix 1. List of Characters 197

Appendix 2. Oral Performances 199

Glossary of Key Hindi Terms 207

Notes 211

References Cited 223

Index 233

Illustrations

2.1. Raja Nal and Dumenti seeking help from women with an infant 34
2.2. Raja Nal fighting the demons in the forest of Lakhiyaban 41
2.3. Dhola, son of Raja Nal, meeting his bride Maru in the garden of her father's kingdom 51
2.4. The Gate of Budh Singh falling on Dhola as he enters the fort to claim his bride Maru 52
3.1. Ram Swarup Dhimar as Raja Nal, circa early 1960s 68
3.2. Ram Swarup Dhimar and his troupe 70
3.3. Matolsingh Gujar and his drummer 81
4.1. The goddess and the singer of *Dhola* 97
5.1. Dancing girl 131
5.2. Woman in purdah 132
6.1. A Jat Landlord of the nineteenth century 155
6.2. Nat acrobats of the nineteenth century 157

Tables

Table 1. Oral Performances Consulted in This Analysis 200
Table 2. Commercial Cassettes Consulted in This Analysis 205

Preface

More than thirty years ago, on a hot, humid monsoon day when the men of the village known as Karimpur[1] in Mainpuri District in western Uttar Pradesh could not work in the fields, they gathered in the village dharamśālā (pilgrims' way station usually attached to a temple) to hear Ram Swarup Dhimar (Kahar, Water Carrier by caste),[2] a resident of Karimpur, sing *Ḍholā*. I later learned that this was a long oral epic segmented into eighteen or more identifiable episodes, each usually performed in one night. Because the men knew of my interest in various kinds of oral performance, I was invited to attend (and was the only woman present, camera and tape recorder in hand). Little did I know then that I was beginning a quest that would last more than thirty years to understand what I heard that rainy day.

I saw a man, probably in his late thirties, clad in his everyday *dhotī* (a piece of lightweight cloth that men wrap around their waist to create pants) and shirt, playing a *cikāṛā,* a simple stringed instrument, accompanied by a drummer on a *ḍholak* (see cover). The singer was clearly an expert, telling a story to a fascinated audience as he mixed song with prose sections. As I have since learned, Ram Swarup shares a lower-caste identity with the majority of *Dhola* singers. Some months later, I saw this same performer with his "company" performing *Dhola* as a folk opera on a neighbor's verandah. Here he was dressed as Raja Nal, the epic hero, while others became women or his male helpmates. I had little sense of what I saw and heard, the poetry then being beyond my Hindi skills, though I was able to follow much of the prose narrative portions. But the story was complex and confusing, its history unknown. I could find no reference to what I was hearing in the scholarly literature, though I soon found that I could buy chapbooks (cheap pamphlets, usually of twenty-four or fewer pages and selling, literally, for cents) of *Dhola* in any local book stall (and still can, though now one is more likely to be able to buy a commercial tape cassette of an episode of *Dhola*). As I went on to explore other village oral traditions, and social change in north India more generally, I kept returning to *Dhola* as time and circumstances permitted.

On return trips to Karimpur in 1974 and 1984, and then regularly throughout the 1990s, I began attending any *Dhola* performance I could find, eventually hiring Ram Swarup Dhimar and other singers to perform for my tape recorder and, beginning in 1989, video recorder, sometimes on the verandah of the house where I resided, sometimes in the dharamsala, sometimes in another village or at someone else's house. Later I worked with Komal Kothari in Jodhpur with a singer, Matolsingh, and tracked other singers through the Braj region. A foray into the archives of the British Office Library in London led me to nineteenth-century publications of versions of *Dhola,* also in chapbook form, as well as to a greater understanding of the relationship between its performance region and its history.

Since *Dhola* is never performed as a continuous story, I have recordings of only twelve episodes. I do have one of the commonly performed episodes sung seven times by four different troupes, plus numerous episodes on commercial tape cassettes from another dozen singers, including one set of twenty-one cassettes that contains most of the epic. I also have numerous chapbooks, including complete sets of the epic by the two most prominent writers of the latter part of the twentieth century. The performers and other local storytellers can narrate a summary of the whole epic, although even these renditions run many hours, and their audiences seldom demand the infrequently performed episodes.[3] *Dhola* is driven by audience demand, not by ritual, although there is an odd reference to singers who worshiped Raja Nal. That *Dhola* is not tied to ritual is important, because the singer is not constrained by a fixed text that must be accurately performed for ritual purposes.

This book is broken into two sections. After a brief introduction, part 1 includes a vastly condensed retelling of the epic itself, followed by a brief literary and cultural history of the epic and the region where it is performed. Chapter 3 illuminates epic performance through the life stories and styles of two renowned *Dhola* performers. These are Ram Swarup Dhimar, my initial guide to *Dhola,* and Matolsingh, one of the most renowned *Dhola* singers of the 1980s. This chapter highlights their more rural (Ram Swarup) and more "refined" (Matolsingh) performance styles. Part 2 contains four analytic chapters that focus, respectively, on the goddess, on women and issues of femaleness, on caste, and on Raja Nal's identity and human-ness. A concern for order and chaos pervades all episodes of the epic, along with a concern for hierarchies of body, geography, psychic identity, and social structure. Each chapter also focuses on different episodes as the singers highlight different issues in some places and not others. Through lengthy excerpts from actual performances, I seek to convey the actuality of performance and the vivid imaginations, nuances, and humor that make this story so compelling to its rural audiences.

None of this would have been possible without the singers who worked with me, especially Ram Swarup Dhimar (Watercarrier by caste) of the village known as Karimpur. Matolsingh Gujar (Shepherd by caste) and his troupe from the village Ghamani, Bharatpur District, Rajasthan, also extensively shared their love of *Dhola* with me. Other singers included Mangu Lal and Nanhe Lal, Kachis (Farmers by caste) of Farrukhabad District, Uttar Pradesh;

Mangtu Lal, a Chamar (Leatherworker by caste) of village Jalhaka, Haryana; Pandit Shankar Lal, a Brahman from a village in Aligarh District, Uttar Pradesh; Suman, a Chamar from Mainpuri District, Uttar Pradesh; and two other singers from Karimpur, Ram Swarup Kachi and Mata Din Garariya (Shepherd by caste). Raghubar Kachi, also of Karimpur, although not a singer of *Dhola*, shared his knowledge of the story with me on numerous occasions. Two of these singers are blind. At least two are now deceased. The materials collected from these singers are archived at the Archive and Research Center for Ethnomusicology, American Institute of Indian Studies, New Delhi, and at the Archive for Traditional Music, Indiana University, Bloomington, Indiana.

I owe much gratitude to Komal Kothari, who provided moral support, contacts with singers whom I did not know, and a place to record Matolsingh and company. Ram Narayan Agrawal and colleagues at the Braj Kala Kendra in Mathura shared their knowledge and writings on *Dhola* with me. Carol Babiracki patiently instructed me on the language of writing about music: chapter 3 owes much to her careful insights and readings. Jishnu Shankar, of the South Asia Center, Syracuse University, put his considerable skills at Hindi to translation and sorting out nuances of meaning when the tapes challenged our ears. He also gave wise counsel that aided in my development of the chapter on the goddess. Shubha Chaudhari and staff at the Archive and Research Center for Ethnomusicology in New Delhi were patient with my requests and sponsored several occasions when I could test my ideas. They have also worked with Globalsound, of the Smithsonian Institution, to make recordings of *Dhola* available via the Internet, and hence obviating the need for a CD with this book.

My biggest debt is to Umesh Chandra Pandey of Karimpur, who transcribed, translated, arranged for singers, brought tea, and generally supported this project throughout. Others who helped with either transcriptions or translations include Rajani Pandey Dikshit, Guddu Pandey, Nita Pandey, and Nanhe Khan, all of Karimpur; Ragani Despande and Vikas Goswami of New Delhi; and Sonali Sathaye and Vikas Choudhary, graduate students at Syracuse University. Vandana Tivary provided vital assistance in the final summer of revisions. Sunil Khanna and Laura Derr accompanied me on various searches for *Dhola* singers. Vanit Nalwa of New Delhi contributed an invaluable last-minute historical connection from her family's folk history. Ann Grodzins Gold, Lindsay Harlan, and Kirin Narayan, as well as numerous audiences over the past decade, provided invaluable comments on the manuscript itself.

My family, but most especially my husband, Richard Olanoff, will be grateful that *Dhola* has ended for us, at least for now. I especially appreciate their forbearance in the final summers of writing, when vacations disappeared and dinners were scant.

Note on Transliteration

Proper names are given in common English transliterations, without diacritics or italics. Hindi terms (in the dialects of Braj or Kanauji) and the names of epics and books are given with diacritics on the first instance only, following the rules set by the Library of Congress. Place names are given in their English equivalents. Words such as purdah that are found in the Oxford English Dictionary are not indicated as foreign words.

The term *Dhola* has three meanings. In this book the name of the epic appears in italics. Raja Nal's son's name appears as Dhola, in roman type. When the word refers to the musical melody-type to which the epic is commonly sung, dhola appears in lower case.

Part One. *Dhola*

1 Introducing *Dhola*

What will be is powerful	*honi ho balvān*
And what is in one's fate cannot be changed	*aur karamgati taṛe na ṭare.*

(WA 84:239)[1]

Sitting on a dung heap, considered a mad man, Raja Nal, the hero of *Dhola,* sums up one of the most potent messages in *Dhola,* a north Indian oral epic sung in the Braj region in what is now western Uttar Pradesh and eastern Rajasathan. *Dhola* is ultimately about Raja Nal and his acceptance of the nature of human mortality after his metaphoric descent into madness when, for six months, his body blackened with sores from leprosy, he has no social interactions. Having lost everything—kingdom, friends, kin, wife, and even his relationship with the goddess—and seeking neither wife nor kingdom, Nal accepts what will be. This pivotal point marks the beginning of Raja Nal's return to wife, kin, friends, kingdom, and goddess. While he struggles constantly with what life gives him, Raja Nal must also, at times, accept the rule of fate and his human-ness. His predicament, although couched in the language of Hinduism, is that which all humans face: Raja Nal is fighting to make the life that he envisions, but at times must admit that he has no control over what befalls him. *Dhola* is thus a tale of being human, of being mortal, of loving the goddess, but ultimately of being subject to the rule of fate or "what will be will be."[2]

Dhola is also about belonging to one of the many castes that make up India's hierarchical social system, of issues of achieved versus ascribed status, and of the powers of women—Raja Nal's two wives, Motini and Dumenti, as well as the goddess Durga. No battle is successful until Raja Nal calls upon Motini or the goddess to save him. Thus *Dhola* also contests the more dominant discourses of Hindu India, particularly the Sanskritic textual traditions. Recent scholarship has focused on such contestations by women (e.g., Raheja and Gold 1994), but there has been little consideration of lower-caste male visions of the Hindu world. Through most of the twentieth century, scholarship on India remained caught in a view promulgated by the British and other early European scholars who saw Hindus as trapped by beliefs in both fate and caste. A classic version of this scholarly orientation is that of the sociologist Barrington Moore, who commented on the "willing acceptance of personal degradation" (1966, 340) among the Indian peasantry owing to their rigid adherence to the cultural norms of caste (and women's roles), images still promulgated in popular discourse (and by my undergraduate students). *Dhola* challenges such views of the "inert masses" and demonstrates instead that the "illiterate folk," or as Gramsci (1971) put it, "organic intellectuals," use their oral traditions to comment on and sometimes to contest the traditional social order, whether the caste system, norms for women, or life itself.

Locally known as "our *Māhabhārata,*"[3] *Dhola* is a long oral epic, sometimes said to contain thirty-six or more episodes (Suman 1962), although most chapbook renditions give us a more modest eighteen or so episodes. Local scholars believe that it was composed some two to three hundred years ago by a man named Madari in honor of the goddess of Nagarkot.[4] *Dhola* is primarily about the goddess, usually identified as Durga, who is its patron and primary benefactor to both singer and hero. The goddess, and the wives of the hero, Raja Nal, often working in tandem, are those who resolve all conflicts, and bring battles to a conclusion. But *Dhola* also portrays the multi-caste world of rural north India, drawing on stereotypic views of individual castes to depict characters drawn from the real lives of its rural audiences. Finally, *Dhola* is about being a king, and being accepted as a king by those already so recognized. And thus it has ties to the history of the Braj region where it is found, a region controlled for most of the seventeenth and eighteenth centuries by kings belonging to the Jat caste of agriculturalists.

The hero of *Dhola* is Raja Nal of the kingdom of Narvar; he is known to most Hindus both as Nala,[5] the husband of Damayanti (called Dumenti or Dumaiti in the dialects of the regions where *Dhola* is sung) and as the central character in the episode known as the *Nalopākhyāna* from the *Mahabharata.*[6] Both Raja Nal and Damayanti (hereafter Dumenti to distinguish the heroine of *Dhola* from the heroine of the *Mahabharata*) do in fact play primary roles in *Dhola,* but with significant additions and variations to the version of their story that we find in the *Mahabharata.* Most critically, in *Dhola,* Nal is married twice, the first time to Motini, an *apsāra* (heavenly nymph) from Indra's heaven, and the second time to Dumenti. Raja Nal and Dumenti then have a son, Dhola, who is married to Maru, daughter of Raja Budh Singh (whose kingdom varies but is usually named as Pingul or Marwar). The addition of Dhola and Maru, in fact, marks the joining together of two famous stories, that of Nala and Damayanti and that of Dhola and Maru, hero and heroine of a Rajasthani ballad often dated to the sixteenth century (Vaudeville 1962; Williams 1976).

Dhola, as an oral epic with relatively few written versions and those all in chapbook form, takes part in a hierarchy of forms of discourse that define it as "low," rural, peasant. As one singer in a modern commercial cassette says as he begins his story, "Now I will tell the story of *Dhola* in *deśī* (country) language." There is no doubt that *Dhola* lacks any claim to being a privileged discourse, one attached to dominant groups with access to the power to define the value of other discourses (Stallybrass and White 1986; Ghosh 1998). Barely a "cheap book," it exists on the fringe of society, sung mostly in rural areas by illiterate males usually of lower caste. Nevertheless, *Dhola* works to subvert the ranking of discourses propagated by the dominant ones, and the hierarchies of social norms and rules found in those dominant discourses. Constructed out of desi or rural language, filled with profanities and vocabulary not common to the elite, *Dhola* has an earthy quality that suits its populist view of the world from below. As Mikhail Bakhtin commented, "In the world of carnival the awareness of the people's immortality is combined with the realization that established authority and truth are relative" (1968, 10). In *Dhola,* in contrast, an awareness of human mortality is combined with a realization that established authority and truth are relative.

Interpreting *Dhola*

Over the years, as I have listened to *Dhola,* and read versions of it, I have become increasingly fascinated, indeed entranced, by this story. For despite being named for a hero-son, "Dhola," who is not in fact the primary hero of the story, it is rather an epic about the goddess and the powers of women. It is also about being human. This is why the identification of the Sanskritic hero Nala with Raja Nal is so basic, because Nala, too, was, more than anything, a human. Raja Nal's human-ness is continually reiterated in *Dhola,* and it is the intersection of this humanity and the goddess that continually undergirds this story. The argument in this book is framed by these two concerns: the exploration of the story begins with an analysis of the goddess and ends with an analysis of Raja Nal's human identity.

Stories are a way to make sense of the real world: they express deeply rooted cultural themes (Narayan 1989). A series of cultural themes are woven through the various episodes of *Dhola,* with the importance of any one theme to a specific episode varying widely: some episodes are about goddesses, while others focus on issues of status, and still others on unjust gods. Intersecting these themes are hierarchies of body, geography, social order, and psychic identity: as Stallybrass and White note, "cultures 'think themselves' in the most immediate and affective ways through the combined symbolisms of these four hierarchies" (1986, 3). The rural males who have composed and sung *Dhola* through the centuries are actively "thinking their culture" through their explorations of these hierarchies as they relate to the threads of five cultural themes or concerns that run throughout *Dhola.*

The most encompassing theme is a focus on social order versus chaos, on people and events in their proper places, on kings ruling justly and being rewarded versus ruling justly and being banished. Disorder is caused by a period of distress, in Braj (the dialect of the region known as Braj where *Dhola* is most frequently performed) distress is termed *aukhā,* related in idea if not etymology to the Rajasthani *vikhāu* (Zeigler 1973). This time of disorder is caused when the king, as head of the kingdom and sustainer of the moral order, loses that position, as indeed Raja Nal does. The result is a confusion of order and a mixing of castes, with the king himself becoming a refugee, dependent on others, having no land or power. Since caste is dependent upon Hindu constructions of the body and of social space (geography), there is a continual "thinking" about the meaning of body, clothing, and appropriate social spaces as the singers explore questions of order. In *Dhola,* this disorder is caused by the injustice of Indra, angry over Dumenti's choice of Raja Nal as her husband, and the curse of Motini, angry that Nal broke his promise not to marry again. Yet even though he makes a very human error, Raja Nal eventually sees himself as the victim of a fated injustice, and he can only regain his kingdom when he accepts that fate, what one does, controls all. And only through service to the master can one regain one's power, and hence rightful position as a king. Raja Nal, complainingly, must also learn to serve others.

A second pervasive theme is that of devotion to the goddess, here Durga, a goddess who, when worshiped, will right wrongs and see that fate is played out. Worship of Durga is contrasted to the wrongful worship of Kali, who sides with the enemies of Raja Nal. Kali is shown to represent selfishness and the sacrifice of humans (a major theme in the Rajput traditions to which *Dhola* and its singers are antagonistic), both elements that transgress the norms that *Dhola* lays out. As the Other, Kali is also associated with various sects of yogis who are thought in *Dhola* to misuse their powers for egotistical reasons. Thus another subcurrent is the battle between the competing forces and attractions of Durga and Kali, and of the Rajput (the "enemy") connections with both sacrifice and Nath yogis. These, combined with the "vaishnavized" Durga of *Dhola,* also raise issues of allegiance to the two opposing Hindu traditions, one associated with Vishnu (often termed "Vaishnavite") and one associated with Shiva (Shaivite).

A closely related theme concerns the powers of women, most especially women's control of magic, magic learned from the yogis (and from Bengal or from both). Women who are married and whose use of magic is in the service of their husbands' families are extolled whereas those who are unmarried and use magic for their own or their kin's selfish reasons are condemned. Women's control of magic is opposed to men's control of swords in battle, a role denied to women, and to their status as *pativrats,* women devoted to their husbands.

Appropriate and inappropriate female (and male) behavior, especially related to sexuality and the ways in which bodies are coded through clothing, also appear as issues again and again. Unlike many Indian epic traditions, *Dhola* is not misogynist (Smith 1989): rather than an antipathy toward women, or even a general disinterest in them, here the "females of the species," both human and divine, play central roles.

A fourth theme has to do with identity, especially caste identities, and with status as ascribed through birthright or won through achievement, as well as with the stereotypic behaviors and mannerisms associated with various castes. Our hero, Raja Nal, is born in the forest, raised by a Merchant, reunited with his father, the king of Narvar, disguised as an Acrobat, only to be banished from his kingdom to become a wanderer in the forest, a charioteer, a "mad man" and leper, and an Oil Presser, all before regaining his right to his kingdom. As he moves through life, the cultural associations, behaviors, and social spaces linked to various castes whose identities he adopts are delineated, as are those of the castes with which he comes into contact. Hence *Dhola* portrays a multi-caste world where each caste has certain rights and obligations that allow its members to act in particular ways and spaces, and not in others. The epic singers have Raja Nal and Motini manipulate these caste identities as they take on disguises in order to defeat their enemies, manipulations that are critical to the epic story.[7] Other castes play out their allotted roles in ways that are stereotypical or clichéd.[8] But most important is the question of whether one is defined by one's birth or by what one achieves in one's lifetime. While the answer seemingly is birthright by caste, Raja Nal's own ambiguous caste status, and that of the rulers of the area where *Dhola* was and is performed, leave this a truly open question. Tied to caste are issues of marriage, especially marriage with the right "kind" of being. With its focus on women and castes, on order and chaos as created through marriage, and recognition of one's true identity, *Dhola* captures the ambivalence surrounding ascribed versus achieved status in Indian society.

Finally, *Dhola* is about being human or divine, about belonging to the world of mortals subject to fate or to the world of immortality; it is also about the proper attitudes toward life of those who inhabit the fated world. Raja Nal, as the always-human hero, known throughout India and in all versions of his story as "human," captures the essence of human-ness. As one local scholar put it, "the 'root' [of the story] lies in the *Mahabharata*. It is just Nal's character that the folk poets have elaborated on in their own fashion" (WA 94, 15). But it is exactly the fact that Nal is human that pervades his character in both the *Mahabharata* and *Dhola*. It is this root of the story that is so essential to Raja Nal's eventual recognition of the meaning of life, as noted in the opening lines above.

Most critically, *Dhola* challenges the dominant understandings of the Hindu world: it is popular in one of the most densely populated regions in India and, in the centuries that it has existed, has been heard by many millions of rural north Indians. I argue that it has been much more relevant to their lives than the Sanskritic texts adopted by the British, with the aid of a Brahman priesthood, as the core of Hinduism. As such, it has also, until schooling began to spread a more classical Hinduism among the densely populated rural villages of Braj, been heard and listened to and thought about by many more Hindus throughout the history of this region of India than texts widely thought to be the core of Hinduism, such as the *Bhagavad Gita.* Thus I challenge the reader to consider what our understandings of Hinduism would be had *Dhola* been among the dominant texts nominated by Western scholars as representing Hinduism. Would the pervasive understandings of women and of caste that dominate Western and elite Indian thinking about Hindu society be different?

2 The Story of *Dhola*

The Banishment of Manjha (*Manjhā Kā Nikālā*)

Characters

Raja Pratham of Narvar
Rani Manjha, most beloved of Raja Pratham's 101 wives
Narad, heavenly sage and adviser to the gods
Dharamraj, a god, literally "the king of righteous behavior"
Indra, King of the gods
Nilgagan, the god who takes birth as Raja Nal, never to be defeated in battle
Brahman Pandit, astrologer
Sweepers, outcastes given the most impure and inauspicious jobs
Durga, the goddess to whom Raja Nal is devoted
Lachhiman Seth, a Merchant (Banya) by caste

There is a king named Pratham and his 101 queens. He is very powerful and his palace is magnificently adorned. From the turrets, flags flutter in the winds, and the walls and ceilings are covered in gold. But Raja Pratham has one sorrow: he has no sons. One day, as he is sitting on his roof with his favorite queen, Manjha, two birds fly by on their way to the nearby lake. Pratham claims that they are geese[1] while Manjha says that they are crows. Arguing, they finally bet on the birds' identities. If Pratham loses, he will be banished from his kingdom for twelve years, and if Manjha loses, she will be required to chase crows off the roof for many months as penance for her wrong guess.

Calling a servant, they send him off to the lake to learn the identity of the pair of birds. But before he departs, Manjha secretly draws him aside and tells him that whatever is the truth, he is to say that they are geese, for Pratham dare not lose the bet. Hurrying to the lake, the servant finds a pair of crows.

One of the dilemmas in this telling of *Dhola* is how to present a story that can take thirty or ... nights to perform, with the translated text from any one night running over one hundred ... of pages. My answer is twofold: I asked Raghubar Kachi, a knowledgeable storyteller and ... long. *Dhola*, though not a singer of the epic, to tell me the story: this rendition was about six ... ersions Using it as a base, I further condensed the epic story, while noting key pieces from s... words. I that had been omitted by this teller. I also reverted now and then to a specific sin... telling realize that the folklorist will shudder at the audacity of my telling the story, but little more that comes near the brevity needed here (aside from one overly condensed version ...ized as my than a recitation of the names of episodes). Thus the resulting story must be version of *Dhola*, not that of any one singer or teller of the tale.

Returning to the palace, he tells Manjha that indeed she was correct, but she again urges him to lie to Pratham. For some time Manjha chases crows off the roof of the palace.

In an earlier life Pratham had forgotten one hot dry June to give water to 101 cows, and he was cursed. In his next life he had four daughters, but he killed them and buried each one in a corner of his garden. These four daughters cursed him, saying that for seven births he would not have a son. Now one day, as Pratham is going out to hunt, he passes a Sweeper woman in the street. She averts her face from the sight of the childless man, saying that she will be unable to eat the whole day because she has seen him. And despite Pratham's efforts, she does not eat that day. Pratham then decides to leave his kingdom for the meditation grounds in the forest. He asks Manjha to rule in his place, but she refuses, insisting that she go to the jungle with him. There, they come upon a sage who has been meditating so long that white ants have eaten away his body, and only a heap of mud remains. Pratham and Manjha sit down, one at each side, and after several days he opens his eyes. Seeing Pratham, he is very angry, proclaiming that his twelve years of meditation have been spoilt. He finally agrees to give Pratham the boon of a son, but only after Pratham returns to Narvar, donates 101 cows with horns decorated in gold and silver to Brahmans, bathes in the Ganges, and holds a major sacrificial ritual.

Pratham donates the 101 cows, bathes in the Ganges, and performs the sacrifice. But as the sacrifice (*yajñā*) ends, the drums sound and the throne of Indra, king of the gods, is shaken. Angered, Indra sends the sage Narad to discover who is disturbing the world. Narad comes to the garden of Narvar and, as the day is ending, decides to rest there. He lights a fire, and when the smoke reaches the sky, Manjha and Pratham are dismayed. There must be someone who has not eaten at their feast, so their sacrifice is not complete. Pratham runs to the garden, and Narad immediately recognizes him as a childless man. Narad refuses the invitation to the feast, saying that he never takes food from the house of a childless man. Crying, Pratham runs to the palace where he tearfully tells his story to Manjha.

Manjha commands him to be silent, saying, "I am a *sati devī* (i.e., I am a reincarnated woman who committed sati in her previous life). If I am known a *pativrat* (a woman who worships her husband), then I'll give food to this E." Running to where he was sitting, she bows her head. Narad trembles as recognizes her as a sati, and commands her to speak. She says, "Please con nd eat at our palace," but Narad refuses. She responds, "Then I'll touc ur feet," and immediately Narad leaves his body, for when a sati touch feet, his body is spoiled. Manjha grabs his feet and holds on, saying, "I leave. If you go to heaven, then I'll go to heaven." Narad reaches the throne of the god Dharamraj and begs, "Please king, help me. My old body has been snatched by Manjha, and until she gets a child she won't let go."

Dharamraj opens his astrological chart and says that Pratham's fate is not to have a child for seven lives. Narad exclaims, "But I cannot have her on my feet for seven births! I'll not be able to go back to my body. Please tell me a way out."

But Dharamraj can find no solution and calls together all 33 crore (330 million) gods and goddesses. He asks the gods to save Narad's body, and the gods say, "But aren't you king of the world? We only obey your orders." So Dharamraj decides to send a god to Manjha's womb, but every god refuses with folded hands, saying, "Humans eat off food and cereal, but we have godly bodies and live off the smell of flowers and travel through the air." Only one god, Nilgagan, does not protest. Dharamraj says to him, "My son, you are the most obedient. Go and save Narad."

Nilgagan replies, "I will go, I am not scared." Then he asks for the gods' blessings and receives a boon: no one in the world will be able to beat him in battle. Then the gods push him down and he becomes a grain of rice, which is given to Narad who is told to mix it with 100 more grains and give one grain to each queen. But when each of the 101 queens is given a single grain of rice, each is offended by the meager offering and all but Manjha throw the grain away. Tying her grain in her sari, Manjha eats it only after bathing.[2]

Several months later Manjha's sari is blown about in a high wind and the one hundred queens realize that she is pregnant. They quickly confer about the dishonor that will befall them if she has a son and they do not, and they decide to bribe the Brahman Pandit to lie to the king about the nature of the child about to be born. Calling the Pandit, they offer him jewels and gold to tell a story to the king that will result in Manjha's demise. Despite his wife's horror when she realizes the source of his new wealth, the Pandit goes to Raja Pratham and explains to him that the astrological charts predict that the child about to be born will only cause the destruction of the king. Believing the Pandit, Pratham calls for his two Sweepers to take Manjha to the forest and kill her, bringing back her eyes as proof of their deed.

So the Sweepers take Rani Manjha away into the dense dark forest of Shantiban (Peaceful Forest). Then one Sweeper says, "Take off all your clothes so that I may take them back to the king. I will take your eyes after I have killed you." Rani Manjha pleads, "I will give you whatever I have, but please let me live. Take the eyes of a deer." And she gives him a ruby ring. Just then, some god hears her and places a deer at that very spot. The Sweepers kill the deer and take its eyes back to the king, leaving Manjha alone in the forest.

Manjha has not a shred of clothes left, but her hair quickly grows and covers her completely, and a thick impenetrable hedge of thorns surrounds her. These events are immediately known at Hinglaj,[3] the abode of the goddess Durga. Durga, who is sleeping there, wakes up at once, and she says, "Oh *langurs* (black-faced monkeys, her assistants), don't wait a moment. Go to Kajari (Black) Forest and quickly catch a brown lion. Some trouble has befallen Rani Manjha." The Mother, with all her assistants, riding on her brown lion, quickly comes to the thorn thicket protecting Manjha. She cuts the umbilical cord and sends her monkey helpers for the milk of a tigress.

A few days later the goddess leads the Merchant Lachhiman Seth astray, and he comes near the thicket hiding Manjha and the babe. Upon hearing a child crying, he becomes fearful. He calls out, "Who are you, are you a ghost or a human?" Hearing this human voice, the queen replies, "I am a human, Father. I have just given birth, and I am in trouble. I don't have a shred of clothing, but my hair has grown long to cover my body." Then the Seth says, "You have called me father, you are my child by *dharma* (religious duty). Come and sit in my cart. Wrap yourself in my turban." He throws her his turban, and she joins him in the cart. On the road he meets an old Saint (Narad in disguise) who gives the child three names: "Vipati," because he has been born in a period of distress; "Nal Banvari," Nal of the forest, because of his birthplace; and "Nal Chhatravedi," Nal under the canopy of kings.

Moving quickly, they soon reach Dakshinpur where the Seth's wife sees the woman in the cart and thinks, "He has brought a co-wife!" When he explains that it is his dharma-daughter, she lovingly brings her inside and treats her with great affection (WA 68:11; WA 84:207; WA 89:7–9; WA 94:6–8; Shankar Lal 1987).

The Battle of Shantiban (*Śāntibān Kī Laṛāī*)

New Characters

The Merchant's two sons, Raja Nal's "adopted" uncles
The Tortoise deity, Kachua Dev

Nal grows quickly, since he is of the lineage of Raghuvansi (of the god-hero Ram). While the other Merchant boys make scales and pots out of clay, he makes a sword and a horse. Finally, the Merchant sends him to school, but when the teacher asks him to write a and b, he writes c and d. He is always one step ahead of what the teachers are teaching him. So the Merchant takes him out of school and gives him a bow and arrow. Practicing with his bow and arrow, he shoots all the birds in the area, until the lanes are filled with carcasses. When the villagers complain, the Merchant takes the bow and arrow away, and gives him a slingshot. He uses the slingshot to break the clay pots of the women at the well. When they abuse Nal's grandfather the Merchant, he tells them that he will buy them all brass pots.

One day when Banvari is about seven years old, he demands to go hunting in the forest. His mother, Rani Manjha, forbids him to go into the forest of Shantiban. So the boy looks for game in the nearby forests, and eventually wanders into Shantiban. Now Raja Pratham has also come to Shantiban to hunt, as it is his favorite forest. Sitting atop his decorated elephant, he sees a tiger and shoots it in the neck, but as the tiger falls it veers straight into the elephant, knocking it off its feet and throwing Pratham to the ground on top of the tiger. About to shoot a boar, Nal sees the pile, and grabs the tiger and cuts its head off. Astounded by the actions of this young boy, Pratham asks which king is his father. Nal replies, "I am not the son of a king. I am the grandson of the Merchant Lachhiman Seth." Pratham looks at the boy and sees that he looks like Manjha, but he cannot believe that she and the babe have survived. Then Pratham says, "If you are the son of a Merchant, how dare you enter Shantiban. And how dare you kill my game. And why are you so fearless?"

Nal looks Pratham up and down, and replies, "I have saved your life, and you want to do battle with me? You can do battle with me, but I shall win."

Pratham ponders his options, and says, "Okay, but take this reward," and he lifts from his chest the red breastplate that he had received as part of his dowry from Manjha's father and puts it on Nal.

When Nal returns to Dakshinpur, Manjha immediately knows that the boy met his father that day. She anxiously asks Raja Nal, "I hope this doesn't mean that you killed a man today?" But Nal assures her that he had saved the hunter, that no harm had come to him, and that Nal had received the breastplate as a reward.

Then the Merchant decides that he should hold a sacred thread ceremony for his adopted grandson and invites Raja Pratham to the ceremony. When Pratham arrives, he takes the boy onto his lap and laments the fates that have taken such a son from him. Durga, who hears this lament, mocks him from the rooftops, saying that if he had had more faith in his wife and less in the Brahman, he would have a son. Meanwhile, Manjha is hiding in purdah with the women of the household, unable to eat until her husband, the visiting king, has eaten. Making up excuses, she manages to maintain her pativrat, her respectful worship of her husband, without anyone realizing who she is.

The Merchant is determined to teach this boy, who loves horses and swords, to be a good trader, so he sends him across the seas with his own two sons on a trading mission, each with their own boat. One day they come to a small island, covered in forest. Raj Nal insists on stopping there, though his uncles remind him that there are no inhabitants and no harbor. So they leave Nal, who wanders on the lovely beach. He discovers that many pairs of swans live there. So he takes his merchandise off the ship and sets up shop on the beach. The swans love the smell of the goods in Raja Nal's shop. As they eat it, they also shit. In their shit are pure white pearls. Raja Nal collects the pearls until he has an enormous store of them. Going to a nearby village, he hires laborers to bring cow dung to his beach and hires women to make cow dung cakes. Each cake is filled with pearls. Throwing everything that is unnecessary off his ship, Raja Nal fills it with cow dung cakes.

When the uncles return, they howl with laughter on seeing the ship filled with cow dung. They remark that a merchant weeps at the loss of even five paise, and here Nal has traded valuable goods for dung worth maybe one hundred rupees! When they ask Raja Nal why he has bought the dung, he says, "My mother used to have trouble making bread for me every day. Everyone made arrangements for flour, but no one arranged for fuel. I purchased the dung as fuel for my mother."

That night, as Raja Nal is sleeping, the uncles steal four or five dung cakes to use as fuel to cook. When they break them open (usually a cake is broken into smaller pieces to use as fuel), they find the pearls inside. Greedy and immoral, they want to take over the ship filled with dung cakes, so they pick up the sleeping Raja Nal and throw him overboard. But instead of falling into the sea, Raja Nal lands on the back of the tortoise-god Kachua Dev, who quickly takes him to Dakshinpur to await the arrival of the ships.

When the ships land, Raja Nal insists that his horde of cow dung cakes be locked in Lachhiman's treasury.

Another time the Seth and his sons, with Raja Nal, are out in their ship, searching for more goods to trade. On some island they find a beach where a beautiful girl is bathing and playing games with her cowry shells. As the strange men approach, she grabs her belongings and flees, leaving behind one cowry shell out of a set of sixteen. They take the shell back to Dakshinpur, and the Seth decides to offer it to his king. Putting it in a plate decorated with beautiful flowers and fruit, he takes it to Narvargarh. When Pratham sees the plate with the cowry shell, he becomes very happy and tells his prime minister to give ten villages to the Seth. Then Raja Pratham takes the shell to the Rang Mahal (literally, Palace of Colors) where his hundred queens live. They are outraged: "What, you have given him ten villages for only one shell? Where are the other fifteen shells? Will you give him ten villages every time he brings a shell? You will have nothing left!" Listening to his queens, the king has the Merchant locked in jail.

When the news reaches Dakshinpur, there is much commotion. When Raja Nal hears that his grandfather has been jailed, he is determined to go to Narvar to free him, although Manjha begs him not to go. Finally, Manjha agrees, saying, "When you greet the king, you must bow your head. Remember that he is your elder and bow your head." She is afraid that Pratham will see that Raja Nal resembles Manjha. So Raja Nal takes a sword and leaves for Narvar. When Pratham sees him, he knows that here is the boy who killed the tiger in the jungle. When asked why he has come, Nal says that he has come to free his grandfather and that he will find the other fifteen cowry shells within six months. If he doesn't, then Pratham can kill the grandfather.

A maidservant sees the boy with Pratham and runs to the Rang Mahal, where she tells the queens that they should do something immediately, because Pratham is showing great love to a boy who looks just like Manjha. They send for the boy and know, without a doubt, that he is Manjha's son. One prepares a cup of poison and starts to give it to the boy. But Durga sees what is happening and prevents Raja Nal from being poisoned by the queens. Raja Nal goes back to the king and says that he will return within six months to free his grandfather (WA 89:9–10; WA 02:6–7).

Motini's Marriage (*Motinī Kā Byāh*)

New Characters

Behmata, the goddess of fate, she who determines one's fate at birth
Motini, an apsara (heavenly nymph) raised by a demon
Bhumasur, the demon father of Motini
Somasur, brother of Bhumasur

With the Seth in jail, Nal and the two sons of the Seth return to the boat, hoping to find the maiden and the other fifteen shells. Eventually they reach the beach where she had been bathing, and Nal leaves the ship, which is to return for him in six days after delivering its cargo. Sitting on the beach is an old woman throwing rings of rope (*jūrī*) into the sea. Nal doesn't know that this is Behmata, the goddess of fate. He asks what she is doing, and she replies that she is making marriages by twisting two ropes together and tossing them into the sea. If they sink, the marriage will be brief, but if they reach the other side then the marriage will last a lifetime.

Nal begs the old woman to make a marriage for him, but when she asks his caste, he says that he is a Merchant. Behmata replies that she cannot make marriages for the Merchant caste, only for those of the Warrior caste. Nal becomes very angry, so she finally agrees to make his marriage. The first twisted ring of ropes sinks quickly. Again angry, Nal asks for a second marriage "that will last my whole life." She makes the second ring of ropes, and it reaches the far shore. Then Behmata tells him that his first marriage is to take place immediately. Nal asks, "How?" And Behmata replied that they would travel to his first bride. She makes a flying boat and sits in it with Nal in her lap. In minutes they fly hundreds of miles till they arrive at a stone fort. At the fort, Behmata leaves Nal.

Nal wanders around the fort, looking for an entrance. He bemoans his fate: here he is at the home of his bride-to-be, but he cannot enter! Then he remembers Durga. His cry reaches Durga in her palace, and she orders her monkey helpers to immediately saddle her lion. With her retinue of ghosts, monkeys, and other assorted goblins, she reaches Nal after just one and a half moments. She questions, "Son, what is the matter?"

Nal responds, "I pray to you today because I am so close and yet so far. I cannot find the door into the palace!"

Durga said, "Oh son, you are right by it." And she orders her monkey helper to kick the boulder that was in fact the door, a boulder weighing many hundreds of pounds. Raja Nal goes inside and finds Motini sleeping peacefully, covered by a five-colored shawl. So he wraps himself in a sheet and stands like a pillar, waiting for her to awake. Motini opens her eyes and sees him there, disguised as a pillar. She immediately recognizes him as a Warrior, but when she asks him who he is, he responds that he is a Merchant. Disbelieving, Motini challenges him to a game of gambling played with cowry shells (*sarpānse*). Nal pulls out the cowry shell Motini had dropped on the beach, much to her surprise. But she adds the other fifteen, and they bet their shells to the winner. Raja Nal quickly wins game after game because he is, after all, a true Kshatriya (warrior), and only such men are truly good at gambling.

Suddenly Motini stops, as she hears the sound of her father, the demon Bhumasur, coming back from feeding in the forest. "Quick," she says to Nal, "you must leave, as my father eats humans." But Nal refuses to depart, so she turns him into a parrot and puts him in a cage. Bhumasur comes quickly, like a typhoon, and easily moves the boulders weighing hundreds of pounds. The skulls that are piled in the palace from earlier feasting on humans say, "A human has been here today." And Bhumasur can smell a human. When he questions his daughter, who is actually a heavenly nymph from the god Indra's kingdom whom he has kidnapped as a young girl and raised, teaching her all that he knew, she repeatedly denies the presence of any human.

The next morning Bhumasur is ready to depart again for the forest when he notices the parrot hanging in the cage. "Daughter," he said, "I will eat the parrot before leaving." Motini weeps, saying, "Father, I have made a pet of this parrot and now you want to kill it. Please don't eat it." So he again goes into the forest, and Motini changes Nal back to his human form and they play some more. This time Nal bets that, if he wins, Motini will be his, and if she wins, he will be hers. He figures that either way, they will be together. And he immediately wins, and in this way Motini gambles away all that is valuable to the demon. When evening comes the demon returns, and the skulls again tell him that a human has been in his palace. But Motini denies it, and he can find no one.

In the morning, as the demon is leaving, he says, "Today I will eat the parrot." Motini is furious. Taking the cage with the parrot, she dashes it to the ground, meanwhile turning the parrot into a pearl that she puts on her hairpin. That night the skulls again tell Bhumasur that a human is present. This time he makes Motini swear that there is no human. He takes her to the ocean where she must submerge herself[4] and take an oath that no human is present. She takes an oath saying that she has no one except her husband-god over her head (i.e., Raja Nal), and so she is able to trick the demon.

Bhumasur is certain that he has been tricked—that somehow the human is on her head. So he asks if he can oil and comb her hair. She allows him to do so, but first she takes Nal off the hairpin and turns him into a spider which she puts on her curtain. Then the demon lovingly fixes her hair, but finds nothing. So he goes off to the forest, but returns early, saying, "I have not licked the curtain for three days: I shall lick it today." So she changes Nal from a spider into a parrot whom she hides in her blouse. Finally, one day the demon comes in over the walls, rather than through the boulder entrance, and discovers Motini gambling with Raja Nal. She quickly turns him into a parrot once again and hides him in a pile of bricks. Convincing her father yet once more that she is alone, she then asks when she will be married. "Never," the demon replies. "Once I visited Raja Pratham whose queen, Manjha, was pregnant: you would have been married to his son, Raja Nal. But Rani Manjha has been killed. So there is no one. There is no one to marry you and no one to kill me."

Motini then asks, "Father, if there is no one to marry me and no one to kill you, tell me one thing. Where is your life kept? Then I can look after it and guard it." So the demon tells Motini, "There are seven rooms. In the seventh room is a golden cage hanging from a hook. In it is a crane. The day the crane dies, I die."

The next day after the demon went into the forest, Motini gives Raja Nal the keys to the seven rooms. Upon opening the first room, they find the wife of the demon, so large that her head is in the sky and her feet in the bowels of the earth. Shaking in fear, Nal realizes that she is guarding her husband's life. But, once again, by putting Raja Nal in a tiny box, Motini is able to trick the wife and get to the second room. Here they find a seven-edged sword that once belonged to Indra. Only Raja Nal has the power to control that sword. Taking the sword in his hand, Raja Nal opens the third room where the four brothers of the demon await him. Raja Nal immediately remembers Durga, who at once comes to fight the demons. When she has killed three, the fourth, named Somasur, whose nose was chopped off, asks to be spared, saying that he will worship Nal. So he is spared. In the fourth cell is the magical flying water horse (*jaldāriyā*) that was also Indra's. Only Indra and Raja Nal can ride that horse. In the fifth cell is a golden whip worth one and a quarter lakhs of rupees. In the sixth cell is Shesh Nag, who has been captured by the demon and placed there to guard his life. Raja Nal frees the grateful snake. In the seventh room is the golden cage with the crane. As Raja Nal puts his hand on the cage, miles away in the forest, the demon begins to tremble and starts running back to his fort. Motini says, "Break one of its legs," and Raja Nal does so. Then he breaks the second leg, but even without legs the demon keeps running. So he breaks the bird's wings, breaks them both. And the demon enters the fort. Then, as the demon drags Raja Nal to the ground, Motini breaks the neck of the crane.

Motini then asks Raja Nal to let her cry for a while, for she has killed her own father. And she cries a lot. They then purify the area with cow dung to prepare for their wedding. Motini talks to Raja Nal: "Husband, please listen to me carefully. I am willing to marry you on the condition that you never marry anyone else. If you marry anyone else, I will leave you. Very bad things will happen to you. You must also remember that I am a daughter of the gods, and I cannot bear a child for you. Think about this carefully and, if you still wish to marry me, swear on cow dung that you'll never marry again." So Raja Nal swears that he will not marry again.

Then the goddesses Durga and Behmata come, with all their ghosts and followers. Behmata sings *gālī* (songs of abuse toward the boy's family sung by the women of the bride's family at north Indian weddings). And the marriage canopy is set up and the marriage held. Motini gives Raja Nal the necklace of eighty-four snake gems that had been found in one of the rooms of the demon as dowry, along with the seven-edged sword of Indra and the flying water horse. The next morning Raja Nal gives the kingdom of the demon to the brother with the chopped-off nose, and he and Motini return to the shore to meet the ship of the Seth's sons (WA 84:233–235; WA 89:8–11, 18–20; WA 90: 22–24; WA 94:11–13, 29–31, 02:2–3; Shankar Lal 1987).

The Battle of Patal Lok (*Pātāl Lok Kī Laṛāī*)

New Characters

Basukdev, the king of snakes and ruler of the Patal Lok, the underworld
Basuk Dev's daughter, who later takes birth as Dumenti, daughter of Bhim Sen
Mansukh Gujar, Raja of Siyanagar who becomes Raja Nal's best friend and main helpmate

As soon as the two uncles see the beautiful wife of Raja Nal, they are driven by lust and begin to plan how to make her their wife. Motini is suspicious of their behavior and places the necklace with the eighty-four snake gems around Nal's neck, telling him not to remove it until he reaches his mother's house. But as Motini and Nal sleep, the two uncles pick up Raja Nal and drop him overboard into the sea. Nal is able to grab hold of the anchor chain, but the two wicked uncles take sticks and beat his hands so that he is forced to let go. And he falls down to Patal Lok, the underworld of the snake king Basukdev.

On the ship the two wicked Merchant uncles try to seduce Motini, but she reminds them that they are the maternal uncles of her husband and therefore she is like their real daughter. She asks where her husband is, and they tell her that he is coming by a different boat, but she doesn't believe them and weeps like Sita in Lanka. Then she curses them so that their ship doesn't move. Narad Muni and Durga both realize that there is some trouble on earth, and Narad comes to the uncles. They explain that none of the machinery on their ship will work, that they are stuck in the middle of the ocean. Narad tells them that they have committed a great sin and that they should bow their heads to Motini and beg her forgiveness: only then will their ship move.

When they reach the shore, Motini speaks to the magical flying horse, asking him to wait by the seashore for eight days for Nal to return, adding, "No one has yet been born who can kill my husband." And the horse agrees to wait even for eight months, saying that no one can harm him or use magic against him because he is protected by Indra's blessing.

Meanwhile, in Dakshinpur, Manjha has been weeping so hard that she has become blind. When the ship docks in Dakshinpur, the Merchant women come to greet the new daughter-in-law, but Motini refuses to disembark because they are performing rituals that are Merchant rituals, not Kshatriya rituals. So the women call Manjha. Motini catches the feet of Manjha, saying, "Why are you weeping? I am your son's wife. I am not the daughter of a Merchant. Stop your tears." But Manjha refuses to accept Motini as her daughter-in-law.

Now the two wicked Merchant uncles are very worried because the six months that Pratham had given them to find the missing cowry shells have passed, and they have nothing to give Pratham. So they decide to offer Motini to Pratham instead. They go to Motini and tell her that, in their family, it is the custom that the wife first go to worship Raja Pratham, and then she can worship any god. They bedeck Motini in the finest of clothing and leave for Navargarh. As they leave, Motini sneezes. In a dried tree, a single bird rests. A sadhu walks down the road. These are all bad omens.

After one and a half days they reach Narvar and take the palanquin directly into Pratham's court. Pratham asks, "So six months have passed. Do you have the missing cowry shells?" The Merchant says, "I am bringing you instead a young woman, more beautiful than Rani Manjha." And he takes off the veil, and Motini sits there in great shame. Upon seeing her, Pratham is immediately entranced, and says that he will make her his head queen. But Motini refuses, saying that she will be head queen only when he has found a Pandit who can tell the "story of Nal" (*Nal Kī Kathā*).[5] So Pratham gives her the palace of Manjha to live in. Once there, she finds a picture of Manjha, and Motini knows that it is her mother-in-law.

Meanwhile, having fallen into the ocean, Raja Nal reaches Patal Lok, the land of the snakes. There he finds himself surrounded by snakes, all ready to attack him because he is wearing the necklace of snake gems, each gem coming from the head of a snake that had been killed on earth. But then Shesh Nag, the snake that had been forced to guard the life index of Bhumasur, recognizes Nal, and says, "Wait, he is the one who freed me from the demon. Please don't kill him." And he takes him to his father, Basukdev. Basukdev makes Nal his *dharam bhāī* (brother by religious duty), and the two men exchange turbans.

Then, while Nal is walking in Basukdev's garden, he meets Basukdev's daughter. This lovely snake-maiden immediately falls in love with Nal and desires him as her husband. When she entreats him to marry her, he replies, "But I already have one non-human wife! I can marry you only if you take birth as a human!" So the lovely snake-maiden decides to take birth as human so as to marry Raja Nal.

Meanwhile, she hands him a flower, saying, "Smell this." Raja Nal smells the flower, and suddenly his whole appearance changes: he is an old man, dressed like a priest. "Stop," he shouts, "return me to being a young boy. I don't want to be an old man."

"Smell the flower again," replies the snake-maiden, "and you shall return to your normal self. But keep the flower, so that you can transform yourself into an old man if need arises." Then the snakes take Nal to the edge of the sea, where he finds his magical flying horse awaiting him. As Raja Nal and the horse approach the small kingdom of Siya Nagar, they come upon a lion standing over a man whom the lion had dragged off his horse. Raja Nal grabs his sword and kills the lion, and Mansukh Gujar[6] is saved. The two agree to be friends and come to each other's aid. Then Nal returns to Dakshinpur to find his wife and mother.

When Nal reaches Dakshinpur he disguises himself as an old Pandit. The Merchant uncle asks him, "Where is our nephew, Nal." And Nal replies, checking his astrology books, "He has died." Then the Pandit is taken to Manjha, who says that she is dying without her son. Nal tells her not to think this way. "I am sure that you will meet your son. First, take me in your arms." So Manjha takes the old man in her arms and milk flows from her nipples, and

Nal drinks it and touches her feet. She no longer is blind. (WA 84:235; 89:11, 20; 90:23–24; 94:13)

The Story of Nal (*Nal Kī Kathā*)

Pratham searches everywhere for a Pandit who can tell the story of Nal so that he can win Motini. He sends messengers to Banaras, but they find no one who knows the story of Nal. Then he finds one Pandit who says that he knows the *Nal Purāṇ* and demands a gift of five villages. They start out from Banaras, stopping only for the Pandit to smoke hashish on the way. Everyone gathers in the court, and the Pandit begins to speak. But it is not the story of Nal that he tells. Motini sends the gatekeeper to tell Pratham that it is not the story of Nal and that if he doesn't find a Pandit to tell it soon, she will kill herself with a sword.

So the constables search far and wide. One day, a constable comes upon an old Pandit (Nal) near the sea. This Pandit says that he can sing the Nal Puran! So the constable tries to pursuade the Pandit to ride on his horse with him, but the Pandit insists on going on foot, saying that he is not the kind of Brahman who is a beggar or who farms or who goes to lower castes or who is in the control of others. Then Nal goes quickly to Narvargarh. Red flags are flying above the palace, and a dancing girl is performing in the court. An astrologer is lecturing on different religious beliefs.

The Pandit insists that, before he can tell the Nal Puran, everyone in the kingdom has to be in court. So they call the hundred queens who, with Motini in their midst, come to the court.

The Pandit starts, "There was a King Pratham of Narvargarh. He had a queen who was killed by a Sweeper." And Pratham says, "But this is my story." Then he hears that Manjha had not died and that she had a son, and cries, "Where is that boy, he is my son." Every once in a while the Pandit stops and says he cannot continue the story. At this, Motini weeps and begs him to continue. Then the Pandit tells of the battle in Shantiban and the discovery of the cowry shell. King Pratham cries, wondering where his son is. And he tells of searching for the cowry shells, of the demon who tries to destroy Nal, and of his marriage to Motini. And the queens are sitting there thinking, "Now we'll all be killed." And the two Sweepers who had saved Manjha also worry that they will be punished.

Then the old Pandit relays the story of the wicked uncles who threw Nal overboard. Hearing this, Pratham wails loudly, certain that now his son is gone forever. The Pandit asks, "King, why are you weeping? There is more to the story." Then he tells of returning to Dakshinpur and coming to the court. Then Pratham asks, "Where is Nal now?" And the Pandit replies, "The story of Raja Nal is being told by the son to the father." And he takes out the flower and smells it, and becomes a young man again and grabs his father's feet. Pratham wants him to move immediately into the palace, but Raja Nal declines, saying, "I'll come only if you dig a pit, and in it lay the hundred queens and sprinkle them with curds and then loose hunting dogs on them. And you kill the Pandit who lied to you. And you double the wages of the two Sweepers." Manjha also refuses to reside in Narvar, saying that she had been living in a Merchant's house and must first bathe in the Ganges[7] (WA 89:20–23).

The Battle of Kampilagarh (*Kampilāgaṛh Kī Laṛāī*)

New Characters

Phul Singh Panjabi
Sarvati, the daughter of Phul Singh Panjabi

Manjha is reunited with her husband, Raja Pratham, but insists on bathing in the Ganges to remove the sin of living with the merchants for twelve years. As the procession is readied for its departure, Manjha's maid hurries to Raja Nal to tell him that his mother is leaving. As he leaves his palace, his sword clanking and his stride like a lion's, he sees innumerable inauspicious omens—a crow crying in a dry tree, a crane alone and bereaved without its partner, a single deer. His mother begs Nal to accompany her to the Ganges, but Pratham refuses his permission, telling Nal to remain in Narvar. Then Motini arrives and tells her mother-in-law that it is indeed crucial to bathe, for otherwise the kings of the fifty-two kingdoms will insult Narvar. Her sin must be washed away.

So Pratham and Manjha depart, with Pratham saying to his son, "Nal, you must stay here. I am no less brave than you. Stay here comfortably." The king's procession moves quickly, arriving at the Ganges in just three days, pitching tents at its bank. Also there are the kings of the fifty-two kingdoms. One, Phul Singh Panjabi, has an army with men built like wrestlers and no one can defeat him. He announces that his wife and daughter will bathe first. Pratham says that Manjha will bathe first. All this talk leads to the unsheathing of swords. Pratham says, "I have not come here to live as a slave nor to ask for any land. I shall bathe in the Ganges and then depart."

Then the battle begins: nine hundred of Narvar's soldiers are killed and four thousand of the Panjabi's. Three times, Pratham's army repels that of the Panjabi. Finally, Phul Singh retreats to his tent where he tells his daughter of his losses. But Sarvati, his daughter, reassures him, saying, "Why do you worry while I am here? We will bathe first." And they ready themselves for a fourth advance, this time accompanied by the sorceress Sarvati. She speaks magic words and changes Pratham's army into stone. Pratham is tied up and Manjha put in a cart. Then Phul Singh tells her that he has heard that she, Manjha, bears especially brave sons, and he desires a son from her womb. Manjha tells him that she will bear him a brave son only when day turns into night. Then Manjha is taken to the prison where she has to keep crows off the roof, and Pratham is taken to the flourmill to grind grain day and night. Nine jailers await his slightest falter, ready to beat him instantly (WA 75:106; 85:302–305; 89:12–16, 25–26; Shankar Lal 1987; Kailash and Laturi 1988a).

Battle of Phul Singh (*Phul Sinh Kī Laṛāī*)

New Characters

Kali, a powerful Hindu goddess, here associated with Phul Singh Panjabi
Chando, the mausi (mother's sister) of Sarvati
Jalandhar, the leader of the Nath yogis with whom Motini battles

Back in Narvar, Motini dreams that her in-laws are jailed, but Raja Nal refuses to believe such a thing. Motini taunts him, saying, "Husband, I did not think you were so weak. Or perhaps your mother has sinned, and the child from her womb was someone else's. Husband, you stay in the palace; I will fight the Panjabi." Eventually one poor Brahman, who had been sitting on a rock at the edge of the battle, makes his way back and tells of the debacle at the Ganges. Sending for Mansukh, Raja Nal readies his army. Motini, too, prepares to go, but Raja Nal rejects her wish to go, saying that he would be laughed at by the kings of the fifty-two kingdoms if he brought a woman with him to battle. So Raja Nal sets off with an army of twenty-four thousand Jat soldiers to free his parents.

That night, at their resting place, Motini catches up with them. Using her magic, she transforms herself into a handsome soldier with all the necessary weapons. Seeing this proud warrior, Raja Nal asks Mansukh to introduce him, but Mansukh replies that his friend will shake hands with no one.[8] Motini knows that she cannot shake hands with her husband and wonders how to proceed. Finally, Mansukh convinces her to shake Raja Nal's hand, and Raja Nal immediately becomes angry, "Mansukh, go to hell. Here we are ready to battle, and you have me shake hands with a woman!"

Mansukh replies, "Calm yourself. This poor man has come to help, and you are insulting him by calling him a woman again and again. His hand is soft because he is a Merchant!"

Later that day they reach the bank of the Ganges. There a stone is inscribed with a message from Sarvati: "If any man moves beyond this stone, he will be blinded." But Raja Nal doesn't notice, and he and Mansukh and their army continue on. They suddenly find themselves blinded. They cannot see one another. Raja Nal cries out, "My royal throne is gone; my life in the palace is gone. A bad time has come to me, fate is opposing me from all sides. How can I free my parents when we have been made blind?"

Mansukh quickly replies, "Raja Nal, if we had brought Motini with us, she could fix it so that we could see."

Then Raja Nal remembers his wife, "Oh, daughter of the demon, take care of me. Oh, daughter of the demon, take care of me." Hearing these words, Motini comes to them and speaks magic words, restoring their sight. Able to see again, Raja Nal starts back to Narvar, saying, "It doesn't matter if my parents live or die, I don't have enough power to free them. If we try to free them, we'll only be blinded again." But Motini picks up Sarvati's magic marker and throws it in the Ganges. Then she informs Raja Nal that he doesn't have the power to free his parents, but that if he'd listen to her she would free them. "Tell me," Nal replies.

So Motini reveals her plan: she, Raja Nal, and Mansukh will become Nats,[9] Acrobats, a lower-caste group that wanders from town to town and whose women are often thought to be prostitutes. But in order to successfully deceive Phul Singh and his court, they will have to look and act like genuine Acrobats—shaved heads, loincloths, different names, and lots of tricks. But while Motini shaves Raja Nal's head, she makes herself beautiful, so that the Panjabi will lust after her. She also changes their names: Raja Nal is Pestle, Mansukh is Mortar, and Motini is Chutney. Motini then calls her demon father's brother, Somasur demon, to come to help them. He brings items that Acrobats own—dogs, cocks, and buffalo, a drum, cymbals, and juggling implements.

As they ready themselves to enter Kampilagarh, the fort of Phul Singh Panjabi, Motini warns Nal and Mansukh not to lose their tempers, not to talk back. But Raja Nal responds, "If someone says something once, I won't care. I can bear it a second time. But the third time, I'll break his head!" Motini then decides to leave their weapons behind, lest Raja Nal err into violence.

As they make their way toward the court, the Cowherders leave their cattle and the Water Carriers their buckets and well, all entranced by the beautiful Nat and her juggler. Phul Singh himself says that he has never seen such a beautiful Acrobat, although he notes that the eyes of the men are red (a sign of a warrior by caste) and they seem ready with their bamboo sticks.

Worried that these Acrobats are not true Acrobats, Phul Singh's prime minister convinces him to offer them food, for jugglers would eat from his kitchen whereas pretenders would not. So Phul Singh insists that they eat at his court that day, despite Motini's warning that her jugglers often act up, drink a bit too much, smoke too much pot, and even indulge in opium. But Motini is able to elude the dishonor of eating an enemy's food through a clever deception. When she serves Mansukh, the demon uncle, and Raja Nal, she gives the first two large helpings, and serves Raja Nal only a small torn piece of bread and hardly a handful of lentils. He immediately rises up and starts a fight over his meager helping, dumping all the food on the ground in his anger. With all the food spoiled, they can eat none of it. Phul Singh notes that no Kshatriyas would fight over food like this: they truly are Acrobats.

When Phul Singh arranges to visit Motini at their tent that night, she puts the two men where she had claimed to be sleeping, and Phul Singh, grabbing the hand of "Motini," comments on her lack of bangles and then about her shaved head, before he is beaten and stripped naked by Raja Nal and Mansukh.

Finally, the beautiful Nat and her helpers perform their tricks. Nal climbs a rope that disappears into the sky; he is seen no longer. Suddenly parts of his body fall to the ground—a leg, an arm, a torso—until his whole body lies in pieces before Phul Singh's court. Seeing her dead husband, Motini insists that he be cremated and that she commit sati. Phul Singh has a funeral pyre built; Motini sits on it with the pieces of Nal on her lap, and the fire is lit. Suddenly both emerge, alive and unscathed.

Through a variety of tricks, Motini, Raja Nal, and Mansukh manage to ward off the obstacles in their way and gain access to the jail where his parents and nine hundred other prisoners, including a 7½ foot Bengali who had his nose cut off by Phul Singh, are held.[10] Phul Singh and his daughter, Sarvati (who has fallen in love with Raja Nal and desires to marry him, even though he is a Nat), must now battle the freed prisoners and their helpmates. Phul Singh has the goddess Kali on his side, Nal has Durga. Fortunately, Motini has been able to convince Sarvati to give her half of her magic in order to be able to marry Raja Nal, so that Sarvati's powers are diminished. Phul Singh's army is quickly destroyed.

As Phul Singh faces defeat, he begs his daughter for help, but she admits that she no longer has magic strong enough to defeat Motini and Raja Nal. But then she remembers her *mausī*, her mother's sister Chando. She calls on Chando who comes from Chandigarh: she blasts Nal with her magic and leaves Motini senseless. She takes Raja Nal and, by tying a magical scarf around his neck, turns him into her witless slave, making him perform duties normally done by women, such as drawing water. A Tamil woman who also draws water at the well realizes what has happened and lures Nal into her hut where she removes the scarf so that his wits return. She then gives him magic to counter Chando. The magic turns Chando into a horse that Nal rides to freedom.

Once again the two armies prepare for battle. Sarvati, unable to help her father on her own, calls her guru Jalandhar from Bengal. He arrives with his fourteen hundred disciples and another battle begins, this time between Jalandhar and Motini. They blast *vīr* (magical sayings/powers or "arrows") at each other, but Motini has the power of only thirteen vir, whereas Jalandhar has fourteen vir. He defeats her and takes her with him to his ashram in the jungle where he desires to marry her.[11] She pretends to be ill and says that she'd marry him only after the pain in her ribs is cured. Jalandhar sets out to seek a doctor or *vaidya* (traditional medical practitioner).

Meanwhile, Nal is without his wife and calls on the goddess Durga to aid him. She arrives and, with magical glasses, shows him his wife lying ill in Jalandhar's camp. She enables him to fly there on his magical water horse. Disguising himself as a doctor, he enters the camp and begins to treat Motini. She tells him that his price for her cure should be the secrets of Jalandhar's fourteen vir. Nal is to write them down, one a day, and she will learn them. When they have the fourteenth vir, they will escape. This is accomplished, and Motini escapes as a bird (a kite). The fourteen hundred disciples immediately transform themselves into hawks and follow her. She dives into a pond and becomes a fish, and the fourteen hundred disciples become herons and start to search the pond. She becomes a leech and enters the stomach of a buffalo that has come to the pond to drink, and thus she reaches the Oil Presser's house. Jalandhar's disciples manage to buy the buffalo from its owner and prepare to cut it open. But Motini, in turn, escapes through its dung, once again becomes a kite, and flies away. When attacked by the fourteen hundred disciples, she becomes a necklace worth nine lakhs that falls around the neck of a princess. She tells the princess not to give up the necklace. The yogis become Acrobats, enter the king's court, and, as a reward for their performance, demand only the necklace worn by the princess. The king finally agrees and the princess, forced to give it up, slams it to the ground where it breaks into thousands of pearls rolling across the floor. Motini, in one pearl, is hidden in a crack in the floor and escapes the pecking of the fourteen hundred cocks now eating the pearls.

Finally free, and having the power of the fourteen vir, Motini attacks Jalandhar and kills him. But Pratham, anguished at the dishonor that has befallen him, takes his own life, submerging himself in the Ganges. Manjha readies herself for sati. Nal escapes a marriage with Sarvati but must seek the sandalwood for his mother's funeral pyre in the forest of Lakhiyaban (WA 74:106; 85:302–305; 89:14, 17, 25–26; Kailash and Laturi 1989; Shankar Lal 1987).

Dumenti's Marriage (*Dumentī Kā Byāh*)

New Characters

Dumenti, the daughter of Basukdev reborn as the daughter of Raja Bhim
Raja Bhim of Samudsikal

Rani Kamla, wife of Raja Bhim
Raja Indra, the king of the gods, an irascible and often immoral character

The daughter of Basukdev was reborn as Dumenti, daughter of Raja Bhim of Samudsikul. When Dumenti is twelve years old, Bhim's wife, Queen Kamla, says to him, "Our daughter is now of age. It is time we found her a husband." Raja Bhim ponders the matter, knowing that his daughter possesses sixteen qualities unmatched on earth, and decides that only Raja Indra, king of the gods, is a worthy husband. So he calls a pair of geese, saying, "Oh King: take this offer of marriage to Indra." The geese do not wait but hurry to do the king's bidding. But on their way they meet Dumenti, who questions where they are going. The geese answer that they are off to heaven and are taking her marriage invitation to Raja Indra.

"But that's impossible," responds Dumenti. "This marriage with Indra will never take place." The geese wonder at this: Indra has thirty-three crores of gods, all with mighty weapons, ready to battle in a moment. And the marriage will not take place? Dumenti continues, "You should take the invitation to Narvar, not Indrapuri. Take it to Raja Nal."

"A man, instead of a god?" asks the goose.

Dumenti insists that she wishes to marry the human of Narvar and writes a second invitation, sealing it with her turmeric-stained handprint, and also attaches it to the neck of the goose. Then the geese depart for Indrapuri, aided by soft gusts of air. The geese are pleased that today they will meet the gods. But what do they see on their journey? A deer chasing a fox, a water buffalo leading the cowherd.[12] They are worried by these inauspicious signs but continue nevertheless.

When the geese reach the court of Indra they present him with the invitation, and he puffs up like a flower blossoming before their eyes. He calls the gods and tells them to prepare for a wedding. Then Indra sees the second letter around the goose's neck and demands to read it also. Indra is stung by the second invitation: one daughter and two invitations, and one to a mere human! He suggests that the geese return directly to Samudsikul, not stopping in Narvar, but before that they should rest for a few days and feast on pearls.[13] As the geese rest and feast, Indra frets: "What if they do stop in Narvar? That bastard Nal was born with his umbilical cord cut. He can't be trusted at all." So he calls the gods to send strong winds and rain in the path of the geese so that they will lose their way and not reach Narvar.

The winds and rain are so powerful that the geese lose their bearings. Then the wind pushes them to the ground, and they land in a garden: the day is dark with the storm. Unknowingly they landed in Narvar. Water is everywhere, and, in its midst, they see some drowning mice. The goose-wife insists on rescuing the mice, despite their own predicament, claiming that if you do l happen to you, but if you behave badly, misfortune will befall ck up the mice and tuck them under their wings, where the) the warm dry feathers.

...ng, when the goose flaps his wings, feathers and flesh fall to ground. The mice had eaten the wings of the geese. Unable to fly, the geese sit by the pond, the goose-wife crying with wrenching sobs. Soon Raja Nal arrives in the garden, despite Motini's protests that he not examine the damage to his garden for she had dreamed that only trouble would come of this visit. Nal finds the strange birds, with no wings, sitting there. Then he sees the letter around the goose's neck and, picking up the geese, puts them on his horse to carry back to the palace. Then he turns his back to read the letter. In it, Dumenti reminds him of their meeting in Patal Lok and her promise to be reborn as a human. But Nal's magical horse, received as part of his dowry from Bhumasur, is angered that Nal has turned his back, and questions him. When the horse hears of the marriage offer, he is furious, saying, "I have come in Motini's dowry: she is my sister. If you do this, she will kill herself. You cannot marry again." But he cannot convince Raja Nal to give up the idea of marrying Dumenti.

Returning to the palace, Nal discovers that he doesn't have a single real pearl in his kingdom and must ask Durga to send a rain of pearls for the geese to feast on. The geese decide that Nal might be acceptable as a bridegroom after all, for who but a god could cause such a rain of pearls?

Nal is obsessed by the thought of marriage to Dumenti and finally decides to seek the help of Mansukh. He sends a messenger to call Mansukh from Siya Nagar, and Mansukh rushes to Narvar, despite seeing menacing omens on the way. There he is greeted by Nal, who asks again and again, "Are you my true friend?" Mansukh assures him that he is. When Nal finally tells of the marriage proposal, Mansukh is dismayed, knowing that Nal has promised on Ganges water not to marry a second time. "Motini will kill herself," he reminds Nal, "and what will she think when she learns that I am here?"

"No," Nal exclaims, "do not go to the palace. You will dress me as a bridegroom here in the garden. Rani Motini must not know." So Mansukh dresses Nal in gold, with the marriage threads around his head. And the marriage procession of two, Nal and Mansukh, prepares for departure. Indra would be accompanied by 330 million gods, but Nal will have only Mansukh as he dare not tell anyone else.

But when Nal calls the magical horse of Indra to carry him to Samudsikul, the horse refuses, crying that he cannot bear to leave Motini. Finally Nal convinces him to go, since he has promised, but the horse then refuses to carry two—Nal and Mansukh. The horse says that his first rider was Indra; his second was the demon Bhumasur; his third Raja Nal. He will have no other riders. "I am not a donkey, after all," he says, "and you cannot keep heaping on one quintal and then another and another." Finally, the horse agrees to let Mansukh hold onto his tail, which won't be so bad when they fly as the horse's legs will stretch behind. Mansukh isn't pleased but has no choice, so the odd threesome prepares to leave Narvar.

At midnight, as they are leaving, the horse neighs once, and Motini immediately awakes and calls her maid, "Please see where my husband is. His horse neighed. He must be returning home."

The maid hurries out and finds Raja Nal and Mansukh in the garden. "Where are you going," she asks.

"To hunt," Raja Nal responds.

"In the middle of the night?" the maid asks. Then she notices the marriage threads and the gold bangles that adorn Raja Nal. Raja Nal claims that they really aren't bangles but a bandage covering a wound. The maid soon realizes that arguing with him is useless, even though she reminds him of the many times that Motini has saved his life and his family. Eventually she rushes back to the palace to Motini. "He is wearing a marriage crown and is going to Samudsikul," cries the maid.

Motini's heart is broken, and she weeps uncontrollably. Then she goes to the garden, a pot of Ganges water in her hand. Upon seeing her, Raja Nal turns away, ashamed to look at her. Motini says, "Look, I told you at the very beginning that you should not marry me. I am a daughter of the gods. I cannot bear children. You promised, taking an oath on Ganges water, that you would not marry again. Now you have betrayed me." Weeping bitter tears, Motini begs him repeatedly not to marry for a second time. Mansukh also asks Raja Nal to reconsider, but Nal refuses.

As Raja Nal departs, Motini's body falls from the palace ramparts. Mansukh and the horse look back and see her soul depart her body. Both sob uncontrollably. Then Raja Nal, too, looks back and is desolate. Memories of Motini flood him. The life of his palace is gone. He asks Mansukh to bring her to the garden and to bring a bright shawl to cover her, one embroidered with pearls. As he goes to light the pyre, the horse begs, since he is Indra's horse, to let Motini speak to them once. Reminding her that life is ultimately only wind and water, Indra's magical horse revives her. She immediately turns her back on Raja Nal and speaks to the horse, saying, "Let me tell you a secret from the Nal Purana. I was meant to play this part and leave. Don't you let my husband down, oh horse. And don't think that I have betrayed him either. My body is no longer here, but I will remain in his service twenty-four hours a day." Then she speaks to Raja Nal, "You will be betrayed a second time, my love. When you bring a second wife, you will bring Shani (the god of ill luck) with you. You will go from door to door begging." Then she departs again, and the funeral is held immediately so that Raja Nal and Mansukh can attend the wedding in Samudsikul.

In Samudsikul, the sky is filled with the arriving gods. From a palace balcony, Dumenti searches for Raja Nal. Then she hears a loud neighing and knows that it is Nal's horse. Meanwhile, Raja Bhim has given Indra twelve jewels as an initial wedding gift. When Raja Nal arrives at the edge of the city, he refuses to go farther until he, too, is given a gift. Recognizing the insult, Dumenti begs her mother to give the stranger standing by the sea a gift of one jewel to Indra's twelve, saying that when he realizes he has been insulted again, with only one jewel to Indra's twelve, he will leave. Wondering at her strange daughter, who isn't satisfied with one marriage party, the mother eventually coaxes the king into a gift for the stranger by the sea. "After all," she says, "he is a mere human being and will leave when he realizes we have insulted him."

Raja Bhim, atop his grand elephant, goes to where Mansukh and Raja Nal, and the horse, form Nal's marriage party. "Look sons," he says, "I feel sorry for you. There are just the two of you. There isn't even a dog in your procession."

Raja Nal is angered and responds heatedly, "Listen to me, Raja Bhim. There is no evading destiny. This marriage was decided by the gods long ago. We left Narvar in ruins (i.e., Motini dead) to be here, and you talk to us this way!"

Raja Nal and Raja Bhim continue to exchange insults. Finally, Bhim agrees to let the matter be decided by Nal, Indra, and Dumenti. When Raja Nal enters the inner court, Indra is astounded. Who is the man with the puny horse? Narad assures him that these are all invited guests, the only difference being that Bhim invited Indra, and Dumenti invited Nal. But looking around, Indra is worried. How dare this human challenge him? Then Indra asks Narad to have both his and Nal's turbans placed on the throne. Let Dumenti pick the turban of her chosen husband. Bhim agrees to the plan. And in the palace the queen and her retinue urge Dumenti to choose Indra's turban, so that she can live in heaven and ride on flying machines!

The next morning Dumenti enters the courtyard riding an elephant. Oh, she is so beautiful! Probably at the moment she was born, no one else was born in the whole world, for she is so wondrous. Nal sits calmly, his feet touching the ground as befits one born a warrior. The two turbans rest on the throne: Indra's glimmers with the entire milky way sewn into it, whereas Nal's is old, threadbare, stained with turmeric. Initially Dumenti is distracted by the glowing jewels of Indra's turban, but then she realizes it is the illusion of wealth. She picks up the turmeric-stained turban and holds it to her breast, leaving the star-studded one on the throne.

Indra weeps on discovering his fate and cannot be consoled by Narad. Then Narad urges him to win through trickery, saying, "We the gods have been doing it through the ages; it is our way. Your standing among the gods will increase if you win by cheating." Indra leaps to his feet and grabs his turban, saying, "I refuse to accept this verdict. She must garland her chosen husband. I will accept only that." And Indra calls Bhim to him and says: to avoid a fight that the few humans would surely lose to the multitudes of gods, Bhim must ask Dumenti to garland her husband. When Nal is told of the new plan, he replies stoically, "Let her garland who she will. But I tell you, this dishonest Indra will not accept the outcome."

Dumenti's mother pleads with her to choose a god this time, saying that humans are just insects to the gods. "If you marry with the gods, you will be called a god yourself." But Dumenti replies, "Mother, even if I face nothing in this world but misfortune, I will still choose Raja Nal as my husband. Oh amma, stop pleading for the gods. You do not know the whole story. Oh amma, accept my pativrat, my devotion to my husband."

So Dumenti chooses her husband again. This time Indra turns himself and all the 330 million gods into figures identical to Nal. Dumenti gazes with wonder at the multitudes of Nals. But with the help of the goddess, she is able to identity the one Nal who is human, whose feet touch the earth, whose garland is wilted, whose eyes blink. Recognizing Raja Nal, she garlands him. Again Indra is furious. Taking his followers with him, he leaves immediately for heaven, committed to seeking revenge against Raja Nal, that mere human who was chosen over himself, king of the gods, by the lovely Dumenti (WA 94:17–19, 22–27; 02:6–14; Shankar Lal 1987).

Nal's Time of Distress (*Nal Kā Aukhā*)

New Characters

Shukra, the god worshiped on Friday, often a helpmate of Shanidev
Shanidev, the god worshiped on Saturday, known to be allergic to oil seed
Daughter of Raja Biram
Lakha Banjara, a gypsy who finds Dumenti alone in the forest

Indra is very angry that Raja Nal has won Dumenti, so he sends the gods Shukra and Shanidev, and also the planets Rahu and Ketu, to create great distress for him. As they approach Narvar, three towers of the fort collapse. When Raja Nal asks Dumenti about this, she says, "Yes, for twelve years you will be in misery. There will not even be grain for you to eat."

Now Nal is really upset! When he goes to the stable all his horses are dead. Gold is black like ink, and the jewels have turned to coal. He has no food—not even enough for a single meal. And he has not a single cent. For three days Nal and Dumenti go hungry. Then they beg in Narvar, but no one gives them anything. Nal tells his queen, "I can defeat brave men and kings, but I cannot defeat gods like Shukra and Shanidev."

Dumenti replies, "Whatever god has written in your fate, no one can change that. Don't think about it because everyone gets difficulties at some time. Remember that Dasharath (Ram's father in the *Ramayana*) was distressed when his sons were sent into the forest. And Ram, who is head of the gods, was distressed when the demon Ravan kidnapped his wife Sita. So have no fear of this. If you just sit and weep, you will accomplish nothing." Then at midnight, Dumenti wakes Raja Nal and suggests that they leave Narvar. So quietly they steal out of the kingdom. Nal speaks to god, "Oh Bhagvan, you are great. You can do anything. Once I was a king; now I am a beggar. You can change mustard into a mountain in just one second. And you can turn the mountain into a sea."

Then Raja Nal and Dumenti reach Siya Nagar, the kingdom of Mansukh Gujar. Nal and Dumenti go into the garden, and word is carried to Mansukh that they are there, in torn clothes. When Mansukh reaches the garden, Nal explains that Shukra and Shanidev have caused these problems. Mansukh himself weeps and promises that he will feed and clothe Raja Nal and Dumenti. He has food prepared and taken to the royal couple on the roof, but the minute that Mansukh leaves, the food is spoiled. Again they go hungry.

That night Raja Nal and Dumenti are in a room provided by Mansukh when Dumenti notices that the hook on the wall has just swallowed the necklace worth nine lakhs that had been hanging from it. Quickly they slip away, knowing that in the morning they will be accused of stealing the valuable necklace.

Next they go to Raja Nal's sister's place at Ayodhya. Arriving there, they enter the garden. It happens that the Gardener is from Narvar, as he had been included in the dowry of Nal's sister. Phoola Mali[14] recognizes Raja Nal's sword, and asks, "Who are you?" Given their tattered clothes, he does not recognize Raja Nal and Dumenti. Then the Mali touches the feet of Raja Nal and says, "Don't go to your sister yet. There are seven kinds of fruits in my garden. Pass your time here." But as soon as Phoola Mali leaves to tell Nal's sister of her brother's arrival, the garden dries up. Nothing edible is left. The leaves wither. The fruits shrivel.

Now when Raja Nal's sister hears of his arrival, she is very happy, asking, "How many horses are with him? And chariots?" But Phoola Mali tells her that the couple is alone, in torn and dirty clothes. His sister is furious: "When he was wealthy he never came near me. Now that he is a beggar he dares to come!" And she orders a palanquin, gathers up two breads and a small pot of buttermilk, and goes to the garden where she accosts her brother. "You, eat this now and then turn your back on this place." And Nal and Dumenti leave quickly for the jungle.

There in the forest they come upon a beautiful temple built by some unknown king. Once they enter the temple, Shukra and Shanidev cannot follow them. They regain their wits and are comfortable in the temple. But as it grows dark, Dumenti wishes for a light and asks Nal to use the *dīpak* mantra to light a lamp for them. The king in a nearby city sees the lights in the temple and comes there to find out what saint is visiting. He serves them every kind of good food and they eat heartily. But Shukhra and Shanidev are awaiting their chance.

In the morning, when Nal and Dumenti step out of the temple to do their ablutions, Shanidev is waiting. And Shanidev immediately causes them to wander some more. After fifteen days, during the monsoon month of Savan (July–August), they come upon a group of girls who are bathing and singing *malhār* (songs connected symbolically to the month of Savan). The girls invite them to join in their festivities, but Dumenti refuses, saying that they are starving and filthy and that the mood of Savan isn't pleasing. Then, in another month, it is Chait and the farmers are harvesting their fields.[15] Dumenti asks the women working in the field for five stalks of barley for her husband who has had no food. The women laugh and ask her why she is traveling with such a husband. One woman says, "I have four unmarried brothers-in-law. Why don't you come home with me? They aren't like this old man." Then one of the women takes pity on them, and says, "You watch my child, and I'll get food for you." But as soon as she places the child in Dumenti's lap and leaves for her house, the child dies owing to an illusion created by Shanidev. When the woman returns, they quickly hand over the babe and depart. Once they leave, the babe comes back to life.

Later they see fish in a ditch and are able to catch some and make a fire with wood from the jungle. As the fish cook, Raja Nal volunteers to go for water. Immediately the fish jump from the pan into the ditch. When Nal returns, Dumenti claims that she has eaten both fish. On they go. They see two partridges (actually Shukra and Shani in disguise) and manage to catch them and roast them. Now Dumenti goes for water, and the partridges fly from the pot. Raja Nal chases after them and tries to use his dhoti as a net, but the partridges sweep it up and leave him naked. When she returns, Dumenti tears her sari into two and shares it with Raja Nal.

They walk on for another whole year; Chait comes again, and the ground burns their feet. Shanidev thinks, "Who will believe that Raja Nal is in true distress if his wife is still with him?" And he casts a spell on Dumenti. That morning she begs Raja Nal to find water, despite the fact that they are in a dense jungle with no sign of water anywhere. She says, "Husband, if you can't

Figure 2.1. Raja Nal and Dumenti seeking help from women with an infant. Woodcut from a nineteenth-century chapbook, Todarmal 1879, *Nalcaritāmrita arthāt Ḍholāmārū.*

get water, then collect wood for my funeral pyre." So Raja Nal takes his broken pot and goes for water. Dumenti sleeps, and while asleep is carried by Shukra and Shanidev many miles away and left in the bush.

Meanwhile, Raja Nal comes upon a snake with its head pinned to the ground by an arrow while a fire slowly circles in on the spot where the snake is trapped. The snake calls out, "Raja Nal, save me." Raja Nal is perplexed: how does the snake know who he is? And what can he do? The snake goes on, "You are under the curse of Shanidev and your brain is addled, but you have the mantras of water, fire, and light." Nal realizes that this is true and speaks the water mantra which puts out the fire. And then he thinks, "If I have this knowledge, why are my queen and I so thirsty? I could drown us in water!"

Then the snake says, "Now I must bite you and kill you. The arrow which pinned me down was shot by Ajaypal, your maternal grandfather. In revenge I must kill you." At these words, Raja Nal begins to cry and his tears drop on the snake. The snake cries out, "You are not the real Raja Nal. The real Raja Nal would never cry,"

But Raja Nal cries, "I am the real Raja Nal." And he thinks that the honor of seven generations is ruined.

Then the snake says, "Listen carefully. I am your life index. But today I shall bite you because you have sinned. First, your grandfather shot an arrow at me. Second, in the fort of the demon you promised, using Ganges water, that you would not marry again. Motini cursed you that you would become a leper. I will bite you to make you a leper." And the snake bites Nal and then shields him with his hood until Nal regains consciousness. Raja Nal's body is festering, pus oozing from the sores.

The snake sends him in the direction of Amrit Pond, where he bathes and his sores disappear, only to reappear the minute he leaves the pond. Meanwhile, Raja Biram's daughter arrives there and finds the pond contaminated by the leper. She calls her guards and has him jailed in a dried well. There he remains for months and months, until he is able to call upon his dharam bhai (brother by religious vow), Basukdev, and get the snakes to bite the king's children. Each time one is bitten, they need a *baigi* (exorcist) to perform the snake bite curing ritual of Ḍānk and thus cure the child.[16] Only Raja Nal can perform this ritual. In this way Raja Nal eventually earns his freedom and is taken by the sage Narad to Kashipur.

Meanwhile, Dumenti is alone in the forest. She comes upon a caravan of Banjaras (gypsies). Its leader is Lakha Banjara, and he volunteers to care for Dumenti. She makes him swear on five handfuls of Ganges water that he is her father and she the daughter. So she goes with him, but soon discovers that he seeks to marry her by force in spite of the vow he made with Ganges water. Now Dumenti is there in the forest, where there is neither temple nor house nor village nor city. She prays to the gods for help. Narad Muni is instantly ready, as is Durga. Durga's monkey helper sets a fire on all sides of the Banjara camp, and the Banjaras are unable to extinguish it. Then Narad Muni comes disguised as an old Brahman and tells Lakha Banjara that he has sinned, and only when he has touched the feet of that woman (Dumenti) will the fire go out. So the Banjara prays for forgiveness and swears to have nothing more to do with this woman. Narad Muni advises him to take her to her father at Samudsikul.

Raja Bhim is horrified at the return of his daughter, saying that she has shamed his family enormously by being returned alone by gypsies. But she tells of being left alone in the forest, and he forgives her and rules with peace (WA 84:234–237; WA 02:5–14; Shankar Lal 1987).

Dumenti's Second Svayambar (*Dumenti Kā Dusrā Svayambar*)

New Character

Raja Tikam of Kashipur

Narad takes Raja Nal to Kashipur. There Narad goes to the king of that place, Raja Tikam, and says that this man (Raja Nal) who is called Bavariya, the Mad One, is a good chariot driver. You should employ him. Raja Tikam resists but Narad insists, saying that this chariot driver can cover thousands of miles in a short time. All Tikam has to do is to pay him one ser (less than two pounds) of cheap millet a day and leave him alone. Narad also explains a significant problem that will occur: Bavariya will become angry once every six months and will kill twelve thousand people. Tikam starts to tremble on hearing this for, counting himself, there are exactly twelve thousand people in Kashipur! Narad says that as long as Bavariya is left alone and has no conversations or social intercourse with others, they will be protected. So Bavariya begins to live, alone and socially ostracized, in Kashipur.

Raja Bhim is anxious that Dumenti remarry, and she insists again that she be allowed to choose her groom. So once again letters are sent to all the kings on earth and in heaven, including Indra, who thinks, "This time I'll get this woman, for Raja Nal must surely be dead, not having had any grain or water for twelve years." And the kings begin to arrive, with no sign of Raja Nal. Then Dumenti asks her parents if any king has been omitted from the list of invitees, and they realize that Raja Tikam has not been invited. So Dumenti immediately sends a letter to Kashipur, worded thus:

> Oh exalted one who are like Shiva; please maintain our dignity,
> Let me be the one filled with petty weaknesses; you remain as deep and calm as the ocean.
> Oh exalted one who are like Shiva; please maintain our dignity,
> Let me be the one filled with petty weaknesses; you remain as deep and calm as the ocean.
> I am like a poor person now; please make sure that I don't lose my husband,
> They have given it the name of svayambar; when you look at the letter, don't just sit there.
> I will wait for you till four o'clock.

The messenger is sent off on the best camel Raja Bhim owns, and in two to three days reaches Kashipur. Tikam reads the message and at once readies his army. But his generals question him: "You want to go nine hundred *kos* (about five hundred miles) in two to three days? You'll not reach half the distance in that time." And then he remembers Bavariya—he is supposed to be able to travel huge distances in a short time. So he calls Bavariya and says that they must leave immediately. Only three days remain before the svayambar. Bavariya knows that he must act in some way, so he demands to see the horses Tikam has readied. When he sees them, he rejects them right away, and starts his own hunt for horses. Two days later he finds two horses, almost dead, belonging to the Grain Parcher. He buys these horses and takes them to the palace. Tikam is dismayed at his new charioteer. But because he is afraid that Bavariya will kill twelve thousand people, he helps to massage the horses' legs, his finery getting covered in pus and blood. Finally, they sit in the chariot and take off for Samudsikul.

Once they start Bavariya speaks the magical mantra, and the horses fly through the sky. Arriving at the court of Raja Bhim, Bavariya drives the decrepit horses right onto the carpets where Indra is sitting. Narad Muni intercedes and convinces him to put the chariot elsewhere. Bavariya unrolls his blanket and sits quietly, without a care in the world, on a dung heap behind Raja Tikam's chariot. He says this: "What will be is powerful, and what is in one's fate cannot be changed."

Dumenti is fearful that Raja Nal has not arrived, so before she chooses her husband she asks her father to have the assembled kings put to a test. All the fires in the kingdom are to be extinguished, and the kings are to be asked to cook. Raja Bhim does as she asks, and no fire remains in Samudsikul. Then the kings are asked to prepare food. The outcry is overwhelming! None of them can find fire. There is no fire anywhere in the kingdom. Hungry, they complain bitterly. Bavariya asks for some flour and water, and they laugh, "Is he really crazy? Will he eat it raw?" Then he speaks the fire mantra, lights his fire, and cooks his food. Hearing that someone is able to cook, Dumenti is overjoyed, for she knows that Raja Nal is somewhere in her father's court.

As Dumenti leaves to garland her groom, her mother urges her once again to choose a god for a husband. Dumenti doesn't listen. In the court, she looks everywhere for Raja Nal. Finally, she prays to the goddess who shows her where he sits, disguised by the leprosy that has eaten away at his body. To everyone's dismay, Dumenti garlands the crazy leper. And then she and Raja Nal prepare to leave once more, for their twelve years of the aukha of Shanidev are not yet expired and they do not wish to bring disaster to any of their kin (WA 89: 27–29; WA 02:5–14).

The Battle of Bhamartal (*Bhamartāl Kī Laraī*)

New Characters

Raghu (later renamed Raghunandan) the Oil Presser and his wife (Telin)
Raja Budh Singh of Marwar (or Pingul)

It is again the month of Chait (April–May), and the hot sun burns the ground and Dumenti's bare feet. Slowly the old leper and his companion move through the forest. One day on the forest path they come across an Oil Presser rushing to a nearby village where he hopes to sell mustard oil. His wife is a very domineering woman and has ordered him to sell some oil that day or else! He knows that if he comes back with nothing sold, she will refuse to feed him. And if he is even an ounce short, if what he earned doesn't equal what he has taken in oil that morning, she will beat him with a pan. So he is quite reluctant to stop when Dumenti calls out to him. "Please Oil Presser, can you spare a few drops of oil for this poor leper?"

Raghu, the Oil Presser, refuses, wanting only to get on with his sales. But Dumenti persists, so he finally gives a small handful of oil to spread on the sores of the leper. Then he goes on to a village where he unsuccessfully had tried to sell oil for several years. And he sells oil at every house. The money piles up, but the pot of oil remains full! At the end of the day Raghu returns to his village with his full pot of oil and his turban piled high with coins. Arriving at his hut, he discovers that his wife is visiting elsewhere, so he leaves the full pot of oil and the money tied in his turban on a cot where she will find it. Then he goes to seek her out.

The Telin (a female Oil Presser) returns from another direction and finds the full pot of oil and the many coins. Anger burns in her! "That sister fucker,[17] he has now taken up gambling!" She grabs a nearby pot to clobber him when he returns. Eventually Raghu returns and his wife raises the pot to beat him, when he whines, "No, look at what I earned today."

"What you earned," she scoffs. "What you won gambling!" Raghu is eventually able to tell her the story of the leper whom he had met on the road in the forest that morning and of his successful sales all day. But his wife is angry yet again. "What, you left the Baba (holy man) in the forest? You didn't bring him home with you? Hurry, we must find them." And she drags her husband into the forest to show her where he had met the Baba and the woman.

Luckily Raja Nal and Dumenti had not traveled far, and Raghu and his wife soon find them in the forest. The Telin presses them to come to their home. Raja Nal is reluctant, for, after all, he is a Kshatriya. How can he live with Oil Pressers? How would they eat? They couldn't take food from such a low caste. But Dumenti, tired and worn and burned by the sun, is anxious to accept the Oil Pressers' invitation, so he finally agrees. They follow the Oil Pressers back to their village. Shanidev and Shukhra watch these events with despair, for once Raja Nal enters the Oil Presser's hut, Shani's power will be offset by the mustard oil to which he is allergic. They even disguise themselves as policemen and try to grab Raja Nal before he enters the Oil Presser's gate, but the strong Telin pushes them off and shoves her guests inside.

Once at the Oil Presser's, Raja Nal hangs his sword on a hook. Raghu asks him to begin pressing oil, while the Telin gives Dumenti a winnowing basket and a pile of oil seeds to clean. The Telin is amazed when Dumenti cannot perform this task, wondering what kind of mother she had had who had taught her nothing useful! She thinks that Dumenti must be of a very low caste.

That night Raja Nal presses all the mustard seed in the hut. A whole year's worth in one night. Quickly Raghu becomes wealthy. He soon owns 360 oil presses, as well as horses, elephants, and camels. He builds a house as lavish as a palace and has as much wealth as the king.

Now the king of that place is Raja Budh Singh. He is well aware of the wealth that the Oil Presser has amassed and knows that one day he will have to acknowledge it. Finally, he decides to celebrate his son's sacred thread ceremony, and he invites the fifty-two kings to the ceremony. He also invites Raghu, now called Raghunandan in honor of his new prestige, and all his employees. Only Raja Nal is left out of the invitation. When reminded that an old man also worked for the Oil Presser, Budh says that he is unimportant.

On the day of the ceremony, Raghunandan is warmly greeted by Raja Budh and given a seat of honor on a stool in the center of the court. The other fifty-two kings wonder who is being honored in such a way, as they sit on carpets on the floor. Raja Budh has warned his family not to say anything about the Oil Presser, for it would bring dishonor to his family if the fifty-two kings discover that he recognizes a mere Oil Presser in such a fashion. Then the entertainment begins, and Raghunandan's followers are lavish in giving donations to the singers and dancers. Acknowledging the donor in song, the dancing girls identify Raghunandan as an Oil Presser, horrifying the assembled kings who immediately leave the court, dishonored.

Meanwhile, since everyone else is at the feast, Raja Nal is left to take the 720 bullocks that run Raghunandan's 360 oil presses to Bhamartal for water. Angry at the insult of not being invited to the king's feast, he lets the bullocks run wild in the pond, churning up the mud. The 700 guards who are left fight with Raja Nal, until only two are alive. Nal takes an iron rod, ties it around their necks, and returns to the oil press.

When Budh discovers what has happened at Bhamartal, he is outraged. But first he has to free his two soldiers. No one is strong enough to unbend the iron rod. Finally, it is suggested that the Oil Presser's servant can free them. Raja Nal returns to the pond and faces a dilemma. If he bends down to untwist the rod, he will bow his head to his rival kings. So he kicks the rod and unbends it that way, saving his honor. Now Raja Budh is amazed: who is this servant of the Oil Presser? He creates a test: to shoot an arrow at a fish from 450 paces. Raja Nal easily shoots the fish, but the other kings all swear that it was their arrow, not his. So Raja Nal shoots an arrow at 700 paces. Budh is still unwilling to accept him as a king. So with his Oil Presser friends, Raja Nal returns to the press.

Then Raja Budh calls Raghunandan to court for gambling. Raghunandan is fearful, for he is a man of low caste and only Kshatriyas know gambling. Budh very cleverly tells the Oil Presser that he'll teach him to gamble and that at the beginning they won't make any serious bets. Budh slowly teaches him, always letting him win. Then one day he announces that they can now gamble for real stakes. In just one day Raja Budh wins all the oil presses, the bullocks, the horses, and the elephants. Nothing remained. Raghunandan returns to the oil press that night sorrowful, ready to flee the kingdom immediately. But Raja Nal entreats him to stay one more day, to use the cowry shells that Raja Nal will give him, and to bet his Telin. "He will need your Telin," Raja Nal proclaims, "none of his queens can press oil."

Returning to court the next day, Raghunandan does as Raja Nal suggested. And he wins. As he rolls the shells a second time he speaks Raja Nal's name aloud, and Budh Singh grabs his wrist: "What did you say?" Then Budh insists that Raja Nal come to gamble. Raja Nal goes to the court, and the two kings bet on the unborn child in each of their wives' wombs. Whoever has a daughter will marry her to the son born to the other[18] (WA 94:243–245; 89:30–32; 90:1–2; Shankar Lal 1987).

Battle of Phul Bagh (*Phūl Bāg Kī Laṛāī*)

New Characters

Dhola, infant son of Raja Nal and Dumenti
Maru, newborn daughter of Raja Budh Singh

Both Raja Nal and Raja Budh return to their wives and threaten that they must have a son. Neither wants to accept the demeaning role of having to give a daughter to the other. At midnight Dumenti gives birth to a son, Dhola. And Budh's queen delivers a girl, Maru. Budh is dismayed and forbids any announcement in his kingdom. Meanwhile, Behmata, the Goddess of Fate, has *satiyā,* the auspicious symbol used to mark the birth of a son, put on every house in the city in honor of Dhola's birth

Raja Nal sends a messenger to Raja Budh asking that a date be set for the engagement and marriage rituals, but Budh only responds with yet more tests for Raja Nal. Most important, he must press 360 maunds of mustard oil in one night and fill a tank at Budh's palace. Raja Nal quickly organizes a tank to be built and a pipeline run from the press to the palace. That night the tank is filled with oil (WA 90:3–4).

The Battle of Lakhiyaban (*Lakhiyābān Kī Laṛāī*)

New Characters

Bhil "tribals"
Chudaman, the leader of the demons inhabiting Lakhiyaban
Pushkar Sultan, Brother of Raja Nal

Figure 2.2. Raja Nal fighting the demons in the forest of Lakhiyaban. Woodcut from a nineteenth-century chapbook, Todarmal 1879, *Nalcaritāmrita arthāt Ḍholāmārū.*

Next Raja Nal must bring black sugarcane from the forest of Lakhiyaban. This is a more daunting task than the first, as the forest is guarded by Bhil tribals and demons. Going alone, Raja Nal mounts his magical flying horse and sets off for the forest. Arriving there, he is warmly greeted by the Bhil tribal girls who sit him on a cot and bring him water. He watches as they put fresh layers of cow dung on their houses and prepare for some festivity. One girl, very enamored of this handsome king, whispers that the preparations are in his honor, for they intend to kill and eat him. Raja Nal is dumbstruck. But he calls upon Durga, who comes with her troops of ghosts and goblins and sets fire to the Bhil camp. Raja Nal mounts his horse, and they move deeper into the forest.

There he finds the demons led by Chudaman, a relative of Bhumasur. When he battles the demons, every drop of blood turns into still more demons. Durga runs off, saying, "This is out of my control: I kill one demon and one thousand more are born."

Only Motini is able to help Nal. Knowing that every drop of blood produces another demon, she tells Nal not to fight with his sword. The demons attack by throwing stones, and stones pile up around Nal and his horse. The sun sets, and so the demons say, "Fine, we'll get him out in the morning." At midnight Motini comes and frees her husband, and says, "Quickly, get some sugarcane and mount your horse." But Nal refuses to steal the needed sugarcane even though Motini again begs him to leave.

When the sun rises the demons search for Nal but become scared:

thousands of pounds of rocks have buried him, but he is not there! Then they find Nal and start throwing stones once again, and Motini makes an umbrella of bamboo over Nal and the horse. Once again, by sunset, they are buried. And again Motini frees them in the night. Motini says, "Mother Durga will return, and then we'll burn them alive." Durga comes and says that she will fight again, or no one will worship her as their savior. So a great war is fought in Lakhiya forest. Nal kills the guards one by one, while Motini flies overhead. The yogis run around the battlefield licking every drop of blood that falls so that the demons cannot regenerate from the drops of blood. Nal wins the battle and has the sugarcane cut. Then he orders the twelve thousand demons to carry the sugarcane to Marwar. In a few days, they reach the town of the Bhils, and the Bhils join in helping to carry the sugarcane.

Now at the edge of the Bhil town, a cow gives birth to a calf and one of the demons picks up the calf and eats it. The cow struggles to her feet and moos loudly, and Raja Nal comes and finds her. The cow says, "Someone has brought demons here, and I was licking my newborn calf when a demon ate it." Nal is enraged, and says, "I'll kill all twelve thousand right now!" And he flies to the front of the line of demons and demands to know who ate the calf. The demons say, "It is someone back there, someone back in the line. Chudaman Demon ate the calf." So Raja Nal comes face to face with Chudaman, and says, "Double his load." The demon cries that his legs are already wobbly, but Raja Nal replies, "If you are so wobbly, how did you eat the calf?" Then the demon laments that his sister, Motini, has destroyed Lakhiya forest.

Raja Nal brings the demons to Marwar where he tells the residents to feed them fodder, a real insult as it is not good food. Eventually the demons, with their loads of sugarcane, reach a river they must cross to get to the fort, but there is no bridge. So Raja Nal has four demons lie down in the river, head to foot to head, and turns them into a bridge the others can walk across. Reaching town at midnight, they unload the sugarcane in front of every door, causing the men of the city to fall over it and bang their heads as they exit their houses in the early morning to urinate.[19] This is the day of Deothan, a ritual that takes place near the beginning of the late fall harvesting of sugarcane, and the worship of sugarcane on Deothan is said to have started when Raja Nal brought sugarcane from Lakhiyaban.[20]

The Oil Pressers are ready for the *bārāt,* the marriage procession of Dhola. Budh laments the fate of his beautiful daughter, who must now go to live in an Oil Presser's house with this foreigner. While the Oil Pressers rejoice in the wedding, Budh's court is filled with sadness. Raja Nal says to Budh, "My problems are now over. Tomorrow I'll go back to my own country." Then Budh performs the *kanyādān.* And thus Dhola gets married.

Raja Nal has one more job. He calls Budh and tells him to destroy the gate to his own castle, that a new one must be built. And the twelve thousand demons stand around demanding to return to Lakhiyaban. Raja Nal becomes angry and speaks to their leader: "In the Bhil town you ate the calf. In exchange for the calf, I am having you killed." Chudaman demon grabs Nal's feet and prays for his sins to be forgiven, saying that his wife will be crying in Lakhiyaban. Nal replies, "And the cow whose calf was eaten is also crying." So they cement the demon into the new gate that marks the main entrance to the fortress. As he is entombed, Chudaman says, "You brave one, what you seek will be. And if I am truly a demon, I will also not falter in my actions. Do what you want (i.e., kill me). Today my wife will cry in Lakhiyaban. And today your son will be married. But remember that a day will come when you will both cry because of me. I will kill him at this very door, and your seed will not survive."

Then the Oil Presser apologizes for not recognizing that his helper was Raja Nal. Raja Nal replies that he should not worry, that he has been like a brother or father and that he was treated well. Then Raja Nal departs for Narvar. At the edge of Marwar, he is met by Mansukh Gujar who has brought an army to accompany Raja Nal, Dumenti, and Dhola. Meanwhile, Raja Nal's brother, Pushkar Sultan, hears that he must return the kingdom to Raja Nal. Pushkar angrily says, "How can I return it now? I have had it for twelve years while he worked in an oil press. The kingdom is mine now." But Mansukh explains that he will have to return it (WA 68:11; 89:37–39; 90:5–6, 10, 11, 17–19; 02: 6–14).

The Battle with Vir Singh (*Vīr Singh Kī Laṛāī*)

New Character

Raja Vir Singh, a very religious man

Meanwhile, Dumenti wants to bathe in the Ganges at Banaras because her body has been polluted by living with the Oil Pressers. So they go to Banaras. On the way they see numerous bad omens. Dumenti wants to heed the omens and not proceed, but Raja Nal insists they go on, saying, "You wanted a bath. Now I am taking you for one."

When they reach Banaras, Raja Nal calls a Pandit to read the astrological chart. The Pandit says that they are leaving a period of bad times only to enter another. Dumenti again begs Nal not to stay in Banaras, but again he refuses. They prepare a shelter and Nal asks Dumenti to nurse her son before taking her bath.

Raja Vir Singh, who bathes daily at the Ganges, is also bathing at that time. He sits on a sandalwood stool and has his holy beads with him. He is an extremely religious man. The queen with the babe in her lap is in the shelter when the wind blows the curtains back. On hearing the queen's laughter and seeing her, Vir Singh loses control. The image of Dumenti sticks in his heart. He thinks, "If I do not get this woman, I will give up my life here at the Ganges." Five heavenly nymphs come to aid him, saying, "Oh son, you have lost your head." They hold his hand, trying to get him to cool off, and tell him that his whole life and family will be destroyed by trying to get Dumenti. But he replies, "Even if the whole world gives me ill will, today I will become engaged to this queen. I am no longer a worshiper of the Ganges."

The heavenly nymphs continue to say that Raja Nal is very powerful, that he has the blessing of Durga and the help of Motini. Motini is older than the nymphs, and they will not be able to help Vir Singh against her. But he still doesn't listen, and instead sends for a chariot in which to steal the queen.

Raja Nal, concerned about the inauspicious omens and the possibility of a crocodile attacking her, makes arrangements for Dumenti to bathe, asking that an iron curtain be set into the Ganges and that twelve soldiers guard her bathing cubicle. But after Dumenti nurses her son, goes to the Ganges, and offers holy Ganges water to the sun, to her god, and to her husband, the heavenly nymphs come, put her to sleep, lift her out of the bathing cubicle, and fly off with her to the city of Bangamgarh. Dumenti is taken to the palace of glass, and Vir Singh is told not to touch her sleeping body, for if he does she will curse him and burn him to ashes.

When Raja Nal discovers that Dumenti is missing, he cries loudly, worried that his son will die of starvation. The flying horse consoles him, saying that if Dumenti is in any of the three worlds, he will find her. The infant Dhola is left with a baba, who eventually throws him into a garbage pile, as he has no food for him.

When Dumenti awakes, she calls upon her older co-wife Motini to save her from Vir Singh, and Motini succeeds after fighting the magic of others as in the Battle of Phul Singh Panjabi. With some difficulty, they also retrieve Dhola from the garbage pit where the baba had thrown him (WA 02:5–10; WA 94: 22–27).

The Marriage of Kishan Lal (*Kiśanlāl Kā Byāh*)

New Characters

Kishanlal, Raja Nal's nephew
Raja Chandrapal of Shankaldeep, Kishanlal's future father-in-law
Chandrakala, Kishanlal's bride-to-be
Two Oil Presser girls
Chandi, a goddess, often ferocious

The women of Ajaypal, Raja Nal's mother's natal home, now a kingdom without men
Gendwati, daughter of Raja Karampal of Bengal

The family then returns to Narvar, where Raja Nal regains his throne. When Dhola is about five, the marriage of his cousin, Kishanlal, is planned. Kishanlal is to be married into a kingdom where all the men have died and thus all the queens are barren. The emissary seeking a groom for one of the princesses there is told that Raja Nal will heed his request for a groom. Dhola begs to be allowed to go along in the marriage procession, so Raja Nal and Mansukh take the two boys and a large retinue of soldiers to the eastern kingdom of Raja Chandrapal to marry Chandrakala of Shankaldeep.

The army moves rapidly through the forests of Bihar, filled with thorns and thick bamboo. On the same road are two young Oil Presser women who have been married and widowed. Desiring to marry the two boys, the Oil Presser girls use their magic to put the army to sleep and to steal Kishanlal and Dhola as they sleep that night. When Kishanlal fights the girls to regain his freedom, they turn him into a black-eyed ox and make the young Dhola a parrot. Early in the morning they meet a Potter out searching for cow dung cakes for his kiln. He urges them to return the two crying boys, saying, "Girls, leave both boys, their parents will die of grief, and you will have sinned enormously." Angry, the two girls use magic to turn him into a donkey and tie his leg to his own donkey's leg. Then they move quickly to the Chandi temple.

Chandi tells the girls that she can't help them, that the goddesses Durga and Sharda always fight with Raja Nal and she cannot win a battle against them. She also acknowledges that she is hungry for a human sacrifice (*bali*), so she offers to take one boy as a sacrifice and let the girls keep the other. But the two Oil Presser girls reject that plan, for which one of them would have a groom?

Back in the forest the army awakes, and Raja Nal and Mansukh learn that the two boys are missing. Searching for the boys, they come across the Potter who tells them that the Oil Presser girls kidnapped them and took them to Chandi. So Raja Nal and Mansukh follow them to the Chandi temple, where Raja Nal catches hold of the feet of the goddess. Chandi says that she will take one of the boys and give the other to Raja Nal. Then Raja Nal faces an insurmountable quandary: if he offers his nephew Kishanlal, he will face enormous shame and dishonor. But if he offers his son, his lineage will end. At this, Mansukh steps in and says that he will sacrifice his son of fifteen days. So Raja Nal asks his horse to please take Mansukh to Siya Nagar, but the horse refuses, saying that he can only be ridden by Indra and Raja Nal. Nal eventually persuades the horse to accept Mansukh for just this one day. And Mansukh immediately departs for Siya Nagar to get his son and bring him back.

When he returns, Raja Nal refuses to make the sacrifice, so Mansukh himself starts to cut the neck of Nal's son. Then Raja Nal calls on Durga and Motini, who both come to his rescue. Durga says, "I will not leave you in any condition to ask for sacrifice during this time of Kaliyug." And with the help of Motini the temple is destroyed, and Chandi is kicked into the underworld.

They search again for the two boys. Motini finds them in the house of the Oil Pressers. Blindfolded and turned into an ox, Kishanlal is circling the oil press while Dhola is in a cage. Motini then chooses to become a Bangle Seller (manihar) in order to gain access to the house. Preparing a basket of beautiful bangles, she enters the house and uses her magic to free the boys and turn the two girls into bitches. Once she has freed the boys, she takes them to the Potter's and there rubs ash over their bodies, transforming them into religious disciples, while she becomes a female sadhu. When the townspeople come to see the unusual sadhu, she turns them all into dogs and donkeys. Then they return to Nal's army.

Eight days later they reach the border of Ajaynagar. Nal is very confused, for looking at Ajaynagar he thinks he has returned to Narvar, despite having been on the road for sixteen days. The shape of the two forts is identical. Then Mansukh realizes that the flags of the fort are different, and they enter the garden. The female Gardener is worried, for earlier the Raja of Bengal had taken all the men of Ajaynagar. Had the wicked Bengalis returned? But Raja Nal assures her that they mean no harm and have not taken anything from her garden. When they reach the market, they find it is empty. Nothing is being sold for there are no men left. The ladies in the palace weep upon seeing them, convinced that the Raja of Bengal has returned. When Raja Nal speaks to an old lady by the gate of the palace, she cries, "You fool. First you imprison my sons. Now you have come for the ladies!"

Raja Nal assures her that they are not from Bengal and asks about her sons, who are named as yogis: Sarbhang, Kishanbhang, and Ratibhang.[21] The three boys had tried to kidnap Surajbhati, daughter of Raja Karampal of Bengal. After winning the first three battles against Karampal, the Raja from Bengal called on his daughter Gendwati to use her magic against them. Immediately every male in the kingdom disappeared, including those in women's wombs. Then the old woman goes on to say that she had a daughter named Manjha who was married to Raja Pratham at Narvar, who had her killed in the forest. Astounded, Raja Nal assures her that Manjha had not died and that he is her very son. But she does not believe him. Fortunately there is a lock in the fort that only the son of Manjha can open. So Nal is taken to the gate, touches the lock, and opens it. The old woman embraces him warmly.

Then Raja Nal convinces Mansukh that they should free the men taken to

Bengal before continuing with the marriage of Kishanlal. So Raja Nal, Mansukh, and Kishanlal leave for Bengal, after convincing Nal's horse to carry all three of them. The young Dhola is left with his maternal grandmother, who is given instructions to take him to Narvar when he reaches the age of eleven.

Arriving in Bengal, they first meet a Potter who tells them that the daughter of the king is eighteen years old and unmarried. When asked why such an old girl is unmarried, the Potter replies that she wanted three husbands: first, the player of a flute in Braj (Krishna); second, the drinker of *bhāng* (marijuana) from the high mountains (Shiva); and third, the brave son of Manjha who had won many battles, that is, Nal himself.

Nal decides to investigate. Leaving Kishanlal and Mansukh at the edge of the forest, he flies into the city where he finds Gendwati on the roof of the palace. There he reveals his identity but tells her that he will not marry her: in fact, he has come to avenge his maternal family. So Gendwati turns him into a parrot and locks him in an iron cage.

When Nal does not return, Mansukh leaves to find him, reminding Kishanlal that the city is filled with magicians. Mansukh himself is captured by an Oil Presser woman and turned into a black bullock. When he doesn't return, Kishanlal enters the garden of the fort. There he meets a Malin (female Gardener) who agrees to buy him food in the market if he will make the garland that she must give to the king's daughter that evening. Poor Kishanlal: he has no idea how to make a garland, so he calls on Motini who comes and makes the most beautiful garland imaginable, filled with gold coins from Narvar, diamonds, and pearls. When Gendwati demands to know where coins marked with "Nal" had come from, the Malin claims that her daughter-in-law had come from Narvar and brought them. Ordered to produce this daughter-in-law, the Malin returns to the garden where Kishanlal waits. There she turns the sixteen-year-old Kishanlal into a beautiful bride, with lampblack on his eyes and rings on his fingers, and takes him to Gendwati. When they arrive at Gendwati's rooftop dwelling, Gendwati orders Kishanlal to take a less prestigious seat, while she takes the more honored seat. Furious, Kishanlal manages to get an honored seat. Then she wants to shake hands with the daughter-in-law, so the Malin urges him to be gentle with his handshake. Even then, when he takes Gendwati's hand, he crushes her to the ground. Gendwati is outraged, but the bahu assures her that the "bride's" strength comes from grazing her father's cattle with the shepherds. The Malin is very concerned, and thinks, "It is very difficult to tell lies without being found out!" Then she leaves Kishanlal there for the night.

From his cage Nal chastises Kishanlal: "The honor of Narvar is destroyed! Why have you become a woman?" Later, on discovering his real identity,

Gendwati turns him into a donkey. Again Raja Nal cries out from his cage: "Now I am truly dishonored. My mustache is shaven. You arrived here a woman and now you are a donkey."

Eventually Motini arrives to save all three: Kishanlal, Mansukh, and Raja Nal defeat Gendwati and return to Ajaypal, bringing with them the missing menfolk. Kishanlal once more sets off to marry Chandrakala.

After the men return to Ajaynagar, Raja Nal seeks the help of his māmā (mother's brother) and nānā (mother's father) in leading the marriage procession. The marriage procession moves into a dense forest, where those at the front see a demon's small platform. Scared, they all move back, but Raja Nal proceeds ahead to battle the demons. As he successfully battles them, the demons become very scared; they begin throwing rocks and threaten to eat the whole marriage procession.

Raja Nal then calls on Motini, who exclaims, "These demons never cease to trouble us!" And she turns herself into Raja Nal's shield. When the demons see Motini standing before Raja Nal, they cry out, "Sister, you are our sister. Why the hell are you so determined to destroy our family? We have already had to abandon Lakhiyaban."

Motini responds, "If you are my relatives, then why are you hurting my people." But the demons respond that they could never cooperate with humans. And so Raja Nal destroys them. He then has the demons clear the forest until they approach the territory of a fierce demon named Chugal. The demons realize that only Chugal can free them, so they demand that Raja Nal fight him. After three days Raja Nal and Chugal are still battling. Motini arrives and, using her magic, quickly destroys the demon. The demons who instigated the battle are required to clear the forest by uprooting the trees with their hands. In this way, Baguri forest is cleared.

They then come to Gukharu, an even denser forest. Unable to penetrate it, Raja Nal has the demons lie on top of the forest, and the marriage procession crosses Gukharu on the path of demon bodies. Then they reach a marsh. When Mansukh puts his foot in it, he sinks immediately. Kishanlal is able to save Mansukh, only almost to lose his own life. So Raja Nal makes a bridge over the swamp with the demons. Some sink, but others survive. In this way, they cross the swamp on the demon bridge. Then the marriage procession arrives at Sankal Island.

A lion guards the island, and Kishanlal successfully defeats it. Another test follows. The bridegroom has to stand in boiling oil and shoot an arrow at a fish overhead. With Motini's help, Kishanlal succeeds. So Kishanlal is married to Chandrakala, and the marriage party begins its return trip to Narvar (WA 68:13; 85:306–308; 02:7–14).

The Marriage of Rewa (*Rewā Kā Byāh*)

New Characters

Raja Mal of Malwa, a Gardener by caste
Rewa, daughter of Raja Mal

As the marriage procession returns to Narvar, those in the procession stop for a night in Malwa, where Raja Mal, a Gardener, lives with his daughter Rewa. When Rewa hears that Dhola is in the garden, she captures him with her magic, turns him into a parrot, and locks him in a cage. When Raja Nal realizes his son is missing, he and Mansukh both assume the disguise of a sage and search the city for him. Eventually they find him in Rewa's cage and call upon Motini to free him. Motini once more becomes a Bangle Seller and goes to Rewa's palace to sell her bangles. Motini is able to talk Rewa into transforming Dhola into a man, on the grounds that she will ask Raja Nal if Rewa can marry Dhola. Motini returns to the camp with Dhola, and they send a formal marriage proposal to Raja Mal. But Raja Mal thinks that his daughter is being forced to marry and wages a battle against Raja Nal. As Raja Mal asks his daughter for her magic to defeat Raja Nal, she replies, "But Father, I want this marriage. I want to marry Dhola, and it would be best if you accept a truce and let us marry."

So Dhola and Rewa are married, the ceremonies lasting a week. Raja Nal is very happy with the gifts and arrangements, and decides not to tell Dhola of his first marriage to Maru, for he knows that the demon Chudaman waits in the gate of her father's kingdom to fall on Dhola when he goes to collect his bride (WA 02:6–14).

Maru's Marriage Fulfilled (*Mārū Kā Gaunā*)

New Characters

Pavan, the flying camel that was included in Maru's dowry; the camel returns daily to Marwar to graze, returning to Narvar every night
Pareba of Mundnagar, sister of Rewa
Taro, sister of Maru
Bharamal, husband of Taro
Raja Ved Singh of Vityagarh
Virmati, daughter of Ved Singh

When Rewa and Dhola return to Narvar, Dumenti tells the new bride to keep her husband intoxicated and always nearby so that he will not hear of his first wedding and leave for Marwar, where the curse on the grooms of

Maru will cause the fort's gate to fall on him. Jealous of her co-wife, Rewa watches Dhola constantly. He cannot pee or shit in private. When he sleeps he is tied to the bed, and Rewa puts his little finger in her mouth so that she will know if he tries to escape. She also destroys most of the animals in the stable, keeping only a few that appear too weak to be mounts if Dhola should try to leave.

In Marwar, Maru laments the fact that everyone but her has a husband. Then she dreams of a beautiful young man sleeping beside her.[22] She asks her mother to tell her to whom she is married. Her mother tells her of Dhola and explains that her gaunā, the consummation of her marriage, never took place. She adds that Dhola would be in danger if he tried to enter the fort. Moreover, she says, he has married a second time. But Maru, in love with the figure in her dream, seeks her groom. She decorates her favorite parrot with gold bands and jewels, and ties a message to Dhola on the parrot and sends it to Narvar, where unfortunately it is caught by Dhola's second wife, Rewa, and imprisoned. But the parrot eventually manages to give Dhola the message, and he is determined to escape to Marwar.

By carving a wooden finger out of wood and putting the wooden finger in Rewa's mouth, and also not drinking the sleeping potion given to him nightly, Dhola is able to escape. Leaving in the middle of the night, Dhola enters the stable to find most of the animals either dead or sick. Only the camel that was part of Maru's dowry remains. It had escaped Rewa's curse, because it flew to Marwar every day to graze and then flew back at night to shit in Narvar. So Dhola and Pavan (the flying camel), along with Maru's parrot, fly toward Marwar. Just as they make their escape, Rewa awakens and, turning herself into a bird, flies after them.

On the way to Marwar, Rewa, using her magic, creates a garden laden with fruits. Glimpsing this beautiful spot, Dhola wants to stop because he is hungry. The camel replies angrily, "Damn it, because of your hunger both of us will die. I travel this road daily, and I have never seen this garden before. Sister fucker, this is an illusion." So they don't stop.

Then they come to the village of Mundnagar where Pareba, Rewa's sister, lives. She is filling her pitcher at the well, and Dhola wants to stop there as he is thirsty. The camel resists, saying that every minute is urgent and that once they reach the Singh River they can stop, for Rewa's magic does not extend beyond that boundary. But Dhola persists, so they stop at the well. Pareba quickly realizes that Dhola has left her sister and tries unsuccessfully to detain him. Shortly after Dhola flies off, Rewa arrives, and both sisters join the pursuit. They catch up with the threesome at the Singh River, just in time to grab the camel's tail. The sisters' magic is very powerful, and slowly they begin to pull the camel back. The camel urges Dhola to take out his sword

Figure 2.3. Dhola, son of Raja Nal, meeting his bride Maru in the garden of her father's kingdom. Dhola is accompanied by the flying camel and parrot. Woodcut from a nineteenth-century chapbook, Todarmal 1879, *Nalcaritāmrita arthāt Ḍholāmārū.*

and cut off his tail. Finally agreeing, Dhola frees them in this way. And that is why camels have short tails.

Eventually Dhola and the camel arrive in the garden outside the fort at Marwar. The daughter of the gardener runs to the palace to tell Maru that Dhola has come. But he must be tested, for many other suitors have claimed to be Dhola.

Maru's younger sister Taro is enormously jealous and is herself married to a man named Bharamal, who has only one eye and one arm. She rushes to the garden to meet Dhola, hoping to convince him that she is Maru, but he sees through her deception. Maru sends her servant women, all dressed beautifully, to test Dhola, but with the help of the parrot he recognizes each one (a Merchant's wife, a Watercarrier, a Gardener, etc.) and rejects them. Maru finally goes to meet her husband, and with the parrot's help he recognizes her. Dhola then challenges Maru to give him water in a vessel made of raw thread in order to demonstrate her truth and virtue. Maru fashions a vessel of wheat stalks and thread that holds water from the well in the garden.

Then Maru and Dhola have to make a plan to enter the palace, for the demon Chudaman is waiting to take revenge on the son of Raja Nal. Dhola tries in many different ways to pass through the gate, but when he tries to fly over it the gate goes upward and when he tries to go under it, it goes down.

Figure 2.4. The Gate of Budh Singh falling on Dhola as he enters the fort to claim his bride Maru. Woodcut from a nineteenth-century chapbook, Todarmal 1879, *Nalcaritāmrita arthāt Ḍholāmārū.*

Finally, Maru calls on Durga who comes with many gods, and an uninvited Indra who hopes to see his enemy defeated. Each of the gods grabs a corner of the gate, and Indra takes a corner, too. As Dhola enters the gate Indra drops his section, but Dhola reaches the courtyard safely.

The husband of Taro is furious that Dhola has succeeded and sends Dhola to kill a crocodile, which he does when Durga empties the pond where the crocodile is living, making it easy for Dhola to kill it.

Then Raja Budh Singh and Bharamal say that Dhola has to get black cow dung from the Kajari forest and clothes from a girl named Hariyal before they can do the consummation ceremony. Dhola prepares to undertake these tasks.

Meanwhile, back in Narvar, Dumenti is very worried, for Dhola has not yet returned. She reminds Raja Nal that although these ceremonies used to take many days, now they only occupy one day so Dhola should have returned by now with his bride. So Raja Nal sends a spy to find out what has happened. On the way to Marwar the spy comes to Vityagarh, the kingdom of Raja Ved Singh. Ved Singh is very arrogant and also quite skilled in magic. Every day at 5 P.M. he asks his subjects if there is a king anywhere in the world who is comparable to him. And they all respond, "There is no king comparable to you anywhere." But when the spy hears this, he is troubled. Then someone notices the stranger in the court and insists that he, too, respond. Eventually the spy says, "Listen, kings like you come and polish the shoes of my king every day. And regarding queens: there is only one, Dumenti. The rest are donkeys. Even Indra came to earth to win her."

Upon hearing this, Raja Ved Singh is inflamed! He sends five men to Narvar to kidnap the queen that night, and the next day he puts her on the auction block in his garden. Sweepers, pimps, Potters, and Washermen all come to bid for the queen. At the very same time Dhola is going to get the black cow dung. On hearing the commotion, he stops and finds his mother on the auction block! He battles with Ved Singh, only to be turned into stone by Ved Singh's daughter, Virmati. Only the parrot escapes to Narvar to call Raja Nal, who comes with his army and that of Mansukh to reclaim his wife and son. Eventually the battle is between Virmati and Motini, with the latter's magic ultimately defeating Raja Ved Singh (WA 02:6–14).

The Battle of Kajariban (*Kajaribān Kī Laṛāī*)

New Character

Hariyal, a daughter of jinns, inauspicious powerful spirits, who is in love with Raja Nal

Taro's husband Bharamal wants to send Dhola for black cow dung, as he knows that the forest of Kajari is guarded by demons. After the battle with Ved Singh, Raja Nal himself agrees to go to Kajariban. There he is greeted warmly by the Bhils and is quite happy, until a girl tells him that he is being prepared to be eaten. So he calls on Motini for help. She sets fire to Bhil Nagari, and Raja Nal escapes to Kajari forest. There Durga helps him to imprison the demons and to get them to carry the black cow dung back to Marwar.

Bharamal is dismayed to see the demons bringing back the cow dung. But he has one more plan. He sends Dhola to get the clothes of the daughter Hariyal. He finds her palace and her room, with the bed decorated in flowers. Tired, he falls asleep there and is guarded by his friend Shesh Nag. But the king's daughter is able to turn him into a parrot and lock him in a cage. So once again Raja Nal comes to his rescue.

On his way to Hariyal, Raja Nal comes upon the kingdom of Raja Keshav of Kishavgarh, whose daughter Keshvani had been devoted to Lord Shiva in order to marry Raja Nal. She eventually is able to capture Raja Nal, who calls on Motini for help.

This time Motini comes and transforms herself into a handsome boy sitting at the well. The women of the town convince Keshvani to marry the boy, who says that he is the younger brother of Raja Nal. But he will marry only if all the women of the town attend the wedding. When they come, Motini turns them all into bitches and sends them back into the town. Then the villagers beg Motini to give them back their women, which she agrees to do only when Raja Nal is returned to his true form.

But Dhola is still in trouble, so Raja Nal calls on Motini one more time. By turning all the inhabitants of the land into donkeys, Motini is able to get Dhola released.

Budh Singh eventually realizes that Dhola's valor adds to his family name and calls him to the palace. All the women of the city are happy, for the king had stopped the custom of gauna (ceremony of a bride's first departure with her husband leading to the consummation of the marriage) until Maru had her gauna, and thus many girls in Marwar who had remained unmarried or were married but unable to join their husbands can now do so. They prepare to send Maru to Narvar, even though a priest predicts that great tragedy will occur.

As Dhola and Maru fly through the sky on the camel, she begs for water. Seeing a well, Dhola goes to get water. Near the well stands a woman with mysterious powers. Giving her a drink, Dhola is caught in her illusion and falls into a stupor. Meanwhile an eagle drops a snake into Maru's lap. When Dhola finally regains his senses, he finds his beloved in dreadful agony, bitten by Basukdev, the snake king. Shepherd boys help Dhola to build a funeral pyre for Dhola and his bride, for he is determined to die with Maru. Before igniting the fire, Dhola asks the parrot and then the camel to carry news of these events to Narvar, but both refuse, saying that all four will burn together. But once again Motini rescues her family and all survive (WA 02:6–14).

The Pond of Magaghi (*Magaghi Tāl*)

The procession with Dhola and Maru moves once again toward Narvar where Nal and Dumenti await them. Everyone in the city gathers to welcome them, except for Rewa, even though Dumenti explains to her that she should not turn her back on her husband.

Before the Devi shrine, Dhola and Maru play sticks (as the bride and groom do when first entering the groom's house, to see who will "dominate" the marriage). Then Maru notices the Shiva shrine with its dried-up pond. Dumenti explains that no one could see the deity therein, because Shiva had closed the doors when a king committed a great sin and was cursed by a sage. But Maru meditates on Shiva and the temple door opens, and Dhola and Maru worship the image. Then she prays to Shiva to fill the dried-up pond. Bowing to their fates, Maru takes Dhola's arm to enter the pond, but he backs away. Maru reminds him that he would then go only to hell, not to heaven.

They then enter the pond, completely submerging themselves.[23] Someone tells the parrot and camel, and both run to the pond. Nal stops them from entering, saying that first the parrot should tell Budhsingh and the camel and the kings of the fifty-two forts. Then they can join Dhola. When all had gathered, Nal decides to join Dhola in the pond with all his subjects (Matolsingh n.d. [a]).

Alternative Final Episode

The Battle of Chandrapal (*Chandrapāl Kī Laṛāī*)

Dhola and Maru have a son, Chandrapal. Dhola rules with great wisdom and gives peace to his subjects. Chandrapal likes to hunt in the forest. One day nine Brahmans come seeking a bride for the daughter of the Raja of Mahendranagar. They think that they should marry her into the family of Raja Nal. The nine Brahmans are amazed by the splendor of Narvargarh. The main reception hall has twelve doors, with eighty-eight pillars, lovely courtesans dancing, and parrots in cages singing the praises of Ram.

They present their letter to Dhola, and the marriage to the king's daughter is arranged. The Brahmans return to Mahendranagar with a multitude of stories about the splendor of Nal's court and the warm hospitality they received there. Arrangements are made to hold the wedding very soon. With only eleven days left until the wedding, the priests from Mahendranagar take the engagement gifts to Narvar. But Nal is distraught, for he learns that arranging this marriage will destroy the lineage of Narvar. The marriage procession is then readied for the trip to Mahendranagar. Dumenti weeps heavily, afraid for her husband and son and grandson. Nal knows that he must fight the demons one more time, this time at the marriage of Chandrapal. Nal calls for his goose to carry a message to Siya Nagar where the aid of Mansukh is requested. Then the goose goes to the underworld to request the help of Basukdev, the snake king. He also calls for Raghunandan Teli.

The procession comes to a wide river, and Raja Nal seeks the help of Basukdev. The snakes make a bridge and the army passes over. The marriage of Chandrapal is held with much lavish display and foods from many parts of the country.

They move off again, and the demon army descends on Raja Nal. Raja Budh fights beside Raja Nal, along with the Oil Presser and Vasuki and Mansukh Gujar. Anger burns in Raja Nal's eye. As Dumenti cries bitterly, wishing that her house could be saved from ruin, Durga enters the fray. The battle rages for days, with death to all. The Oil Presser, Raja Budh, all die. A fire destroys the forest, and no one remains alive (Varma n.d.).

A Brief Literary and Cultural History of *Dhola*

In his book *Haroun and the Sea of Stories,* Salman Rushdie describes the living Ocean of the Streams of Stories. His words capture the history of *Dhola:*

> Different parts of the Ocean [of stories] contained different sorts of stories, and . . . because the stories were held here in fluid form, they retained the ability to change, to become new versions of themselves, to join up with other stories and to become yet other stories; so that unlike a library of books, the Ocean of the Streams of Story was much more than a storeroom of yarns. It was not dead but alive. (1990, 72)

Working with the fluid stories of the oral traditions, epic singers and poets are like the bricouleur made famous by Levi-Strauss (1966). Working with the bits and pieces of their cultural knowledge, they weld together old themes in new packages. Certainly the epic *Dhola* follows this pattern. Local scholars at the local cultural association, the Braj Kala Kendra, in Mathura date it as not more than three hundred years old, while Alf Hiltebeitel (1999) suggests that it develops after *Ālhā, Pabūjī,* and *Devnārāyaṇ,* epics that date to the thirteenth to fifteenth centuries and are most popular to the east (Alha) and west (Pabuji and Devnarayan) of the area where *Dhola* is found.

The story of Pratham and Manjha and Nal's early years and marriage to Motini appears to have no connections to earlier written works, nor have I found clear connections to other folk stories. Nevertheless, various motifs have deep resonances in Indian (and other) cultural traditions, including the use of a life index to kill a demon, the childless king who wins a child through his many sacrifices (King Dasharath), as well as the telling of one's own story to learn one's true identity as well as to reveal it to the father (as do Lav and Kush in the *Rāmāyaṇā*). Some motifs appear in other oral traditions of north India, such as the sorceress who turns an army to stone using magic obtained from Bengal, the "flame" in the corner of the hero's eye that threatens to give away his disguise, or the chains worth nine lakhs (900,000 rupees), all also found in the oral epic *Alha* (Waterfield 1923, 63–66, 89, 128).[24] So while this portion of the story builds on various pieces of cultural knowledge, it apparently is unique as a compilation.

Recently the Internet enabled me to learn of another Nal connection, when Vanit Nalwa of New Delhi contacted me because she had found references to my work on Raja Nal on my web page. From Panjab, her family name Nalwa is said to derive from her ancestor Hari Singh, who had been given the name Nalwa by his mentor, Raja Ranjit Singh, when, as a young boy, Hari Singh saved the king from a tiger when hunting. Her family was told that the name derived from Ranjit Singh calling out, "Nal wa" or "He is Nal" or possibly "Wow, Nal." This incident is also recorded in an *Amar Chithra Katha* comic book telling the story of Hari Singh (Pal 1994). When the young Hari Singh kills the tiger, the Raja announces, "I am giving you the name of Nalwa." A footnote to "Nalwa" states "hunter of tiger" (*bāgh kī śikārī*) (Pal 1994, 7). This suggests that the association of Nal with the hunting of tigers is part of the core oral traditions of north India.[25]

The second section, that of Nal and Dumenti, is one of the most famous and best-known of India's stories, appearing in a variety of renditions over a long period of time. Extremely adaptable, in part because of its separateness as a story even in the *Mahabharata* where it is known as the Nalopakhyana, it has been used as a Jain didactic story (Bender 1951), as a Sanskrit love poem (the *Naiśādhacarita* by Sriharsa; see Handiqui and Bendaraja 1965), as the basis for Pahari miniature drawings (Goswamy 1975), as a Braj poem (Todarmal 1879, 1975; Wadley 1999), as a dance-drama in the kathakali and *yakśagānā* traditions (Freeman n.d.), as a Tamil folk tale (Zvelebil 1987), and much more. There are, nevertheless, many differences between any one of these variants and the one most common to *Dhola,* including the absence of the fatal dice game that leads to Raja Nal's loss of his kingdom in the Nalopakhyana and the role of Shanidev as the helpmate of Indra in his battle with Nal in *Dhola.* The latter portion, that of the Oil Presser, has no written vernacular versions (aside from various renditions of *Dhola*) that I have yet found but is common in oral traditions, where the episode of the Oil Presser might be variously attributed to Nal as here, to Harishchand (Stokes 1880), to Vikramaditya (Wadley 1978), or to King Bhoja (Narayan 1997). Here, however, the ending is different, as Nal is connected to *Dhola* and thus to early Hindi and Jain writings.

Western scholars have linked the story of Raja Nala to Harishchand: in the *Types of Indic Oral Tale* (Jason 1989), both Harishchand, who must sell his wife in the market of Varanasi and also loses his son, and Raja Nala share in the motif of making a ritual error that leads to their loss of kingdom and family (AT 939). The *Mārkaṇḍeya Purāṇa,* in its rendition of the story of Harishchand, actually includes a brief reference to Raja Nala, although he is not named. Here it states: "And the king saw himself born once again in his own race. While in that state, he lost his kingdom in dice-playing; and his wife was carried off, and his son too, and he sought the forest alone" (Pargiter 1969, 49).[26] Ram Swarup Dhimar provides a different connection to Harishchand, saying that Harishchand was an ancestor of Raja Nal (see chapter 3). Women in the village of Karimpur cite yet another link. In songs that lament the troubles that befall those in power, such as to Raja Dasharath, father of Ram, or Harishchand, they often include Raja Nal, as in this example:

It was not the fault of Kaikeyi,
No one knows the consequences of previous actions,
Raja Dashrath has four sons,
Two were exiled,
Yet two were left to rule the country.

And likewise misfortune fell on Raja Nal,
He drove the bullocks of the Oil Presser.
No one knows the consequences of previous actions.[27]

Hence it is clear that the people who sing *Dhola* associate Raja Nal with those who have fallen on hard times, although not as rigidly as the early folklorists' attempts to create universal tale types might imply.

The third section is closely related to the Jain ballad *Dhola-Maru* studied by Charlotte Vaudeville (1962) and Richard Williams (1976), and found today in *Amar Chitra Katha* comic books as well as on Rajasthani silk paintings sold on the streets of Delhi, on stationery featuring Dhola and Maru on their flying camel, and as puppets, again of the camel and its two riders, sold in the *kathputlī* village in Jaipur and stores across the world. The Jain ballad, called by McGregor (1974) one of the first instances of extant Hindi literary works, dates to the sixteenth century, when it was allegedly composed and written by a Jain poet, Kusalalabh, who notes that Dhola's father's name was Nal and alludes to the *Mahabharata* story (Williams 1976). Extremely popular in western Rajasthan and Gujarat, *Dhola-Maru,* from the sixteenth century on, continued to be written and illustrated over the coming centuries. Many later versions of the Rajasthani *Dhola-Maru,* including beautifully illustrated manuscripts, exist in collections in Rajasthan. Composed in medieval Rajasthani dialects, these ballads are still sung by Manganiyar musicians in the western desert regions.[28] Other versions of *Dhola-Maru* were and are performed by *khyāl* (folk opera) troupes throughout Rajasthan since at least the early nineteenth century, and some khyal scripts are also found in manuscript form. The Rajasthani ballad is considered part of the medieval *lok khandakāvya* literature that builds on popular idioms and vernacular lyrics (Williams 1976, 104). The kandakavya literature was a verse-bound story, generally of one or several meters with interspersed folk songs, a style not unlike the *Dhola* considered here. These Rajasthani written versions of *Dhola-Maru* can be seen as original compilations by given authors of lyrics and verses familiar to them or newly created following known metrical and stylistic conventions. Almost surely oral versions of *Dhola-Maru* coexisted, as they do today.

The result is a modern oral epic that also exists in some written forms, woven together from the strands of various written and oral stories and cultural scraps of meaning, as well as different performance styles,[29] each connecting to and reinforcing the themes and issues of most concern to the current author/singer. Most crucially the *Dhola* discussed here cannot be understood without reference to the history and cultural traditions of the Braj region where it developed, probably in the 1700s, as the Jats spread their power throughout what is now western Uttar Pradesh and eastern Rajasthan.

The Historical Context of *Dhola*

The history of *Dhola* becomes more interesting if we consider the political history of the time in which it was apparently consolidated, a period marked by the decline of the Mughal Empire and a new political alignment in the Braj region where it was and is sung. Apparently emerging in the late seventeenth century at the decline of Mughal rule, *Dhola*'s popularity coincides with the rise to power in the Braj region of the Jat caste of agriculturists, a caste that eventually ruled much of the area where *Dhola* was and remains popular.

In addition to the Mughal rulers centered in Delhi, north India was also heavily contested by the Rajputs, the Hindu kings who ruled primarily in what is now the state of Rajasthan. At various times allied with one another or with the Mughal rulers, they maintained independent kingdoms throughout the period of Muslim rule. While they claim and have been given a history by some scholars that proclaims their royal heritage, most scholars would now concur that the Rajputs came from a variety of backgrounds and were anointed rulers owing to their success in warfare. In Rajasthan, even today, the Rajputs, though no longer rulers, are held in high esteem. Moreover, to this day the Rajputs and the Jats, the upstart low caste that rules on the eastern fringe of Rajasthan, remain highly antagonistic to each other.

By the sixteenth century the districts of Mathura, Agra, and Bharatpur (also known as the Braj region and most renowned for its importance to the Krishna cults) were heavily populated by Jat farmers, as well as by Gujars, a caste of herdsmen, and Ahirs, another group of farmers/herdsmen.[30] Further, by the late 1600s the Mughal Empire had begun to disintegrate under onslaughts from Marathas, Afghans, and Sikhs, among others. The Jat landlords of the area sought to fill the vacuum in the Braj region, while Aurangzeb was preoccupied with troubles in the Deccan, on the western edge of the Mughal Empire. Beginning in 1669 the Jats led a series of revolts against the Mughals. Even when defeated in their initial battles, the blood "watered the newly sprouted seedling of liberty in the heart of the Jats" (Qanungo 1925, 38).

The Mughals responded to these onslaughts by appointing the Rajput king, the Raja of Amber (near Jaipur), as military commander of Mathura with the task of subduing the upstart Jats, a task that melded with the desire of the Rajput Kacchwahas to prevent the Jats from gaining independence on their eastern borders. The Mughal-Rajput alliance was only partially successful, and by 1700 the Jats had made the roads south of Delhi unsafe. Eventually the Jats succeeded in looting the Red Fort at Delhi, becoming an increasingly important force in the region. In 1713 the new emperor, Shah Jahan II, formally received the Jat leader, Churaman, in Delhi.

The years following were tumultuous for the Braj Jats, although Churaman's nephew, Badan Singh, was able to establish the Jat headquarters at Dig, west of Mathura, considered by some to be one of the most beautiful examples of Hindu-Mughal architecture, decorated with the spoils of the palaces of Delhi. Here the Jats sought to create a court comparable to the example of Delhi, installing poets and musicians to counter their reputations as "rustic farmers" (Entwistle 1987, 195).[31] Badan Singh was never a feudatory of Sawai Jai Singh of Jaipur, but did accept his authority and went to Jaipur yearly at Dassehra to pay his respects. Eventually he was awarded the title of *rājā* (king), although he preferred the more modest "Thakur" (a man of indeterminate but mid-level caste, usually implying a landowning caste, often Jat).

Badan Singh turned the task of rule over to his (apparently) adopted nephew Suraj Mal, who was involved in building the impenetrable fort at Bharatpur. Suraj Mal successfully united the Jats and headed a rather stable regime in the area south of Delhi in a time of increasing turmoil at the disintegrating Mughal center. Under Suraj Mal, Jat rule extended over the present-day districts of Agra, Mathura, Bharatpur, Dholpur, Alwar, Gurgaon, Rohtak, Meerut, Bulandshahr, Aligarh, Hathras, Etah, and Mainpuri, precisely the districts where *Dhola* is most popular even today.

Suraj Mal's sons fought among themselves and became known for their spendthrift, decadent ways. By 1777 they had only Bharatpur and a few surrounding areas left. In 1805 the British, having taken Agra and Dig, were defeated when they were unable to penetrate the walls at Bharatpur, losing more than three thousand men. The British ultimately took Bharatpur in 1827, ending formal Jat control of the region.[32]

If Braj scholars are correct in thinking that the epic coalesced, or gained affirmation, in this area during the eighteenth and nineteenth centuries, then we are justified in seeking its roots in Jat rule. Although the term *Jat* rarely appears in the epic, one author defines Raja Nal's troops as "the Jat soldiers" (Varma n.d.).[33] Further, a major theme throughout *Dhola* is Raja Nal's attempt to gain acceptance as a Raja, or king. The epic's parallels with the history cited above are intriguing, especially given Jat-Rajput identities and relationships.

Other minor details lend credence to this history. One of the major clans of Jats is called Narwar (Narvar) (Bingley 1978 [1899], 52), and they founded the village of Narvar on the border between Mathura and Aligarh districts, moving there from Aligarh (Drake-Brockman 1984 [1911]). A Jat historian describes an incident in which Kishori, the wife of Suraj Mal, seeks to bathe at the holy lake of Pushkar without permission from the Amber Rajputs. When the Jats and Rajputs battle at Pushkar, the Jats succeed in slaughtering their Rajput enemy (Joon 1967, 168–169). This event captures the core cliché of the episode known as the "Battle of Phul Singh Panjabi," albeit with the territory and characters shifted from a lake in central Rajasthan to the Ganges River, and the Rajputs replaced by another enemy, the Panjabis.

As we shall see in chapter 7, the challenges to the status of a "king," or Rajput, that are the focus of many episodes of *Dhola* are intricately intertwined with the historical importance given the Rajput by the British, especially by the British officer James Tod (1971). Historians have challenged this reading of the Rajputs as having clearly defined genealogical histories, despite their preeminence in a "Rajput Great Tradition" (Kolff 1990, 71). The Indian historian K. R. Qanungo noted that, in the middle ages, " 'Rajput' normally meant a trooper in the service of a chief or a fire lance captain, and sometimes was applied in applause even to a brigand of desperate courage" (1960, 99). Further, there are several links between the Rajput rulers and the yogis, portrayed in *Dhola* as the allies of the enemy. First, Nath yogis were thought to be the power behind the throne of several Rajput kingdoms, especially Jodhpur (D. Gold 1992) and Marwar (White 2001). Second, the Rajput fighters would go to war with their bodies smeared with ashes, marking a common identity of the Rajput warrior and the Shaivite warrior ascetic (Kolff 1995, 266). Thus there is an underlying historical reality not only to Jat history but also to Rajput history that substantiates the claim that *Dhola* is connected to the Jat attempt to gain recognition as kings. That the upstart Jats might relish an epic that challenges the dominance of Rajput authority is not out of the question.

As I sought out singers of *Dhola* in the early 1990s, I was directed to find Jat villages and there to seek out *Jāṭiyā* Chamars, or Leatherworkers who worked for Jat landlords. Indeed, in Harayana I found one Chamar singer, Mangtu Lal, whose primary patrons were his Jat landlords. In Bharatpur city itself, the director of Kala Mandir, a private school located there, affirmed that I would learn about *Dhola* from the Jat community. Thus *Dhola* is sung today for Jat landowners by lower-caste men in the Braj region. And since *Dhola* is more generally about achievement versus ascription, the message of an upstart king who seeks recognition from those who are superior has gained popularity even in those regions lacking a Jat community.

Dhola in the Late Twentieth Century

Beginning in the 1980s, with the advent of inexpensive recording equipment and cheap tape cassettes, *Dhola* started to be produced on audiocassettes for the urbanizing male market of migrant workers. These cassettes can be bought in small shops along all the major highways of north India, as well as in electronics stores in India's many bazaars. On one minor road outside Delhi I found a shop specifically advertising "*Dhola* and *Alha*" tapes. Recently I discovered that the stalls next to the teashops on the Grand Trunk Road, the British-built highway that stretches from Lahore to Calcutta, are lined with cassettes, in addition to candies, cigarettes, and condoms. These shops sell primarily to travelers, especially truck drivers.

Some of the new producers are large establishments with distribution networks that cover a wide region. The electronics market opposite Red Fort in Delhi provides a venue where cassettes can be bought wholesale for redistribution to buyers across north India. Other companies are very small, such as the one in a garage near the home of the singer Ram Swarup that was (in 1985) five inexpensive tape machines hooked to one another to make four copies at a time. Given the different qualities of the recording and copying equipment, as well as the tapes themselves, the quality of the sold product varies enormously.

The smaller local companies do play a significant role, however, for they allow the capture and production of local variants of *Dhola.* These companies sought to provide their audiences with a relatively unabridged version of what they would hear on their verandahs. The dialects of the countryside where *Dhola* has been popular vary dramatically over a short distance. I discovered the importance of this for *Dhola* recordings when I was talking with the owners of the large company Brij Cassettes in Aligarh in the late 1980s. I asked if they had any performances of *Dhola* played with a cikara (a simple bowed string instrument), as they had shown me only those of a performer who played the harmonium (a portable free-reed pump organ played as a keyboard while sitting on the ground). When they said no, but they would like one, I went to my car and got a copy of a cassette that I had recorded of Ram Swarup Dhimar, who lives about eighty miles further east on the Grand Trunk Road. When I played it for them, they commented on the high quality of his singing and instrumental passages, but added that it would not sell in Aligarh as his *bhāśā* (language) was too different. Some singers who do make commercial cassettes are self-conscious about these language differences. One singer comments in his cassette, "Now I'll tell you a story in desi bhasa (that is, in country speech)."

Most of the singers whose recordings I have listened to use the traditional instruments of *Dhola.* But the format—sixty-minute tapes, sometime packaged together as a double or triple set—demands that they sharply condense their performances to fit this new mode of distribution. Many good singers, including Ram Swarup, chose not to record for the local companies, as the meager pay, usually less than a thousand rupees, seemed like little return for their skills.

Other troupes used the cassette industry to reach new audiences and were decidedly more pro-active in modernizing their performances, adding new instruments such as the violin or synthesizer. One such troupe is that of Kailash and his co-singer Laturi Lal. The cassette jacket suggests that Kailash and Laturi are from Farrukhabad, Uttar Pradesh, about eighty miles straight east of Agra on the Ganges River. I purchased their tapes in Delhi and was told by the cassette company there that I would not be able to meet Kailash as he traveled all around and was often in Bombay. I have no way of authenticating this statement. These versions were recorded in 1988 by MAX, a company noted for the small-scale production of cassettes in the regional languages/ dialects surrounding Delhi (Manuel 1993).

What is distinctive about Kailash's performance is his parody of film tunes, using them for the same aesthetic purposes that older singers might use folk tunes (see chapter 3). Where an older singer might use a tune from a traditional martial epic, such as *Alha* to send his hero off to battle, Kailash uses music from a Hindi film, "Hindustan ki kasam" (literally, "The Oath of Hindustan"), music that connotes patriotism and war to its now moviegoing hearers. What we have here is a shift from the use of easily recognized folk melodies, and hence their connotations, to the use of easily recognized film tunes, with comparable connotations and symbolic content.

Kailash sometimes uses film songs in their entirety, as in an example from the episode "Raja Nal's Second Marriage." Here he borrows a film tune associated with marriage that itself was originally a folk song. But to the modern cinema attendee, the mental connection is to the film tune, not the folk song. This is a more extreme use of film songs than the borrowing of a melody but one that recurs in many singers' performances.

Kailash's text also shows a consciousness of modern themes. In one episode he is comparing Nal and Mansukh with Ram and Lakshman. On the bank of the Ganges, Ram starts shivering with cold; growing angry, Lakshman says, "Why are you shaking like your sister's—" He leaves the final word unspoken, but the rhyme is clear: to rhyme with *ṭhanḍ* (cold), the missing term must be *lanḍ* (penis). Here we move into the sexually explicit world of modern cassettes, explored by Peter Manuel (1993) in his chapter on *rasiyaa,* another genre of the Braj region.

Kailash's cassettes show a further attempt at modernity. Packaged as a three-tape set, the title of the episode called "The Battle of Phul Singh Panjabi" is changed to "Panjab Battle." In a soft plastic cover, the illustration is of men with tanks and in khaki uniforms, an image that takes us far from the realms of traditional Hindu kings.

Meanwhile, Brij Cassettes made an effort to produce all of *Dhola,* with one singer, Shankar Lal, a Brahman living on the outskirts of Aligarh, producing more than twenty cassettes of the epic, each marked only by number (1–25). This set obviously aims at a better-off market, as you cannot tell which episode you are buying. The aim is to sell full sets.

Although *Dhola* can be found today in chapbooks and on tape cassettes, its primary audiences continue to be found in the villages of the Braj region, where renowned *Dhola* singers entertain their communities. Let us now turn to two respected performers to gain an appreciation of the epic as performed.

3 *Dhola* as Performed: Two Singers

Performance is essential to *Dhola* because it is through the voices of the singers that the characters are brought to life, usually through the voice of a solo singer. That *Dhola* is about transgressing norms is given even greater impact because, despite the existence of the chapbook versions, the epic lives through performance. One of the principles of performance is identification with characters, the sharing of circumstances. Oral performance is based not on rhetorical deliberations but rather on engaging the sympathies of the audience with the very real human problems encountered by the characters whom the singer brings to life. That *Dhola* turns the world on its head, and then turns it back again, leaves the audience, and performer, continually questioning reality and attachment: when Raja Nal is a low-caste Oil Presser, beaten and continually insulted by the kings of the land, sympathies are engaged, sympathies that remain even when he eventually reverts to kingly status. The success of the tale being told ultimately depends on the abilities of its singers.

No two of the *Dhola* singers whom I have heard over the past thirty-five years have performed *Dhola* in the same way. A variety of stylistic features function both to add texture and symbolic depth to the singers' renditions of *Dhola* and to keep the attention of audiences, who may be sitting far into the night after a hard day of field labor. I feature two of these singers here: Ram Swarup Dhimar of Karimpur was my initial guide to *Dhola* and a consummate performer who manipulates his cikara and the traditional folk song genres of *Dhola* to add enormous richness and complexity to his performance. His career as a youthful runaway who sought numerous gurus marks one tradition of learning *Dhola*. The second singer featured here is Matolsingh Gujar of Kama District, Rajasthan, renowned not only as a singer of *Dhola* but also as a writer of chapbook versions. Educated through the tenth class, though from a rural farming family, Matol shifted to *Dhola* singing when in his thirties. Matol, who died in 1991, sang while playing a harmonium, and his concern for a *Dhola* more accessible to middle-class urban audiences led him to compose what he defines as the real *Dhola* as well as to train his troupe in a mode of singing that borrows from light classical styles while retaining many of the traditional folk song genres of the region. Both men were extremely knowledgeable, indeed passionate, about *Dhola*.

While the performance styles of Ram Swarup and Matolsingh differ, their venues and audiences were similar. *Dhola* is most commonly performed on the outer verandah of its sponsor's house, a semi-public space adjoining the village lane. The family sponsoring *Dhola* may be celebrating an auspicious event, such as the birth of a son, or may be entertaining a marriage party, or perhaps have called the *Dhola* troupe to gain merit with their neighbors. Performed at night and lit by kerosene lamps, the singer needs only a small space for his troupe—perhaps a half circle twenty feet in circumference. Men and children, mostly male, arrive as the music fills the night air and word of the event spreads through the village lanes, from one man's verandah to another. As his audience of men and children expands to several hundred, with a few women on the fringes, in a separate side section for women and children only, or on nearby rooftops, the singer seems charged by the energy of the crowd. He and his drummer and steel tong player need no costumes, only their voices and instruments. Every hour or so the troupe stops for a break, perhaps to drink tea or smoke a cigarette. When the episode winds to a close, usually at midnight or later, the singers send their remaining audience off to their cots, for the farmers must be up by 5:00 A.M. to begin their labors once again. At exciting points in the songs, members of the audience will offer donations and are rewarded by a brief verse sung in their honor. While the sponsor will provide a substantial sum plus food and drink for the evening, the troupe often garners an equal amount in donations from the audience. As demonstrated below, each troupe has its own aesthetics, its own style of singing, some emphasizing music, others humor, and still yet others focusing on the story itself.

Orality and Performance: Ram Swarup Dhimar of Mainpuri District

Ram Swarup claims to have heard *Dhola* as a child when he lived in his mother's village where his family had moved temporarily. A Thakur lived there: if a *Dhola* singer came, the Thakur would house him for six months or a year. Many came, and Ram Swarup listened. He obtained a cikara and taught himself to play. Eventually, at about age nine, Ram Swarup ran away from home with a singer who became his guru/*ustad*.[1] As with any student of a guru, Ram Swarup was expected to honor and respect his teacher/guru as well as to serve him in any way possible. Ram Swarup stayed away seven years, shifting gurus six times. His gurus were Thakurs, Jats, a Potter, and several others of lower-caste status. One lived in Aligarh, several were in Etah District, and one was from Bidaun District to the east of the Ganges River. When one of his gurus would attend a *Dhola* competition (*dangal*) and lose, Ram Swarup would shift his loyalties and services to the winner, whether delivering massages, running errands, or cooking. For this he received instruction in singing

Dhola. Each of the six had different strengths: each had a different repertoire of tunes and was noted for expertise in different episodes of the epic.

Ram Swarup's knowledge of the intricacies of the story is immense. When I asked him one day about Motini's alleged status as an apsara from Indra's court, I was treated to an hour-long narrative of her mother, Indra, Bhumasur's capturing of Motini, and his raising of her. I had heard none of this in any of the performances I had recorded. He is also firm about Nal's heritage: it is not that of the Rajputs of Narvar. Rather, he traces Nal to Harishchand. Harischand had Mahipal, Mahipal had Jay, Jay had Aja, Aja had Dhuj, Dhuj had Pratham, and Pratham had Nal, who had Dhola. There the lineage dies.

After having been away for seven years, he returned home, to his family's amazement: they had long thought him dead. They begged him not to leave again, but he persisted as there was a month-long festival of *Dhola* in Agra and he was to meet three of his gurus there where he would perform and gain renown. But when he reached the fair, he was not allowed to perform; he was not even allowed on the stage. Other competitors asked, "What did this young boy know?" All the other singers, he says, were fifty years old or older and he was perhaps seventeen. After several days he finally explained to his gurus that his parents were counting on his performing. So one of them agreed to give Ram Swarup his fifteen-minute slot. When it came time for that particular man to play, he went on the stage, hands folded (a sign of obeisance), and told the officials that this young boy would play instead. Then his gurus provided backup for him (playing the drum and steel tongs), and he played for two hours, earning from seventy to a hundred rupees from the audience (a lot of money in the 1940s and early 1950s).

Soon thereafter Ram Swarup started working on his own, later forming a *Dhola* company that lasted more than twenty years. The company was a folk opera troupe composed of four musicians, one cook, one "joker," two dancing boys, one man who portrayed Motini (and the other female characters), and one other singer for male parts (Ram Swarup was Raja Nal; see figure 3.1). He was adamant that his company never included women, for then he would have been thought a pimp. Moreover, he would have had to deal with the problems that women and sex brought with them. His company played in various fairs throughout the region, charging ten paise a ticket (one hundred paise to one rupee—which was worth more in the 1950s and 1960s than now). At other times he would perform at weddings, births, and other local celebrations. But the money never went far when split among ten or twelve people, and he claims, "I did it for love of the music." I saw his company perform once in 1968 on the verandah of the house next to where I lived in Karimpur, but the audiotape of that performance is poor and it was long before the arrival of video cameras. By the time I turned my attention more fully to

Figure 3.1. Ram Swarup Dhimar as Raja Nal, circa early 1960s. Photograph courtesy of Ram Swarup Dhimar.

Dhola, his company was disbanded. Nowadays *Dhola* companies are nonexistent,[2] and *Dhola* singing itself has shifted to commercial cassettes, as described in chapter 2. Ram Swarup, now in his late sixties, continues to perform as a solo singer within the village and outside it, whenever a patron (including the American anthropologist) calls him.

In the 1970s, with the increase in cinema shows at the fairs and his own sense of needing a more settled life, Ram Swarup turned back to farming and his growing family. Raised in a period when boys of his caste were married in their early teens, Ram Swarup's life course is markedly different than others of his caste. In his mid-twenties he married a woman many years his junior. His first son was born when he was in his late twenties, his second eight years later, and the last two when he was in his late forties. By 1996 he headed a large household of sons, sons' wives, and grandchildren. One young grandson followed him faithfully on every call to sing within the village, sitting quietly for hours while Grandpa sang. Ram Swarup is especially proud of his grandson's education (he was then in an English medium private nursery school in the village) for he himself never learned to read or write.

Ram Swarup never had a disciple because, his neighbors say, he was jealous of anyone learning the epic better than he. Nor has he made a commercial tape recording, distrustful of the process and of the profits made by others when he would receive minimal pay (in the late 1980s singers were being paid about one thousand rupees per three-hour episode to fill three one-hour cassettes). He did visit me once in Delhi, sleeping in an air-conditioned room, and going to the Archive and Research Center for Ethnomusicology where the tapes I made are archived. He no doubt receives attention and some prestige from singing for me and feels proud of having his voice kept in such a place. He also wanted to visit a big hotel, so I took him to the Oberoi, worried a bit about the possible repercussions, since the coffee house location mandated that we pass by the women gathered around the swimming pool. In what I consider typical Ram Swarup fashion, he was not offended by the scantily dressed white women but rather scoffed at those inane women who were sitting in the sun "drying up" in the June heat (over 100°F). He is a proud, confident man, with a strong value system that he says is based ultimately on what he knows from *Dhola* itself.

Today Ram Swarup works with a younger man, a Tailor by caste, who plays the dholak (drum) as accompaniment and a young nephew who plays the cimta (long steel tongs) (figure 3.2). Except for the period when he had the *Dhola* company, he wears no costume: his attire is the white shirt and dhoti and sometimes headscarf that are his normal garb. On occasion he will sing with a harmonium, as he did in 1989 when I had brought a second troupe to Karimpur to record. Challenged by the unspoken competition, he recruited a

Figure 3.2. Ram Swarup Dhimar and his troupe in Karimpur, 1989. Photograph by Susan S. Wadley.

harmonium player for that week's performances, and the shift was apparent in melodic range and some marks of style (the harmonium player knew the epic slightly and could sing along on some lines, which the cimta and dholak players never did). Harmonium use encourages a more modern style with a wider range of melodies, including the use of film song tunes as well as traditional folk melodies. Everyone agreed, too, that he had won the unspoken competition, that his voice, and his knowledge of the story, were better than the others'.

Ram Swarup's performances are good examples of the current cikara style of singing *Dhola.* In its "purest" or oldest form, the singer uses one melody, called dhola, in performing most of the epic, interspersing his songs with narrative sections that carry the story line and explain the actions. The dhola melody-type is a distinct melody easily recognizable to the rural Uttar Pradesh audiences. Ideally the singer's voice should mimic the sound of the cikara, so that the vocal quality of a singer performing in this style emulates the thin, nasal whiny sounds of the cikara, accompanied by the pulsating dholak and the ringing clang of the steel tongs. (I recorded bits of three singers using this style, but all three said that it was very difficult and none of them did it regularly anymore; Ram Swarup never used it as his core style.) Over time, and probably in reaction to the development of folk drama forms such as *svāng* and *nauṭankī* and, less directly, Parsi theatrical styles, *Dhola* developed a more narrative style, becoming a string of songs linked by narrative, with only some songs sung to the dhola melody.[3] This latter style still persists, but what has changed is the source of the tunes for the linked songs, and the relative proportion of dhola melody to other song forms.

In north India many folk song genres are distinguished by their associated melody-types and their content. Most folk song genres are marked by one or a few melody-types, although the number of associated texts may seem endless. Unlike Euro-American modern classical and popular music, where (usually) each text has its own melody, here a few melody-types are used for many texts. These melodies, then, can symbolically stand for the genre with which they are associated, even with different texts and in strange contexts. Hence a song genre is a complex symbol form, composed of rhythm, melody, verbal content, and also normal context (singer, event, place, etc.). One afternoon Ram Swarup played twenty-eight different song genres for me to demonstrate the melody, verbal texture, and rhythm attached to each.

Two examples from the selections here clarify this issue. One genre melody-type frequently used in singing *Dhola* is *ālhā,* a melody deriving from the martial epic *Alha,* also performed in the region where *Dhola* is found. *Alha,* sung by men, is a story of war and battle: it has a distinctive metrical pattern of twenty-four beats with an emphasis on every fourth beat. When used in *Dhola,* the strict four-four meter of alha connects it to the martial themes and marching of the army. The audience knows alha by tune and rhythm, and associates alha with matters heroic and military, so a *Dhola* singer frequently uses alha as a musical symbol to remind the audience of the heroic king marching off to war.

A second frequently used folk song melody is that associated with the women's genre *malhar.* Malhar are songs sung by women during the rainy season and mark the longing of a married woman for her natal home, and for her brother to take her there. In marked contrast to the sixteen or twenty-four syllable lines that make up most folk song texts, malhar contain many extra syllables with lines of thirty-six syllables or more. Hence the malhar genre is easily recognizable and marks things feminine, things associated with longing and love. A comparable genre is that known as *nihālde,* named after a romantic story popular in Rajasthan. Thus, by using local song genres, the singers use these genres as a symbol that can convey a particular mood to the audience. Hence it is possible for a singer to convey a particular mood or attitude through his choice of a folk song genre that emotionally connects the audience with the original genre and its texts, even if the melody is used for a different or only vaguely related topic in the epic performance (see also Wadley 1989).

Initially these melodies were drawn from the folk song repertoire of the region (e.g., alha, malhar, nilhade), although the dhola melody still dominated. In a further innovation the most recent renditions, especially those on commercial tape cassette, are very self-conscious about the use of the dhola melody, one singer even claiming, as noted above, that now he would sing in a desi (country) style. These singers appeal to their more urban and media-aware audiences by including film tunes along with local folk melodies and the dhola melody. But these film tunes perform an evocative function similar to the use of the folk melody in that they, too, are known by the audience to be connected to specific topics and emotions.

Two brief examples demonstrate how Ram Swarup manipulates song, instruments, and texts. He plays the cikara, using it to mark the melody before each section of song, often not actually playing it while singing. He thus signals the drummer and steel tong player (and the harmonium player if present) of the melody he will be using in the following segment. (Once, when his drum player showed up drunk for a performance, Ram Swarup complained that he could not shift melodies at all that night as the drummer could not follow his signals.) Putting an oral musical performance on paper is not easy. Here I use boldface type to indicate portions sung or spoken with dholak and cimta accompaniment (and sometimes, but unmarked, cikara accompaniment). Frequently, in spoken sections, the instruments are used for emphasis: the cikara is marked by an open parenthesis; the drum by an asterisk (*); and the steel tongs by a crosshatch (#). The named melodic segments are noted. Those used here are *dohā,*[4] a chanted couplet form (in heightened speech) used to introduce new topics or sections; dhola, a sung section usually accompanied by cikara, drum, and tongs; *bārahmāsī,* literally the "songs of the twelve months," a popular melody-marked genre; *lahadārī,* "wavy," a song genre marked by a lengthy and "wavy" rhythm and rhyme pattern; and *vartā,* narrative prose in everyday storytelling style. Humor is found in the narrative spoken segments: I have never heard laughter in the sung portions. On the other hand, the audience does not interrupt the sung portions with comments or queries or laughter. However, monetary contributions to the singer are made only during the sung portions, and the song is immediately interrupted with a *chāp* (literally, flattery), a song to honor the donor.

This segment was sung in Karimpur on April 14, 1984.[5] Ram Swarup is accompanied by Rajju, the Tailor, on the drum, and his nephew, Tilan, on the steel tongs. It is from the episode "Nal's Bad Times," where Nal and Dumenti are banished from Narvar and seek refuge elsewhere. Here they have arrived at Mansukh's kingdom. Mansukh is Nal's best friend and helpmate, and he is distressed at the condition of his friends.

[On hearing that Nal has arrived, in tattered clothing,]

varta: #* Mansukh is overcome with anguish. "My brother is in such great trouble!
Oh god [Bhagvan], what is this?"
(musical interlude of some eight lines)

dhola: **And Mansukh slowly starts out;**
He goes straight to the queen's palace and speaks to the queen.
"Oh Queen, decorate the palanquin; make it ready.
Bring the royal garments from the palace
And dress my *bhābhī* [older brother's wife] in them."
(Break, tuning)

doha: Then Mansukh goes off, taking a decorated chariot.
Taking garments for a man to wear, Mansukh is ready. *#

dhola: **And Mansukh comes into the garden, *#**
(musical interlude of about eight lines)
Mansukh comes into the garden.
(short musical interlude)
He embraces Raja Nal with affection,
"Tell me truthfully, Nal of Narvar,
(very short musical interlude)
Brother, how is it that you are in such distress?
My friend, where is all your wealth?"
(musical interlude of about four lines)
And Nal is consumed by distress, the King of Narvar.
"Oh Brother, how can I tell you simply?"
(musical interlude of three lines)
And because Nal desires a bath,
A sandalwood stool is set down,
And a jug of water is brought,
Into which Mansukh mixes cool water,
(short musical interlude)
And Nal changes his clothes,
And Raja Nal sits in the chariot,
And Bhabhi sits in the palanquin.

varta: And both set out for the palace,
"We will share your curse."
(musical interlude of one or two lines)

dhola: **And Mansukh proceeds slowly.**
Brothers, they reach the border of Bhamarkila.
(short musical interlude)
When Raja Nal reaches the border of Bhamarkila,
Kashamira bows her head.

And Nal is given a new cot:
On it sits Nal of Narvar.

varta: Meanwhile, Mansukh tells his queen,

dhola: **"Prepare food quickly, make it ready now,**
The day is drawing to a close,
and who knows when the poor one last ate!"

(very short musical interlude)

dhola: **The queen prepares the food and Mansukh thinks to himself.**

varta: **What does he say? Maina Mansukh says, "If we serve him the food, he won't eat it because of embarrassment [*śaram*]. So it is best if we leave them alone on the roof. We can put the food there. Then they can serve themselves and eat as much as they want." LAUGHTER**

(musical interlude of about three lines)

dhola: **They prepare a table, putting food on two trays.**
And Brothers, the food is ready.
Both Nal and Dumenti are there.
Oh Brothers, the guru of truth is there.

varta: "Send only these two and they will not eat in embarrassment. These two poor ones are dying from troubles." Raja Nal goes ahead up to the roof, and Maina Mansukh slips away behind him. Raja Nal and Dumenti both sit down, and both say, "See our younger brother is clever: we have been hungry for many days because of our troubles. They have filled our trays with all this food, but they did not come because of embarrassment. Let us go, let us rest and serve ourselves and eat." When both of them reach for the food, they see a black snake [cobra] sitting there on the tray. There is no food. Nal says, "Rani, my kingdom has gone and my power has gone; life in a palace has gone. It seems as if a strong wind has come and my fate is broken. Rani, god [Dinanath] took our food away in Narvar, now you and I will not be able to eat [anywhere]. Let us go now. Whatever will happen tomorrow, then it won't be here." As it approaches midnight, Raja Nal and Dumenti talk about their troubles. Then the peg on which a necklace worth nine lakhs hung swallows the necklace. *#

(tuning of cikara)

doha: Meanwhile, Nal thinks to himself,
"Oh King of Narvar, how was he to explain to the Rani?" (*

varta: So what does Nal say? (

barah: **"Oh, what I say is not even a bit of lie."**

masi: **And Raja Nal is in distress, the necklace was swallowed by the peg.**

(musical interlude of one line)

Oh, what I say is not even a bit of lie,
And Raja Nal is in distress, the necklace was swallowed by the peg.

(very brief musical interlude)

Oh, the necklace was swallowed by a peg.
And Dumenti says, "My husband's fate [kismat] is broken.

lahadari: **Oh, they will accuse us of having stolen it,**
Husband, it will be impossible to show our face in Siya Nagar."

(musical interlude of one line)
Then Raja Nal and the Rani both agree,
"Rani, let us run away quickly."

And so they leave Siya Nagar and run into the forest where they are separated, only to be reunited at the second svayambar.

In the section above, Ram Swarup draws on several performance devices. He uses three different melodic lines, the standard dhola, lahadari, "wavy," and barahmasi, songs of the twelve months of the year. This latter genre is narrative in style, and although it has a distinctive melody, it does not mark a particular emotive content as the songs of the twelve months can and do deal with numerous political and other topics. He also uses a doha, a chanted couplet, which I discuss further below. Moreover, he connects to his audience through the humanness of his description of Nal's and Dumenti's predicament. Their shame at being starved, and Mansukh's recognition of their possible embarrassment, elicit an overt response from the audience. This is a situation to which many, who have often been hungry themselves, can relate. This hero is just like them.

The following piece demonstrates more clearly Ram Swarup's control of prose and song. I do not mark the instrumentation here in order to focus more on the relationships between genre and verbal content. From the episode "The Battle of Phul Singh Panjabi," it was performed by Ram Swarup in July 1985 in a village near Mainpuri town (WA 85:302). In this episode Raja Pratham has been reunited with his wife, Manjha, after her twelve-year absence. He also has just learned of his son, Raja Nal, and his daughter-in-law, Motini. Because Manjha has been gone for twelve years, she refuses to enter the palace until she bathes in the Ganges. Motini and Nal are very worried about this venture, as there have been bad omens about the trip. Manjha calls a maid and sends her to Nal to explain that she will be departing soon. This section begins when the maid reaches Nal's palace. The different song genres and speech styles are marked as headings. In this short section, six different song/speech styles are identified by the singer: varta, prose speech; chap, the acknowledgment of a patron; alha, the song genre derived from the martial epic *Alha;* the dhola song genre; *chetvānī,* literally a warning; and nihalde, the genre named after the romantic story of Nihalde. These were given to me by Ram Swarup, who listened to a tape of his performance after it had been transcribed.

varta: Then the maid tells him the story: she says to come quickly.
chap: Sher Singh, resident of this village, gave one rupee.
alha: And [he] rises immediately from his room.
Think of a lion, moving in the forest,

As he goes his boots thump loudly,
And his shield clanks on his shoulder.

varta: What does he see?

dhola: Oh, Nal glances ahead:
A widow is carrying an empty pot.

varta: Nal thinks, "Oh, my mother has called, and these unlucky omens make me very fearful."

dhola: How can one remain in peace when traveling on a road?
A crow cawing in a dried tree,
A crane alone, the pair separated,
Or a twitching on the left side of the body,
A deer alone, a pair of jackals,
Or meeting a shepherd riding on a buffalo.[6]

varta: What does Raja Nal say?

chetvani: When destruction comes to a man,
First lightning falls on the brain,
One's own mother is as ferocious as a lion,
And [one's] father seems like Yamraj,
When destruction comes to a man,
First lightning falls on the brain,
One's own mother is as ferocious as a lion,
And Father seems like Yamraj,
Instantly the wind changes direction,
Instantly the leaves fall from the tree,
Sometimes there is yolk in the egg,
Sometimes birds fly from it.

nihalde: Oh, he goes on, then Raja Nal comes into the palace.
The woolen wrap is spread, he sits on a stool.
The women speak to Raja Nal,
Then Motini notices her husband,
And she embraces Raja Nal . . .

varta: Manjha comes and embraces her son. Nal says, "Dear Mother, tell me everything, why have you called me?"
What does Manjha say?

dhola: "Oh my son, I must bathe in the Ganges.
Son [literally, calf], I have been ordered to bathe in the Ganges.
Oh my child,
My heart's desires will be fulfilled."

varta: Nal said, "Don't have any worry. I will see that you go and bathe."
What does Raja Pratham say?

dhola: "Oh my son, you stay in the fort.
Son, you remain in the fort.
And don't take a step toward the Ganges."

varta: Raja Pratham says, "Oh son, I will not take you with me to the Ganges."
What does Raja Pratham say?

dhola: "Oh, I have defeated Rome, China, and Gujarat,
I also beat Britain, defeated all the kings of India.

I have the blood of the lineage of Raghunath in my body,
I have command of the whole world,
Just as in Mathura, Krishna defeated Kans."

In this section, each of the named genres, sometimes called *rāstā* or road by Ram Swarup, has a unique melody and linguistic texture. The genres are most readily identifiable by their melodic and rhythmic structures but also vary in poetic rhyme schemes, poetic meter, and other linguistically marked aspects.

The importance of these shifts can be easily seen in a few examples. Take the lines, "And [he] rises immediately from his room. / Think of a lion, moving in the forest, / As he goes his boots thump loudly, / And his shield clanks on his shoulder." Here Nal is not going to war but rather to see his mother. But by using alha metrical structures and melodies, the singer is able to convey by more than words alone the heroic nature of Nal as he goes to meet his mother.

Likewise, the mood shifts suddenly as Nal is brought into the women's court where a genre, nihalde, based on a well-known romantic epic is used to seat Nal and for the greeting by his wife. Here, as elsewhere, the message of the epic is conveyed not only by words but also by linguistic texture, melody, and rhythm. Recognizing the importance of texture, melody, and rhythm allows us to move beyond the textual analysis of epic traditions of most Western writers.

Further, the singer uses the different song genres in order to keep the epic characters distinct. This scene has five characters: the maid, Raja Nal, Motini, Manjha, and Raja Pratham. Each shift in character is marked by a shift in genre. Consider just the last few stanzas. Manjha's voice is sung, Raja Nal's (with a short sentence to mark the speaker) is spoken, although the musical accompaniment remains, and then Raja Pratham sings his lines of poetry, which are then recited in an everyday speech style, before he goes on further, once again in song. Epics, unlike songs, are long, and the characters are many. A solo singer cannot rely on different singers' voices to distinguish his characters, so instead changes his own voice to keep them separate. And as Ram Swarup continually reminded me, the story is important: after all, this is a genre that has as its core a narrative of heroic events.

Thus, in singing *Dhola,* by marking changes in voices and situations through shifts in song genres, the moods and characters of events and personae are conveyed. As performed in the latter half of the twentieth century, the shifting of genres is a critical component in developing the characters of the epic personae. With no costumes or props, character can, and must, be conveyed orally. Of critical importance is that this character development is not made merely by words but also through the conscious choice of symbolically charged melodies and rhythms borrowed from the regional pool of genres.

Equally important is the use of conversational speech versus poetry and song. Ram Swarup's spoken style is very informal and one used every day. It is in that sense conversational, as indeed his characters often converse with one another in long prose sections of the epic. In contrast, sung poetry, constrained by verbal and musical meter and rhyme, is more formal than everyday spoken conversation. Bloch (1974) has discussed the formalization of political and ritual language, using concepts derived from sociolinguistics and the ethnography of communication. One aspect of his argument is that ritual language, where choice is denied the speaker once an item is chosen—the Lord's Prayer must be recited with each word correctly placed—has lost its propositional force where propositional force is defined as "the ability of language to corner reality by adapting communication to past perception and connecting this with future perception" (Bloch 1974, 67). However, a second aspect of meaning is illocutionary force or performative force (see Austin 1962), the ability "not to report facts but to influence people." Speech, Bloch argues, that is highly formalized—such as a doha couplet used above or the chetvani—communicates without (or with minimal) explanation. A related theory is that of Wheelock (1980; 1982) who proposes two kinds of speech acts: informing speech (a speaker conveys information to a listener) and situating speech (a speaker creates situations by his or her utterances). Certainly epic prose is more "informing speech" while epic poetry/song is more "situating speech," especially when we consider that it is not merely text but also tune.

Contrast for a moment the components of this epic: there is everyday prose—neither formalized nor constrained by vocabulary, intonation, or rhythm. These explanatory prose sections are very non-formalized. Ram Swarup explicitly calls them "explanations" (*samjhānā*). But by choosing prose for certain segments, Ram Swarup also makes the choice to open the epic up to argument. The interplay between singer and audience (laughter as well as comments and other feedback) in prose sections reinforces this exposure to argument. Here meaning depends on rational discourse, on cornering a bit of reality.

Chanted doha couplets are defined by a fixed linguistic metrical pattern, intonation, and rhythm of delivery: not quite sung, not everyday conversational speech, doha are performed as "heightened speech," which I term here as a *chant*. Consider the first doha in the first selection above: it marks a major transition in the story. Mansukh is ready to depart to meet Nal: "Then Mansukh goes off, taking a decorated chariot. / Taking garments for a man to wear, Mansukh is ready." These lines mark the transition between the palace and the garden where Mansukh will find Nal. They mark, in essence, a change of scene. Critically, as Ram Swarup uses them, doha are usually chanted without musical accompaniment. These chanted sections are highly formalized: their meaning lies in their performative force, not their propositional force. They are markers of scene changes. Yet they are also informing speech. But the fact that the doha message is often repeated in everyday spoken speech suggests that the main message of the doha is to notify a change. Hence doha chants situate not through words but rather through the use of heightened speech. Meanwhile, what they do inform is repeated.

Chanted and sung sections derive their meaning from their performative and situating force. Here other messages are being communicated. The concern is not so much with rational thought but rather to create a mood, paint a word and musical picture, mark a change. Many nonverbal messages are being communicated to aid in creating meaning through illocutionary force—messages via heightened speech, melody, and drum patterns, all culturally understood and decoded (in part at least) by the audience. The type of meaning may differ as we move across the continuum from everyday prose to formalized song, but the weight of meaning may, in fact, be heightened with the addition of nonverbal cues.

It is these skills of music, storytelling, and relating to his audiences that make Ram Swarup a popular *Dhola* singer. As a performer he is fully aware of the different kinds of audiences—those that respond to music or to humor or to story—and he attempts to build each night's performance around the desires of his audience. After a serious fire in Karimpur in 1984 that killed several people and made singing (normally an auspicious event) impossible for some weeks, he agreed to sing on a roof in the nearby town to an audience of a couple of villagers and urbanites who did not know this tradition. I worried that he had had no audience, but he told me, "No, I was the audience this time. I sang it how I wanted to, not for someone else." It may have been the only time he himself was his own audience.

The cikara is associated with a rather traditional form of *Dhola* performance. Below I present a troupe whose primary accompanying instrument is the harmonium. This troupe attempts both to modernize their performance and to make it light classical. Through a variety of performance strategies, they respond to the more sophisticated moviegoers and radio and TV listeners of today while adding additional symbolic meaning to the performance. The leader of this group is also the author of a popular chapbook version of *Dhola*, allowing us to consider issues of orality and literacy as related to performance.

Oral and Written Performances: Matolsingh Gujar of Bharatpur District

I was introduced to Matolsingh of Dhamari near Kama in Bharatpur District through Komal Kothari of Rupayan Sansthan in Jodhpur. Komalda and I shared an interest in *Dhola,* and when I visited him in 1989, he took the opportunity to call Matol, whose troupe was the most renowned in the Mathura-Dig area at the time. Matol arrived with three assistants. For several days Komalda and I recorded their version of *Dhola* in a tent at the back of Komalda's house, interrupted periodically by trains passing by (figure 3.3).[7]

Matol himself, clearly the leader in this group, played the harmonium and sang, although his voice was not as good as his assistants' voices. Unlike Ram Swarup, here the singing was shared among three of the four members of the troupe. Matol was most famous, however, because his version of *Dhola* was the most popular published version in the Braj area. (He told me that it was in print at four publishers—in Hathras, Agra, Mathura, and Jaipur.) A previous published version, by Gajadhar Singh of a village near Hathras, who was in his late eighties in 1989, had fallen into disfavor because it was linked to cikara tunes. Matol's version was intended to be used with the harmonium and the more modern repertoire and was the current favorite.[8]

Matol was a Gujar, a caste of herdsmen and agriculturists. He was born around 1930, which made him just senior to Ram Swarup. He died in 1991 of typhoid. Matol's history differs from that of Ram Swarup. His family was wealthy, owning more than one hundred acres. He was educated, passing the tenth class in 1946, and was employed in a government job as an inspector for the water board. He was drawn to *Dhola* singing much later in life. Matol told of his involvement in various kinds of singing competitions throughout his early years, especially *bhajans* and a form of riddling song called *jhikṛī.* But he came to hate the tension involved in these forms of song performance and turned to *Dhola* as a way to find peace. His father and grandfather had also been *Dhola* singers and had several old manuscripts in their home. Furthermore, singing *Dhola* was supposed to bring one luck in marriages, and Matol was married four times, including one marriage in the 1980s to a young girl in her teens.[9] Apparently all four wives lived in Dhamari with him, although he told of trying to get the oldest, whom he had married while a schoolboy, to leave. It seems that his last marriage was a blatant effort to sire a son after his adult son had died in his twenties, and indeed he had a six-year-old son at home when he spoke to me. He found it extremely difficult to sing the final episodes in which Nal and Dhola die, and he did so only rarely because of the weight of emotion and sorrow in the scene.

Eventually he visited all the places named in the epic—Narvar, Pingal, Marwar. He also read the Sanskrit version of the Nala-Damayanti story, and presented me with a textbook that uses an English version authored in the 1800s as a way of teaching English prosody. Starting in 1954 he began to publish his version of the epic, rendering the text into strictly defined meters and clarifying the poetic forms. He enjoyed playing what are best called verbal games: he

Figure 3.3. Matolsingh Gujar and his drummer in Jodhpur, 1989. Photograph by Susan S. Wadley.

proudly showed me one section where his name and village were incorporated into the text as the first letter of sequential lines. (Thinking of those scholars who pour over texts by long dead authors, and find such hidden codes, I appreciated Matol's ability to point out his games to me!) Further, his written text contains his philosophic statements about the world in which he lives, based on the bhakti religious system he embraces. The printing process is also constrained by the allowable page lengths—multiples of four—so that every episode must be twenty, twenty-four, twenty-eight, or thirty-two pages long. The consequential episodes were sold singly, initially for a rupee or two, or bound together as a book. (I have located eighteen episodes by Matol [bound into one volume] in print, as well as some other stories and songs.) The result is that the poetry is printed with the singing style sometimes marked but with the narrative threads that link songs almost absent.

Matol said that Gajadhar's printed version was filled with trash: none of the poetic devices were regular or correct and not even the story was right. So he wanted to do it "correctly." As an educated man, with some fame in the region, and knowing the value placed on writing, Matol was careful to emphasize the value of the printed word and often disparaged the skills of his illiterate companions. He argued that what he wrote was what he sang, although even the briefest comparison shows this not to be the case. His vision of correct performance was so tied to the written word that when he first began to sing for Komalda and I, he was reading from his printed pamphlet but soon shifted away from this rigid text (where the interspersed narrative portions are all but eliminated). Moreover, his companions often sang long portions that were not in the text or altered the text significantly. (Matol complained that Harman especially could not memorize what he had taught him.)

Before looking briefly at Matol's sung and written *Dholas* I will introduce his troupe: Harman, the youngest member (in his mid-thirties in 1989), is, like Matol, a Gujar by caste. He was from Matol's village where he worked as an agricultural laborer and did sharecropping. Although illiterate, he was a superb performer who had learned much of what he knew from Matol. Harman played the cikara and sang. In his hands the cikara was more than an instrument: at times it became a sword or a baby cradled in its mother's arms or a bird flying off. As our recording session wore on, Harman took over more and more of the singing, pleasing his audience if not his leader. Another member of the troupe, Chote Lal, a Gujar in his mid-forties, played the cymbals and sang. Seated slightly behind Matol, he was not as key to the performance as Harman. The final member was a crippled Brahman drummer, Lakshman, in his early thirties. (I knew of several blind *Dhola* singers, and one of Ram Swarup's favorite drummers was blind: performance is an option for the physically challenged in an agricultural community.) The performance style of Matol's troupe differs dramatically from that of Ram Swarup's, and differs as well from what Matol himself has written. Below I present two examples from the episode of Motini's wedding, focusing on the differences between *Dhola* as it is sung and as it is written. Note that, in contrast to the performances of Ram Swarup, Matol's troupe is far more interactive, with key lines sung at times by all three singers. The performance also plays with music differently, and the song segments are much more repetitive than those of Ram Swarup's troupe; also lacking are the instrumental interludes played by Ram Swarup on the cikara. As such the performance of Matol's troupe responds to a different musical aesthetic than the section presented above, one that leans toward a light classical rendition rather than a more traditional folk rendition.[10]

The first example begins as Nal is brought to the fort of the demon, Bhumasur, to find his future wife. Behmata has brought Nal there and deserted him before Nal can make his way in: initially he is unable to find a door.[11] Since there is more than one singer, I have marked the singers by initials (M = Matol, H = Harman, CL = Chote Lal). As in the example from Ram Swarup above, I have used boldface type when all the instruments are used simultaneously. When used as accents, the instruments are marked as above with an asterisk (*) for the dholak, a crosshatch (#) for the cimta, and the addition of the letter *h* for the harmonium (the tape recording does not allow the cikara, played rarely by Harman, to be identified).[12] Capital letters indicate an interjection from another speaker. Because Matol died shortly after the transcription was completed, I was unable to identify the names of the melodies used here, except for those already known to me or to residents of Karimpur.

m (chant): [Nal says] Oh, show me my wife, h*# Motini.
h: **My mother of the lion [nahar vali maiya, i.e., Durga].**
Oh, show me my wife, Motini
mhcl: **Oh mother of the lion,**
Listen oh mother of the lion,
Listen oh mother of the lion.
Oh, show me my wife, Motini.
My mother of the lion.
m (spoken): Oh, Brothers, Nal stands looking at the fort, and the mother got her lion ready, and came running at once. Arriving at the fort of the demon, she sees Nal standing there dejectedly, and laughingly Durga says, *# Oh son, tell me, why are you fretting?" She says, "tell my monkey companion,[13] he'll do what is needed. Oh, your heart is breaking—Son, he'll do as you ask." * And she places her hand on Nal's head. And the monkey kicks [the stone] with his leg. Son. Harman. Chote Lal [Matol calls to his associates]. Yes sir. Yes sir.

hcl (sung):	**He kicked the stone, Brother.** **He kicked the stone, Brother.**
m (chant):	Glory be to that everlasting canopy Oh, my Bhagvan, make me fearless. Saying this [Nal] enters the palace.
h:	eeeeeeee [note held, the slowly descending improvisatory tan]
hcl:	**Glory be to that everlasting canopy.** **Radhe Shyam says, he entered inside** **And Nal goes around all four sides,** **He finds there piles of bones.** **He finds there piles of bones.** **And Nal becomes very worried.**
m (spoken):	And Nal goes around all four sides. And he finds there mountains of bones. And that makes him afraid. How is he troubled? There were piles of human ribs. Skeletons. Now the king, the boy, says, "If Bhumasur demon finds any human, he'll catch him and eat him at once. And there are eighty skeletons here." *# And Nal is very worried at seeing them, and says, "Mother did a very strange thing. She gave me enormous trouble. The old woman sent me such problems. Behmata has done this; the old woman has caused me to be killed today.[14]
cl:	Why has she caused me to be killed? How will she cause it?"
m:	Oh, Nal's heart is being ripped by fear. Oh, Nal's heart is being ripped by fear. "I have gotten into real trouble because of my father-in-law [using the term *sasūr,* here an obscenity]."
h (sung):	Aaaaaaaaaaaaaaaaaaaa [holds note, then slowly descending improvisatory *tān*]
mhcl:	**Oh, Nal's heart is being ripped by fear.** **Oh, Nal's heart is being ripped by fear.**
h:	**Oh** [undecipherable]
m:	**Here daily someone is eating humans.** **Here daily someone is eating humans.** **Oh, in what kind of situation has Nal found himself?**
mhcl:	**Here daily someone is eating humans.** **Here daily someone is eating humans.** **Oh, in what kind of situation has Nal, oh Nal, found himself?**
m (spoken):	Oh, who is here? He thinks that you should tell me what to do, Bhagvan. Here someone eats humans every day. Now where shall I go? How will I go? And Nal began to understand one thing.[15] HE WILL SEE. He said, "Let's go above where the wind blows. Oh, we will see, whatever will be will be." Then, Brother, he made ready to escape. He made ready to climb using his heels.
cl:	How did he do it, Brother?
h:	How?
m:	Oh, the boy climbed up using his heels.

mhcl (sung: malhar):	**Oh, the boy climbs up using his heels.** **Oh, the boy climbs up using his heels.** **Oh, in that way he reaches the fort, Brother.** **Oh, the boy climbs up using his heels.**
m:	**Oh, a five-colored bedsheet is spread over Motini,**
hcl:	**Oh, a five-colored bedsheet is spread over the princess,** **Oh, a five-colored bedsheet is spread over the snake woman.** **Oh, what is she doing; oh, what is she doing,** **Oh, the boy climbs up using his heels,** **Oh, in that way he reaches the fort, Brother.** **Oh, the boy climbs up using his heels.** **Oh, in that way he reaches the fort, Brother.** **Oh, the boy climbs up using his heels.**
m:	**So, Brother, going into that hall, what does Nal see?**
cl (spoken):	**What does he see, Brother?**
h:	**What does he see? That she is sleeping on that bed. And Raja Nal thinks.**
m:	**What does Raja Nal think?**
h:	**That you are sleeping on this big bed. Who is sleeping here? What is the trouble?**
cl:	**What?**
h:	**It is possible that it is she about whom Behmata and the Mother Goddess [devi maiya] told me—that it is the daughter of the demon Bhumasur.**
cl:	**Oh, what else?**
h:	**But I don't know this, I don't know who sleeps here.**
cl:	**Yes, [he] must know if it is a woman or a ghost.** (WA 89:10)

Matol's troupe uses many of the same strategies as Ram Swarup, shifting between prose, chanting, and song, but at times joining two or three singing voices and playing more with musical frills. Like Ram Swarup who used it to mark Raja Nal's entrance into his mother's quarters, Matol's troupe uses malhar, a folk genre associated with women, to mark Nal's entrance into Motini's room.

Matol's sung version can be contrasted to his written version published in Hathras. In the printed version (see below) the text is marked for the reader with the prosodic forms used, also marking potential melodies (*cāl, jhulnā, dhuni, malhar,* and *thoṛ*). Malhar is easily recognizable by both melody and metrical patterns as sung, but the key markers are dropped in the text, making the indication of the proper melody all the more important since a knowledgeable singer will know how to adapt the printed line to the expanded melodic structure.[16] Varta is everyday conversational speech.

cal:	And because of his worry [about finding a door], he remembers Durga. And prays, Oh mother Durga, make it possible for me to see Motini.

varta:	This request of Nal reaches the mother's palace, and she takes her monkey helper and lion and places her hand on her head, and the monkey reaches the door and hits it with his foot.
jhulna:	Glory be to that everlasting canopy, And Nal enters inside.
dhuni:	Roaming in all four directions, He finds no signs of a human, Everywhere immense gardens, And here and there huge piles of bones. Oh, Nal's heart is being ripped by fear. "I have gotten into real trouble because of my father-in-law." . . .
thor:	What a good marriage this is! That widow [obscenity] has made me a fool, sending me here to be killed.
varta:	Nal thinks that night is falling and, looking in all four directions, he is thinking . . .
malhar:	Oh, the boy climbed up using his heels, And when he reached the top, he saw a bed covered with a bedsheet of five colors and a woman resting on it.
varta:	He goes forward and comes back, and he goes forward again but his vision is blurred.
thor:	What is this mystery of fate? I imagine that after eating a human, a demon lies there sleeping. (Matolsingh n.d. [b])

Comparing these two versions, we can grasp a sense of the play of music and performance in the first in contrast to the dryness of the second. Clearly the second version is not really meant to be performed as written, without repetition and embellishment. It is, it seems, an outline of a performance, one adhered to lightly and not fixed in any way. Matol himself claims that men buy it to read, not to perform, and that they buy it because of the beautiful poetry. Some elements seem to be Matol's: for example, neither Ram Swarup's oral rendition of Nal's first sight of Motini[17] (or that of three other troupes of whom I have recordings) nor Gajadhar's printed version emphasizes the daily eating of humans that is so prominent here. Yet, in fact, these lines, especially as sung, are highly effective.

There is little word-for-word similarity between the oral and written texts. Indeed only five lines are close to being the same: that about the canopy of god, the line about Nal's heart ripped by fear, and the first two lines of the malhar, about climbing the walls of the fort and the five-colored bedsheet. One performative consistency is the use of the folk genre malhar in both pieces for Nal's climb and the first sighting of Motini.

Another section in the same episode tells of the wedding of Nal and Motini: in the absence of any parents, family, or friends, the goddesses provide for the wedding, with retinues, food, and so on. First consider Matol's written version, as published by Deep Chand Booksellers.

> Bemata and Durga came,
> And Narad playing an instrument.
> With banana leaves prepare a mandap,
> The branches moving gently in the breeze,
> Motini will be a bride,
> And the one from Narvar a groom,
> Narad blesses both,
> Listen, Govind my friend,
> Matol of Dhamri is saying,
> Motini completed circling the fire. (Matolsingh n.d. [b])

This is a remarkably unelaborated discussion of a marriage ceremony. The oral version is dramatically different. With Matol chiming in periodically, this is sung rapidly by Chote Lal and Harman, who sometimes alternate lines.

m (spoken):	Nal says, "Do one thing. Let's get married."
	After he says this, Durga immediately comes riding a lion, oh she comes.
hcl:	She comes.
m:	And also Behmata comes, considering whether Nal and Dumenti should marry now.
	Narad comes playing a flute,
	And Narad Muni said, "Oh daughter Motini, Nal is god of the gods. Do not consider him less. To give enough dowry, I must ask Indra. That is what you'll give [Nal].
h:	will give"
m:	And Motini speaks, "Baba, that doesn't seem right
	Look, this tradition of dowry is completely wrong. And, second, let me tell you some things about this custom of giving and taking from others.
m (sung):	**And I'll tell you one more thing Baba, I am telling you,**
h:	**I will pay my dowry myself.**
	I will pay my dowry myself.
cl:	**Oh Baba, I will pay my dowry myself.**
	Eeeeeee. . . . .
m:	Now what will I give at the door [*darvāzā*]?[18]
	Oh, at the door, what will I give?
	Oh, at the door, I'll give one flying horse.
h:	**Oh, at the door, what will I give?**
	Oh, at the door, I'll give one flying horse.
	Oh, at the kanyadan [gift of a virgin], I'll give a sword,
	Oh, at the door, what will I give,
	Oh, at the door, I'll give one flying horse,
	Oh, at the kanyadan, I'll give a sword,

m: **Oh look, Maharaj,**
I'll pay the dowry myself.
Oh, at the door, I'll give one flying horse,
Oh, at the kanyadan, I'll give a sword,

cl: And for the leave-taking [*vidā,* the ceremony when a groom departs with his new bride] also, I have made arrangements,
And what is that, saheb?

m: Oh, at the leave-taking, **oh, at the leave-taking with the groom,**
Oh, at the leave-taking with the groom, the leave-taking,

h: **eeeeee. . . . . .**

hcl: **My good sir, I'll place a necklace made of seven kinds of gems [on him].**
Oh, at the leave-taking, oh, at the leave-taking with the groom,
Oh, at the leave-taking with the groom, the leave-taking,
Sir, I'll give a necklace made of seven kinds of gems,
Oh, at the leave-taking, oh, at the leave-taking with the groom,
Oh, at the leave-taking with the groom, the leave-taking,
To my god-husband, I'll give, a necklace made of seven kinds of gems,
To my god-husband, I'll give, a necklace made of seven kinds of gems."

m (spoken): Behmata is thinking, now both [Durga and Behmata] chose. Behmata takes the side of Motini [becoming her relative], and Durga takes the side of Nal. Then what happens? Oh now, Behmata says, "Nal Banvari [undecipherable]. Now I am her family member." Heating up water, she bathes [her] with wedding ointments.

m (sung): **Oh, she binds a *kankan* on her wrist,**
Oh, anoints her with tumeric and rubs her with oil,

hcl: **Oh, anoints her with tumeric and rubs her with oil,**
Oh, she binds kankan on her wrist,
Oh, anoints her with tumeric and rubs her with oil,
Oh, she binds kankan on her wrist,
Oh, anoints her with tumeric and rubs her with oil,

m: **Oh, Narad has them perform the ritual of circling the fire,**
Durga comes and sings the wedding songs,

hcl: **Durga comes and sings the wedding songs,**
Oh, Durga comes and sings the wedding songs,
Durga sings the wedding songs.
Oh, Narad has them perform the ritual of circling the fire.
Durga comes and sings the wedding songs.

m (spoken): Now, Brother, the circumambulations of the fire are complete. What does Durga think? Now what should be done?

h: Then a fight breaks out between Durga and Behmata.

m: Why does this happen?

cl: There is a fight.

h: What happened? Behmata says, "I will not give her to someone whom I don't know."

cl: And what else?

h: "There is no one. No barat [marriage procession]. No relatives.
How can I give her to him? He is alone.

cl: I will not give her for your service. There is no one with him.
How can I give her to him alone?"

h: Durga Mother says, "Look, you'll not be able to feed my barat.
My barat is very long. What kinds of preparations will you be able to make to give them food and drink?"
Oh, Behmata says, "There is no lack of food and drink."
Oh, Behmata says, "We have no lack of food and drink.

cl: no lack

h: I have the whole ocean at my disposal."

cl: OH. . . . . . .

h: From the ocean [undecipherable]

cl: What else?

h: This is Bhagvan's [god's] plan.
So Durga gives the order to the monkey to call the whole marriage procession. Then from villages everywhere comes the marriage procession of demons, ghosts, and witches, some beating their chests and crying.

cl: Many Bhairon

h: fifty-six Bhairon

cl: [undecipherable]

h: Yogis

cl: sixty-four yogis, yoginis
It becomes very noisy all around.

m: The barat of Nal comes

h: Saying, "Bring food, bring food, bring food!"

m: Asking what preparations have you made?
What preparations are made?
Oh 250 sweets were made for the ghosts.
How was it made? Oh, how beautiful was that place?
That demon's fort was wondrously decorated by Behmata. How was it decorated?

h (sung): **Oh, beautiful decorations,**
The chandelier spreads enormous light,
Oh, beautiful decorations,
The chandelier spreads enormous light.
Beautiful beds are laid out, covered with deep red velvet.
The perfume of roses is sprinkled around.
Orders are given to serve the food.
Papads are served, laced with *candur.*
They begin to smack their lips.
At that place then, many things are sent for.
And hundreds of leaf plates are made ready.
Now the bread is ready.

cl: What is the food, oh, what . . .

m: What else?

h:	**There are *purīs,* oh *kachorīs, puā,* and *pāpads, śakarapārā,* even *lucchīs* are there; plates of sweetmeats and salty snacks. Other breads are served, along with salty snacks, salty snacks for the demons.**
cl:	What else?
h:	**Along with salty snacks, salty snacks for the demons, *khīṛ***
cl:	Khir!
h:	**Khir, *Rasgullā,* thick creamy *rabṛī*** [sweets], ***Laḍḍu* of *besan*** [chick pea flour].
cl:	Laddu! Laddus made of besan.
h:	**Oh, there is nothing in your hand. What was there four kinds of?** **Four kinds of laddu,** **Laddu were made of besan,** **twisted *jalebīs, peṛā, barfī*** [all sweets], ***Imartī.***
cl:	Imarti!
h:	**Oh imarti, *gulābjāmuns* within the middle of sweet syrup.** ***Kalākand* and *pethās.*** ***Sohan haluā?* Halua, two kinds of halua.** ***Jimikand, mohanbhog, khīrchan,*** **Foods which are made in the month of Savan** [the rainy season month of July–August] **Very tasty!** **Curds, khir and sugar,** **Rice with fenugreek,** **Dishes with lentils of *moong,* slightly sour,** ***Miṭhāī, batāse,* cardamon drops, rabri with sugar,** **Yogurt and khir sprinkled with raw sugar** [*gur*]. **And *urd, masūr,* moth, chickpeas, too,** **And urd, masur, moth, chickpeas, too,** ***Dāl* is also made.** **Eggplant, bitter melon,** **Potatoes also, cauliflower, carrots, radishes, squash.** **Sour chutney, gourds, okra.** (WA 89:11)

In contrast to the slim outline of a wedding as given in the written text, Matol and his troupe present a verbal feast in their performed *Dhola.* In rural India weddings are often fraught with tension, the potential for the marriage itself to be canceled is always present, and the two parties (the bride's and the groom's) are expected to battle while the groom's party, guests at the bride's home, is to be feasted lavishly. Matol and company present these many issues in a superb piece of verbal and musical art, filled with nuance and humor. With Behmata supporting Motini and Durga acting as Nal's relatives, the wedding proceeds. The two argue, here over whether Motini should go with a groom who has no relatives, for he is clearly alone, as well as over the food and other preparations. Durga challenges Behmata to feed her huge marriage procession, filled with hungry ghosts and goblins. But as Harman reminds us in one line, not only is there plenty of food, but it is made "slightly salty for ghosts." The array of delicacies is mouth-watering, as no doubt it is intended to be! The artistry of these "rural illiterate men" is superb.

Pondering Performance Styles

Matol's written *Dhola* and his troupe's performance of *Dhola* could hardly be more different. Borrowing insights from Mikhail Bakhtin (1981) we see a complex heteroglossia at work, a political economy of language and discursive domains where different aesthetic principles function. Matol sees his written texts as authored, and as truer in some sense than his troupe's performed texts. Given his schooling, his presentation to me of an English/Sanskrit rendition of the Nala-Damayanti story, his social rank (not high by caste but relatively high by economic standards), and his pride in what he wrote, it is clear that he values writing above singing. Nevertheless, being a true artist, and no doubt propelled by his companions, he responds to the demands of oral performance by producing verbal art (Bauman 1977) of a very different sort than he writes. The two discursive domains in which Matol works—written printed text and sung performance—each reflect its own languages and symbolic practices, while also maintaining a dialogic relationship with the other.

The written text, as one kind of cultural product, and the oral event, as another kind of cultural product, produce two radically different "texts." The demands of context, the different audiences, the different goals of Matolsingh himself all work to produce texts that are dramatically different from each other. In one, philosophical arguments and strict adherence to meter and rhyme prevail, along with various verbal games played by the author, only with difficulty perceived by the acutely observant reader. In the other, the demands of musical elaboration and humor triumph over philosophy. The narrative thread is fundamental, and the nature of verbal games changes from hidden codes to overt jesting.[19]

Not only do the aesthetic principles of written and performed *Dhola*s differ, but the contrast between the performances of Matol's troupe and Ram Swarup's illuminate some of the range of aesthetic possibilities of *Dhola* as performed. The verbal and musical performances of both Matol and Ram Swarup capture a sense of the rural lifestyles and concerns of their patrons. Unfortunately, for the increasing populations of filmgoers and TV watchers, they present an aesthetic that is ever less in demand. *Dhola* is no longer as "respectable" as it once was even in rural India, a fact about which performers are extremely self-conscious. As a piece of literature, *Dhola* has never been truly respectable to the Indian elite (who seldom know of its existence), no doubt because of its rural, (relatively) lower-caste singers and patrons, as well as its continual questioning of caste and gender hierarchies and norms. The boundaries of respectability are crucially linked to the power and social status of the groups defining respectability (Ghosh 1998, 175). With its challenges to the Hindu norms of a Sanskritic Hinduism, as well as its political challenges to the Rajput political and ideological dominance of the region, *Dhola,* as sung by Ram Swarup and Matolsingh, is an unlikely candidate for high regard from urban elites.[20] It is these social and ideological challenges that are addressed in the following chapters.

Part Two. *Dhola* Interpreted

4 The Goddess and the Bhakti Traditions of Braj

> Now Mother, listen, we the five Pandavas call you.
> You shall reign over all.
> Mother, why do you turn your back?
> My foes have become powerful.
> Mother, your favorite is praying to you,
> Mother, do get ready,
> And take your sword in your hand. . . .
> Durga, your temple is in the mountains,
> You have conquered all evil. . . .
> I'll go to the mother of my country,
> Oh, Mother of the mountains,
> To see that Mother I'll go barefoot,
> Though the blind can see nothing.
> Mother, bless me,
> Here I sit telling the story of Nal,
> Sitting, I tell of him,
> I tell about Arjun and Bhim,
> Mother, I need your blessing,
> As I am telling of brave men and their time. (WA 94:29)

Sung by Mangtu Lal, a blind Chamar (Leatherworker) singer in 1994, this *sumerī*, or remembrance of the goddess, is typical of the opening lines of all *Dhola* performances, for *Dhola* is first and foremost an epic about the powers of the goddess, and of women in general. It is the goddess who guides the performance and the performer, and it is the powers of the goddess that are invoked throughout the epic as she rides her lion to the aid of her devotee.

As Ashis Nandy has noted, Indian society has a strong pre-Aryan matrifocal orientation:

> Though the Brahmanic tradition attempted to limit the dominance of woman in society, the pre-Aryan dominance of woman was retained in many areas of life, particularly in the symbolic system. This undeniably is a matrifocal culture in which femininity is inextricably linked with *prakriti,* or nature and prakriti with *leela* or activity. Similarly, the concept of *adya śaktī,* primal or original power is entirely feminine in India. . . . In other words the ultimate authority in the Indian mind has always been feminine. (1980, 35–36)

Dhola speaks directly to this focus on the feminine, for the epic is fundamentally about the powers of the goddess and of women more generally. That the lower-caste performers of *Dhola* capture a non-Brahmanical, pre-Aryan orientation to the powers of the female is thus not surprising.

In *Dhola* the role of the goddess displays an intersection between the female *śaktī* (power/energy) and *bhakti* (devotionalism that is critical to the devotional traditions of the Braj area and its surroundings). The message of *Dhola* is clear: Durga, an embodiment of sakti, the female powers that energize the universe, shows her grace, gives her *darśan* and her aid, to those who demonstrate love and devotion to her. It is a love and affection similar to that normally thought directed toward the male gods Krishna and Ram who dominate the literature on the bhakti religious traditions of the Braj area. But as *Dhola* makes clear, similar forms of devotion are directed toward the goddess, not seen as a lover or husband, as are Ram and Krishna, but as a mother who loves her child/devotee. A second message regarding the goddess is the affirmation of Durga over Kali. Seen in *Dhola* as the goddess who demands human sacrifice, Kali, often thought to represent the fringes of society and the powers of total destruction, is associated here with the use of magical powers for selfish purposes. In this, she is also linked to various yogi sects that are thought to worship Kali and develop powers that can be used against moral human society. Kali becomes the Other, linked to the real-world Other of the Rajput kingdoms who refuse to accept Raja Nal as an equal.

Invoking the Goddess

The goddess is clearly the focal deity in any rendition of the story of Nal, and a remembrance of the goddess frames all oral versions of *Dhola*. An early publication of the story, the *Nalacaritāmrit arthāt Ḍholā Mārū*, published in Mathura in 1879 (Todarmal 1879), is profusely illustrated: the first image is of the singer and audience before a temple of the goddess who is portrayed with four arms and flowing locks (figure 4.1). The unbound hair is an immediate symbol of the independence of the goddess, showing that this goddess is under the control of no one and is "powerfully free" (Hershman 1977, 276).

In the oral versions it is the invocation to the goddess, the remembrance or sumeri, that provides the introductory frame to the epic performance, which clearly marks *Dhola* as a tradition in honor of the goddess. Framing devices are key to marking the beginnings and endings of oral performances, and they also set the tone for what follows (Bauman 1977). But the goddess is also the patron of the singer. In the lines quoted above, the blind singer twice asks for the blessing of the mother so that he can "sing of brave men

Figure 4.1. The goddess and the singer of *Dhola.* Woodcut from a nineteenth-century chapbook, Todarmal 1879, *Nalcaritāmrita arthāt Ḍholāmārū.*

and their times." A singer named Ram Swarup Kachi (Farmer), also blind and from the village of Karimpur, begins one performance with these lines:

> Brave Lata, you should be victorious.
> Give me a boon,
> I am begging you for four things,
> Beat, throat, voice, and knowledge. (WA 74:109)

While the singer asks for knowledge and ability, he also asks the goddess to order the performance: Ram Swarup Dhimar, featured in chapter 3, sang the following lines in concluding his sumeri in 1984.

> Mother, all demons are slaves to you,
> The war is against all demons,
> Today turn your chariot toward the singing pavilion,
> All the leaders are sitting,
> Order me where I should start *Dhola.* (WA 85:302)

And in a sumeri that shows true sensitivity to modern times, the invocation on a commercial tape cassette concludes with these lines: "You will have to protect me, Oh Mother, time and again, in my telling of *Dhola*" (Kailash and Laturi 1988b).

Discussing sumeri in an interview, Ram Swarup Dhimar claimed that the sumeri is like taking a bath and changing one's clothes before going somewhere. He used the example of a wrestler who takes off his regular clothes and puts on a loincloth before wrestling. In the same way, a singer will say, "Please god, help me." He added that when someone needs help, he can touch the feet of his parents: in the same way, a singer should pray to god not to say any dirty or vile word. The sumeri also seeks to put the singer in the proper frame of mind, one that will allow the power of the goddess to be channeled through the performer so that the resulting performance is more than ordinary. And invariably, in oral performances of *Dhola*, the deity called upon is the goddess around whom the epic focuses.

In a few instances the performance may close with a frame noting the departure of the goddess:

> Oh god who loves the poor,
> *Dhola* is very long and time short,
> Your wish is complete,
> Now the woman of the mountain (*parvatvālī*) will depart,
> Give something to the singer, now Bhagavati will leave,
> Young and old have both listened. (WA 68:9)

Ram Swarup Dhimar concluded one performance with this closing frame:

> Audience! I have sung what you asked. A break has come in *Dhola.* You young men go to your homes and spread your cots to sleep on. (WA 84:239)

This is not to say that male gods are not present in *Dhola.* Sumeri may include remembrances of the powers of male gods, as in these lines from "The Battle of Kishanlal," by Ram Swarup Kachi, that refer to the epic the *Ramayana* and its monkey-hero, Hanuman, who destroyed the kingdom of the villain Ravan:

> Hanuman, Bajrangbali,
> Please do good things for us. You destroyed the boastful pride of Ravan,
> You set fire to Lanka. (WA 85:307)

The written versions of *Dhola* differ: many times the opening lines call upon Krishna or Ram, without the addition of the lines above that invariably invoke the goddess just before the story itself begins. But even when the printed page invokes a male god, the same author, when singing, invokes the goddess, as Matolsingh did in 1989 when performing with his troupe in Jodhpur.

But the goddess plays a role that is far larger than that of supervising the singing of *Dhola.* In the oral renditions, with very few exceptions, when Raja Nal finds himself in trouble, he invariably calls upon the goddess, usually identified as Durga, or his queen, Motini, to save him. A few singers sometimes invoke Ram or Krishna, though it is only Durga who rides to Raja Nal's rescue. Typical is this example from "The Battle of Phul Singh Panjabi." Nal's wife, Motini, has been captured by the Nath yogi Jalandhar, and Raja Nal does not know where she is. He calls upon the goddess:

sung:	Memories of Durga come into his heart. In his heart, he remembers Durga. . . . You came in Lakhiyaban[1] with your langur (monkey, Hanuman) And filled your *khāppār* (pot/bowl)[2] with the blood of demons. And Durga did not wait even a moment, Hearing the voice of Raja Nal in her ear.
spoken:	As soon as she hears the voice of Raja Nal, she wakes up in her temple. She calls her devotees, and has her lion brought immediately, draped with a green cloth. And what does Durga do?
sung:	She rides at the head of four buffalo, With all kinds of powerful ghosts, male and female. Uncountable ghosts are clapping, And she has sixty-four yoginis, Durga moves with her army. Durga comes, To the border of Kampilagarh, And reaches Nal.
spoken:	He says, "Look, Mother has come." (WA 85:302–304)

In this passage the combination of bhakti, love for the goddess and her love for her devotee, and the potentially more destructive powers of the goddess are evident. Nal calls to her: she responds with an army.

That the singers have an attitude of devotion to the goddess is clear. One of the prominent written versions is by Gajadharsinh Varma, who writes:

> Oh Mother, you always help your devotee (bhakt).
> I am also poor so please save my honesty. Oh Mother and Devi of Dharagarh. Please don't be late.
> Come with your lions, a crown on your head.
> Bring fifty-two *bhairon,*[3] *kaulā,*[4] and langur with you.
> Oh Mother, come soon because our foe is angry and full of pride.
> If you eat there, then drink water here. I am waiting for you. Oh Sarasvati Mother, come on my throat. If I forget some part, then help me to remember.
> Give me that kind of line which will attract an audience.
> Oh Mother of Hinglaj, you also come quickly.
> You also bring fifty-two bhairon, fifty-six kaula, and the langur with you.
> Please save my honesty right now.
> I have heard that you are kind. (Varma n.d.)

Unlike the surrounding Braj region's emphasis on the bhakti of Krishna (especially among the higher castes), in *Dhola* we find the goddess, the mother, as the object of devotion by her children. This devotion lacks the erotic element of much Krishna bhakti and instead marks the merging of shakta traditions that "infused with popular bhakti devotionalism continues to be a vital religious force" in north India (Erndl 1993, 36). The devotee, often thought to be blind and needing to be led, demonstrates his devotion to his mother/lover. To return to the opening lines of the blind singer above, the blindness he invokes is both real and metaphoric: it is not uncommon for the devotee to be spoken of as blind, blind to the ways of the world and the powers of the goddess, unable to see the true nature of things. Women's songs to the goddess capture a similar theme, as in this song by Brahman women from Banaras:

> On the door of the mother, a blind man is calling,
> Give eyes to the blind, but after consideration.
> He must do your worship in your courtyard. (Hume 1990, 686)

To the devotee, singer, and audience, the goddess is the mother to whom one should be devoted as a child would be to a real mother: in response to this devotion, the goddess will ride to her devotee's rescue.

The Goddess in North Indian Religious Traditions

The goddess who is invoked in *Dhola* varies, though without doubt Durga dominates. As Raja Nal's mother says to the daughter of Phul Singh Panjabi, "My son is by birth a breaker of jails, by hitting and fighting he'll empty your kingdom. And fighting on his shoulder is Mother Durga" (WA 94:25). Most scholars of Hinduism contend that the prominence of the goddess dates to the first Sanskritic text to focus on the goddess, the *Devī Māhātmyā* from the sixth century C.E. Thomas Coburn writes, the *Devi Mahatmya* "establish[es] not only the autonomy and independence of the goddess, but also the *de facto* dependence of the gods on her" (1984b, 169). Most important, the *Devi Mahatmya* celebrates a goddess who is not a feminine form of masculine deities, but a female power in her own right (Coburn 1991). In effect, it elevates the goddess and portrays all power as belonging to a single goddess (Hume 1990, 430). The result of these developments is that the goddess "is subsequently understood to be a continuing salvitic presence in the world" (Coburn 1984b, 159).

Durga is the goddess named throughout *Dhola* by Raja Nal when he faces overwhelming problems. In one of the myths of the *Devi-Mahatmya,* Durga is created by the gods when faced with the demon Mahisa who, after heroic austerities, has been given the boon of death only from the hand of a woman. Mahisa then defeats the gods; when they assemble to seek revenge, a mass of light and energy emanates from their fiery energies and coalesces into the body of a beautiful woman. She then proceeds to kill Mahisa (Kinsley 1986, 96). As David Kinsley further notes, "She [Durga] is created because the situation calls for a woman, a superior warrior, a peculiar power possessed by the goddess with which the demon may be deluded" (1986, 97). The goddess who is created violates the model of the Hindu woman portrayed in Brahmanical texts (see chapter 5 below). She is not subordinate to any man; she does no household duties; she excels at male duties, such as fighting battles; and she is not submissive. Later texts focus even more on Durga's ability to control the universe. By the time of the eleventh to the twelfth century *Devī-Bhagavata Purāṇā* (Gupta 2003, 64), Durga's association with military prowess is consolidated and becomes known for giving one success on the battlefield. One story, no doubt related intertextually to Raja Nal's various moments of need in *Dhola,* portrays Ram as despondent about ever winning his wife Sita back; the sage Narad advises him to worship Durga to ensure his military success (Kinsley 1986, 109). Further, a number of manuscripts of the *Mahabharata* have the Durga *stotra* inserted just prior to the *Bhagavād Gītā.* The Durga stotra begins,

> Krishna spoke (these) words for the sake of Arjun's well-being:
> "Having become pure, Oh great-armed one, being about to engage in battle,
> Recite the Durga Stotra for the sake of conquering (your) enemies." (Coburn 1991, 27)

Thus, by the medieval period, the goddess is an establishment goddess (Kinsley 1986, 96), who takes on a role of protecting the cosmos and guarding dharma that is similar to the role of the god Vishnu. And similar, in a manner, to that told to Arjun by Krishna and invoked by Ram on the battlefield, Raja Nal turns to Durga whenever he seeks to win a battle, although, as we have seen, Durga, for Raja Nal, is often only an intermediary to his own first wife, Motini. Nevertheless, the forms of the goddess invoked by Raja Nal and his singers are all associated with Durga, a Durga who has a vegetarian flavor more commonly associated with followers of the gods Vishnu, Ram, and Krishna than with the followers of Shiva and his retinue of ferocious goddesses.

Over time the goddess is drawn into Hindu sectarianism, especially Shaivism and Vaishnavism. Those proclaiming Shiva as their great god have incorporated the goddess through the process of spousification (Uma, Parvati, Sati) (Hume 1990, 148). Drawing the great goddess into traditions associated with Vishnu is more difficult, and devi as Durga is adopted as a late feature of Vaishnavism (Hume 1990, 147). Yet the devotional elements that characterize north Indian Vaishnavism are present even in the *Devi-Mahatmya.* Continual stress is placed on the efficacy of worshiping the goddess, and the dire personal and social consequences of its neglect.

Dhola is known and performed in the Braj region on the borders of Uttar Pradesh, Haryana, and Rajasthan. This area is famous as the center of Krishna bhakti, for it contains the villages where Krishna was thought to be born and brought up. As a movement in the Hindu tradition, bhakti more generally involves anti-hierarchical ideas, in particular the denial of the necessity of the Brahman priest as intermediary: rather, any human being can reach out to god and receive his or her grace (Dimock 1966). The love and service of the devotee are thought to be transformed into the mercy and boons of the deity (Wadley 1975, 84). The Braj Vaishnavite traditions surrounding Krishna form a central part of Vaishnavism as practiced today (and carried abroad by the Krishna Consciousness movement), and scholars have focused almost all their research in Braj on the Krishna traditions (Vaudeville 1976; Entwistle 1987; Haberman 1994). Yet the goddess plays an important role in Braj religious life. Two points about the role of the goddess in the Braj region are critical to understanding the role of the goddess in *Dhola:* the underlying Shaiva and Sakta elements found in the region and the Vaishnava homology made between Radha and Durga.

Goddess worship is an ongoing tradition in the Braj region. As Alan Entwistle remarks,

> After the fall of the Gahadwalas [twelfth century], Vaishnavism in North India ceased to enjoy the patronage of the prevailing dynasties. Saiva and Sakta cults, deeply rooted in the villages, were fostered by the Jogis of the Nath Sampraday. They were followers of the Tantric[5] traditions that played such an important role in the development of popular Hinduism in the mediaeval period. Local goddesses became associated with manifestations of female divinity described in the Tantras and Sakta Puranas. (1987, 302)

These local goddesses, worshiped especially by women and the lower castes, never lost their popularity, despite the increasing dominant elite male Vaishnava traditions from the 1500s on. Mathura is thought to be one of the four *śakti pithās* (sites of the goddesses' powers) in Uttar Pradesh (Hume 1990, 46); and Mathura is included on the list of 108 pithas throughout India that are the sites of the goddesses' powers (Sircar 1973). A Mahavidya Devi temple is a key locale in Mathura, while the worship of the Sami tree, representative of the goddess, is frequent near the entrance to Krishna shrines (Vaudeville 1976, 206). Strong strands of Sakta and Tantric influence continue in everyday rural religious practice, as calendars of rituals for rural communities in the region attest (see, for example, Wadley 1975; see also Vaudeville 1976). All-night *jāgaraṇs,* or wakeful-singing, in honor of the goddess are especially prominent among the lower castes. Vaudeville remarks on a Devi shrine and festival at the site of Nari-Semri, near the town of Chata, where the joint deity is thought to be the *lok-devī,* the protectress, of Braj (1976, 206). A quick scanning of the lists of festivals in the Census of India for both Mathura and Agra districts shows more than twenty festivals in each of these two districts in honor of the goddess each year, with a total estimated attendance in the early 1960s of more than one hundred thousand. Nevertheless, the learned Brahmans, especially those of the Krishna-oriented Vallabha sect, were antagonistic to goddess worship.

One of the goddesses who is considered a form of Durga is Vaishno Devi, whose shrine is located near Katra in Jammu District in northwestern India, although she is never mentioned in *Dhola,* perhaps because her popularity is recent. In 1950 her shrine received some three thousand pilgrims yearly, while in 1990 it received more than two million pilgrims (Rohe 1997).[6] Many think of Vaishno Devi as a form of Durga (Rohe 1997). Vaishno Devi represents a more extreme Vaishnavism of the goddess, for here only vegetarian offerings are now accepted, despite prior traditions of animal sacrifice. Vaishno Devi's vegetarianism represents the increasing influence of Vaishnavism in the region, as well as the increasing influence of vegetarianism in popular culture more generally. In part, especially among Jats, it represents an attempt to achieve middle-class status (Malhotra 2002). (For the Jats, vegetarianism also sets them apart from Rajputs.) This influence is especially predominant in the area where *Dhola* is performed and, as we shall see below, plays a significant role in the battles between Durga and Kali.

Hence the goddess has been drawn into the Vaishnavite traditions. Vaudeville (1982) argues that, under the influence of the goswamis of Brindavan, Kali is all but excluded as a goddess. Instead, the golden-hued, "luminous" Durga, with Radha as her substitute, replaces Kali, who as the primeval mother (and a ferocious goddess who regularly demands animal sacrifice) is forgotten. As a goddess, Durga is transformed into the beneficent mother who can easily fit into the devotional traditions of bhakti: as a female she is thought to be naturally forgiving and a kind mother (Hume 1990, 433). Certainly this is true in *Dhola,* except for those who are Durga's enemies.

In the episodes focusing on Nal and Dumenti, Nal's constant enemy is Indra, king of the gods. At the svayambar where Dumenti is to choose her husband, Nal calls upon Durga for aid. Durga arrives with her retinue of ghosts and goblins. As written by Gajadhar, Indra then asks, "Who is this woman who looks like a murderer?" Then Indra adds, "He can have this marriage because of fright: I cannot get it. I fear this Durga" (Varma n.d.). And, indeed, despite her benevolence, the goddess, with her unbound hair and strange companions, could be a fearsome sight to those who are not devotees.

Yet the singers of *Dhola* portray a positive image of the goddess, one who aids their singing journey and aids their hero in his quest. The audience is continually reminded of the powers of the goddess. Often her exploits in other epic traditions or in other episodes of *Dhola* are recalled at the time that Nal remembers her, as here:

sung: One day she [Durga] was remembered by Shiv Shankar, and snakes wrapped around his neck . . .
One day she was remembered by Ramchandra, and he attacked Lanka;
One day she was remembered by Hanuman, and he set fire to Lanka;
One day she was remembered by Siya [Sita] and she met Ram.
(WA 89:11)

In these ways devotees are reminded that the goddess invoked by Raja Nal has a much broader range of powers than merely aiding this one devotee.

Durga is the mother, to the devotee's child: as a Hindu mother, she is remembered with respect, affection, and love. She responds with a mother's care of her child. A devotee told Mark Rohe of her view of the goddess as mother:

> One must try to establish a relation with the deity, especially with a mother. Once the relationship is there what is there to worry? This relationship is that of love. When you have a relation of love you don't have to ask your mother to feed you or help you. (Rohe 1997, 85)

It is the nature of the mother to take care of her child, and it is this mother, whether goddess or human, who is drawn upon in *Dhola*.

The goddess of *Dhola* is also a very winsome one, as she both laughs at her devotees and cajoles them into acknowledging their mistakes (or when they are unaware of their errors, in the excerpt below, reminds the broader epic audience of their errors). In a performance by Matolsingh, the goddess is very mocking of her devotees. The scene is this: Pratham has been invited to the house of the Merchant, where Manjha and Nal (here called Banvari, "the one of the forest," in reference to his birth) have been given refuge. The Seth is having Nal's sacred thread ceremony performed. His father, Raja Pratham, takes the boy Nal onto his lap, but does not realize that the child is his son and laments what could have been. The goddess then mocks him from the rooftop:

spoken: [Pratham says]
sung: "Oh, all my work is spoilt,
With one son like this in Narvar,
My name would continue,
But my name is submerged,
Oh god!"
spoken: He cries and tears pour from his eyes.
Durga comes on the roof, and the goddess speaks [mockingly],
sung: "Don't you feel bad?
He is the son of this father,

Why do you cuddle him in your lap?
You made your own leave,
Why do you repent?
At home your neighbors told lies,
And made a fool of you." (WA 89:9)

In another scene as sung by Ram Swarup Dhimar, the goddess, here Behmata the goddess of fate, teases Nal when he demands that she make a marriage for him.

sung:	[Nal says] In this way woman, make a marriage for me.
spoken:	So what does Behmata say?
sung:	Oh my son, in which village do you live? Who is your father, who is your mother?
spoken:	What does Raja Nal say?
sung:	Oh Mother, my village is Dakshinpur, My name is Raja Nal, I belong to the Merchant caste, In my house, salt, pepper, and coriander are sold.
spoken:	Then the old woman says, "Son, I don't have marriages for Merchants." (WA 84:235)

Through these devices the goddess is made accessible and motherly, sometimes teasing, sometimes protective, sometimes being the mother who reminds her children of their mistakes. It is Durga, and other forms associated with her such as the much fiercer Hinglaj Devi (whose temple is in Baluchistan in northwest Pakistan) or the goddess known as Kangrevali Devi or Brajesvari Devi (whose temple is located in Nagarkot in the lower reaches of the Himalayas) to whom Raja Nal is devoted. It is Durga, riding her lion adorned with a green cloth while holding her khappar, and joined by her monkey helpers and her troupes of ghosts and demons, who rides to the rescue of Raja Nal.

Durga and Kali

But Durga is not the only goddess who plays a major role in *Dhola.* This is especially apparent in two episodes, those of the "Battle of Phul Singh Panjabi" and the "Marriage of Kishanlal." These two very popular episodes focus the audience's attention on an emerging battle between Durga and Kali, between the benevolent and (here) vegetarian Durga and the destructive and carnivorous Kali. Through this contrast, the singers "think" through verbal images of body, social order, geography, and psychic other. In both episodes it becomes apparent that while Durga rides on the shoulder of Raja Nal, Kali supports his enemies, whether Phul Singh or the wicked Oil Presser women. At one level we can read these episodes as a battle between the two goddesses, and hence as a battle between destructive and more marginal forces (Kali) versus life-affirming forces engaged in restoring order (Durga).

I should note, however, that the boundary between the good Durga and the troublesome Kali in *Dhola* is murky, as when the goddess Chandi, the enemy associated with Kali, is called upon by Maru when Dhola comes to claim her as his bride. Further, Durga is sometimes associated with the Hinglaj temple, a site important to the Nath yogis and Kali. In Hindu traditions more generally, the distinctions between Kali and Durga are not always clear, beginning with Kali emerging from Durga's forehead. And in modern Kolkatta, priests at the Kalighat temple are purposely removing reminders of Kali's Tantric background as they "Vaishnavize her" (Gupta 2003, 62). But in *Dhola,* with its apparent agenda of denigrating Kali and the associated yogis in favor of the more socially acceptable Durga, more distinct lines are drawn.

In narrating (not singing) the "Battle of Phul Singh Panjabi," Ram Swarup Dhimar said, "The Panjabi was an expert warrior, and he was proud of the fact that he worshiped Kali. Durga used to fight with Nal, but Kali fought against him" (WA 94:26). Gajadhar, in his written version, describes this scene in detail:

> Now the Panjabi is praying to Kali, "Either take my life or destroy my enemies!"
> Oh my mother, save your devotee from the enemy . . .
> Kali is chopping and eating and drinking blood, along with her bhairon and yogis.
> From every village they have brought evil spirits and ghosts and they are shrieking [on the battlefield].
> With her bowl for collecting blood in hand, Kali attacks Nal's army . . .
> Motini gains the upper hand when she uses her magical powers from Bengal,
> She confuses the yogis and bhairon,
> She launches her vir (magical powers/spirits) against them,
> And her vir and Kali's vir begin to wrestle. . . .
> Again and again, Kali uses her mantras, making Nal's army unconscious. . . .
> The woman of Narvar [Motini] remembers Durga,
> Asking, "In which country are you hiding?" . . .
> The Old One hears this plea and comes, . . .
> Nal cries out, "Oh Mother, I will not survive Kali this time. Save me now, Behmata."
> Durga again calls her vir, who come racing,
> The Bhavani of Taragarh is happy to help her.
> Durga calls her army. Man-eating vir come instantly. There is Kalua, the ghost, with fire falling from his stomach. She brings him to the battle along with the Bhavani of Taragarh. She also brings Mahakali (the embodiment of all the goddesses).
> When Kali comes before Mahakali, she lays down her pot of blood. . . . Bhagavati is fighting like the Pandavas of the *Mahabharata*. . . . Kali puts her head

> on the feet of Mahakali. Mahakali tells Nal to strike off the head of Phul Singh. (Varma n.d.)

Of special importance in this segment is Durga's calling upon other goddesses for aid, especially the devi Tara. Here Kali is shown as a magician, fighting against the magic of Motini. Durga, as the goddess associated with warriors and battles, is renowned for giving swords that will grant victory to her devotees (as she supposedly did to the Maratha hero Shivaji and also to the Rajput kingdom of Mewar, where the sacred sword granted by Durga is worshiped to this day during the Navarata ritual) (Kinsley 1986, 109–110). Durga is the goddess who fights with swords, as a line from the sumeri that opens this chapter affirms: "Mother, do get ready, / And take your sword in your hand." But when Raja Nal is under extreme duress, when his enemies shift from fighting with swords to fighting with magic, Durga must seek additional aid, for she herself does not have the magical powers necessary to fight for her devotees. Hence, in this scene, she goes to the goddess Tara for aid. Tara, best known for her place in Tibetan Buddhism, is also worshiped as a Hindu goddess in Nepal, Bengal, and Assam, and is known for her magical powers, as a being who "specializes in spectacular, dramatic appearances when her devotees call upon her in dire circumstances" (Kinsley 1997, 94). And, like Durga, "Tara is often said to rescue her devotees from such desperate predicaments as being lost in an impenetrable forest" (Kinsley 1997, 94). Interestingly, in this battle between Durga and Kali, Durga calls upon a goddess most commonly associated with Kali and the Sakta tradition, but one whose characteristics at times resemble Durga more than Kali.

In other episodes Durga gets this magical aid not from a goddess but rather from Motini herself. And in the battle with the demons in the episode of Lakhiyaban, Durga abandons the battlefield because the sword she wields creates only more demons as every drop of blood transforms into a demon (an incident also found in the *Devi Mahatyma*).

On one issue the singers are unanimous: Durga fights on the side of good, whereas Kali fights with the enemies of Raja Nal, as affirmed by these lines from the "Battle of Phul Singh Panjabi":

> Phul Singh was cruel since birth.
> And jinn fight with him by day.
> And Kali at night.
> A comparable pair help Raja Nal,
> Both have equal pairs (of help). (WA 85:302–304)

The many forms of the goddess are marked by the predominance of one of the three *gunas,* or constituent qualities of the universe. The three gunas are *tamas,* darkness, ignorance, and indifference; *rajas,* passion, foulness, and pain; and *sattva,* goodness, virtue, and pleasure. Goddesses in whom tamas dominates are associated with Kali; those in whom rajas dominates are associated with Durga; and those in whom sattva dominates are associated with Laksmi or Sarasvati. All are, nevertheless, representations of the *ādiśakti,* the original power of the universe (Hume 1990, 18, 166). In line with the fact that Durga personifies the quality (guna) of rajas and Kali that of tamas, others have noted that,

> Durga represents heroic power—the power to fight, conquer and punish the demons and anti-gods. . . . Kali on the other hand personifies the unqualified power of destruction, supremely gruesome and grotesque. . . . If Durga or Candi (the Fierce), as She is often called, represents virtuous fury, Kali represents simply fury unrestrained. (Goudriaan and Gupta 1981, 179)

Providing further insight into this battle of the goddesses, I noted above that the connection between the Tantric tradition and the Goswamis of Brindavan in the sixteenth century resulted in the near exclusion of Kali in favor of the golden-skinned Durga. This emphasis on Durga (amalgamated with Radha) in precisely the region where *Dhola* is performed today may also contribute to her winning her battle with Kali. Finally, Erndl (1993) notes that the two goddesses "balance" each other, representing two aspects of the goddess, one gentle and one fierce.

Kali, dark in body, is generally associated with the periphery of society; early in her history she was associated with tribal or low-caste peoples who worshiped her in wild places (Kinsley 1997). Associated today with cremation grounds and battlefields, Kali is often depicted drunk on the blood of her victims. It is she who threatens stability and order, whereas Durga is seen as the preserver of the universe. David Kinsley writes,

> To meditate on the dark goddess [Kali], or to devote oneself to her, is to step out of the everyday world of predictable dharmic order and enter a world of reversals, opposites, and contrasts, and in doing so to wake up to new possibilities and new frames of reference. (1986, 130)

Given that *Dhola* is ultimately about order and the reintroduction of order into human society, it is not surprising that Kali is rejected in favor of Durga, a goddess concerned with maintaining the order of dharma. But another episode provides even further insight. In the "Marriage of Kishanlal," Raja Nal's nephew, Kishanlal, and son, Dhola, are kidnapped by two Oil Presser women whose goal is to offer them to the goddess Chandi,[7] here a representative of Kali. Like Kali, Chandi is known for her fierceness and her easy anger. In the Chandi section of the *Markandeya Purana,* it states that Kali bursts forth from Chandi's third eye. Chandi is also associated with Bhairavi, one of the ten *māhavidyās,* of whom Kali is first and foremost (Kinsley 1997, 191). Like Kali,

Chandi seeks blood sacrifices and, in fact, in the myths about the vegetarian goddess Vaishno Devi, we learn that Vaishno Devi incarnates herself as Chandi, understood as a form of Kali, in order to be able to kill Bhairo who has been stalking her (Rohe 1997, 71). In *Dhola* itself Chandi appears as a bad omen, for as Raja Nal is leaving his kingdom at the time of his banishment, he sees "Chandi bringing a milk pitcher: his throne was lost; kingdom was lost; life in palaces was lost" (WA 90:17).

Here I quote at some length from this episode. The two Oil Presser girls have kidnapped Kishanlal and Dhola, turned Kishanlal into a calf and Dhola into a parrot, and taken them to the shrine of Chandi.

prose: Havan (a fire ritual) is performed, and both say to Chandi: "Let us marry with these two sons. We have stolen them, allow us to marry these two boys." What does Chandi say? . . .
"I don't have the powers to save these sons for you. I can't defeat Nal. Riding on his shoulders, the goddess fights with him twenty-four hours a day."
What does Chandi say? "I am hungry for sacrifice (bali). Cut [sacrifice] one boy here and take the other with you for marriage. . . ."
One girl says, "I would rather live as before, unmarried. There won't be a fair split. So do not take your donation (*bhenṭ*, offering). Or accept two donations from us. But I will not pay you now. Save both these boys [for us] and when we have children, we will give our first children to you as an offering."
Chandi says, "I'll accept that. I will take two in place of one. Take these two with you. But do this: first hide them for eight days. The ninth day will be my responsibility."

Eventually Raja Nal discovers the missing boys and traces them to the Chandi temple.

sung: And Nal comes into the temple,
Raja Nal's head falls with a jerk at Chandi's feet,
And he talks with Chandi,
"Mother, tell me the truth." . . .
And Chandi is not a liar,
Sitting hungry for bali in the temple,
"You have lost your two loving sons,
Cut one and give him to me,
And I'll let you keep one."
Nal thinks regretfully,
Kishanlal is my brother's only son.
And I have only Dhola, . . .
sung: "If I shall cut one to serve you,
The royal throne of Narvar will sink,
If I offer Kishan,
No one will respect me."

Then Mansukh offers to sacrifice his own fifteen-day-old son. He returns to Siya Nagar, his kingdom, and retrieves his young son.

chant: The son of only fifteen days,
The queen embraces her son,
"Take my son,
So that the other sons are saved."
sung: Brother, this happened in the Treta yug,
There are no such friends in the Kaliyug,
Who would sacrifice a son for Devi. . . .

And Raja Nal remembers Durga who comes with her monkey helper, her ghosts, and sixty-four yoginis. Motini also comes.

sung: Raja Nal is holding Mansukh in the temple,
And Mansukh is ready to sacrifice his son.
"I will sacrifice my son."
And Motini reaches there,
And takes the son of Mansukh in her lap.

Durga defeats Chandi in battle, and Chandi cries out,

sung: "Sister, I didn't know that these were your sons,
Sister, I didn't know that these were your sons,
I was deceived in asking for offerings (bhent), . . ."
prose: Then Durga kicks Chandi one hundred yards into the underworld, saying, "I'll not leave you in a place where you can ask for sacrifices from anyone in the time of the Kaliyug."
sung: Well, then the lady of Nal comes,
With her container of magic,
She tears down the temple brick by brick,
Turns that temple into a pile [of brick]. (WA 85:306–309)

In this episode the battle between Chandi, here representing Kali and her demands for animal/human sacrifice, and Durga is clear. Moreover, Durga wins, banishing those demanding sacrifice to the underworld and, with the help of Motini, destroying the temple. Thus, at one level, *Dhola* is also an epic concerned with the appropriate form of goddess worship, including the use or nonuse of sacrifice. This must be contrasted to Rajput epics, where the hero himself is to die as a goat, to make a self-sacrifice (Harlan 2003, 130). The Rajput hero turns himself into a divine attendant or henchman of the bloodthirsty goddess. Raja Nal, as we saw earlier, dies by immersing himself in a rising lake.

The Kachwaha Rajputs who rule in Jaipur have one pair of goddesses who mimic the Durga/Kali scenario found above, as well as a *kuldevī* (literally, "goddess of the clan" or patron deity) story that links their vegetarian goddess to *Dhola*. Jamvai Mata, a vegetarian goddess, is the kuldevi of the Jaipur Kachwahas, but the goddess Shila Mata (the "Stone One"), stands in for her at the Navratri rituals in which buffalo (previously) and goats (now) are sacrificed. Moreover, Shila Mata's magnificent shrine is found in the Amber fort, whereas Jamvai Mata's small temple is on a distant ridge. It is not uncommon for members of the royal family to claim Shila Devi as their kuldevi, and it is quite likely that the public believes that she is their patron deity. Shila Devi is explicitly linked to Kali in some versions of her origin story, as she was believed to be won by the sixteenth-century Maharaja Man Singh when he battled Raja Kedar in East Bengal. Unable to defeat Kedar, Man Singh prayed to Kali who enabled his victory in return for his promise to obtain a stone image of her from the sea and install it in his fort. That stone image, ostensibly of Kali, is Shila Mata (Harlan 2000, 88–81).

Jamvai Mata, however, is linked specifically to Dhola and Maru, sometimes thought to be of the Kachwaha lineage (although there is no historical evidence of such a link). Here is her story, as related by Lindsey Harlan.

> The Kachwaha family is an offshoot of Kush [one of the sons of Rama in the *Ramayana*]. From Ayodhya it moved to Rahitasgarb, then to Nimarana, Dausa, Ramgarh, Amber and Jaipur. Dhola married a princess of Marwar, Maru. He'd married her at Pushkar below the age of five. His parents had met there [to get them married]. His mother noticed that the stars were bad, so she didn't disclose to Dhola that he had been married. [Later, when he found out about his marriage], he marched to Marwar.
>
> [At that time] [a] Meena [tribal] chief ruled Ramgarh. [Dhola said,] "Let me fetch my wife and on return[ing] I'll fight [him]." He returned and fought at Ramgarh. Dhola's army was killed and he was wounded. Maru wept and prayed to her kuldevi. She appeared [to Maru] as an old lady and said that a cow would come and give milk on its own [spontaneously, without being milked].
>
> Maru told Dhola to sprinkle some [of the cow's] milk on himself. He did this [and recovered].
>
> So . . . she [Kuldevi] was called Jamvai. Jamvai Ramgarh was the original name of that place. (Harlan 2000, 81)

Here we have two mythological connections between the Rajputs: the story of Dhola and two goddesses competing for human favors, one related to Kali and one acting like the benevolent mother Durga found in the epic *Dhola*.

Numerous other factors may have contributed to the attack on sacrifice present in *Dhola* in addition to marking a difference with Rajput values. These include the Vaisnavite (and vegetarian) overtones of the Braj region; the increasing pressure against sacrifice from British colonial rulers; the Arya Samaj movement which swept through some Jat communities and regions where *Dhola* was popular in the late nineteenth and early twentieth centuries; and the modern shift away from sacrificial forms of worship in popular culture. Whatever the contributing causes, *Dhola* manifests a clear affirmation of Durga and a denial of the forces of Kali. But there is one other set of players who are also crucial in these battles, and those are the various sects of yogis spreading Tantric rituals and beliefs across the north Indian countryside from 1200 C.E. on. Although most were Nath yogis, various sects of yogis are conflated in *Dhola.* The resulting message is a further attack on Kali, this time in association with the Nath yogis.

The Goddess and the Nath Yogis

The Nath yogis featured in *Dhola* represent the Shaivism that was the dominant cult in north India for many centuries (Vaudeville 1976, 196). As the ancient heartland of Shaivism (White 1996, 98), an underlying layer of Shaivism remains in the Braj region where *Dhola* is performed, one that tends to be ignored (by scholars, not necessarily the general populace!) where this story is found even today (Wadley 1999). Throughout north India, from Maharastra through what was the northwest frontier provinces across the Gangetic Plain to Bengal and Assam, the Nath yogis are represented in folklore, story, myth, shrines, and monasteries, while continuing their presence as both ascetics and householders. Said to derive from the supreme yogi Shiva himself, the Nath yogis, most often Gorakhnath but also other gurus such as Jalandhar, interact with humans—providing sons to the childless, as sometimes happens to Pratham; serving as gurus to women, as with Gopichand's mother (Lapoint 1978; Gold 1992); or teaching magical lore, as in the legend of Guga (Lapoint 1978). Although both ascetic and household yogis are found in the Nath tradition, "yogis who marry are held in contempt by others" (Briggs 1973, 47). While clearly worshipers of Shiva, the Nath yogis also venerate the goddess in her many forms, and a trip to Hinglaj Devi in what is now western Pakistan was thought to be mandatory for all those who sought to perfect themselves, to become adepts in yogic practices (Briggs 1973, 105). Nath yogis are frequently found at devi shrines (such as Nandi Devi in Nainital) throughout north India, where they often serve as functionaries, despite their association with the Shaivite forms of the goddess rather than her more benign, increasingly Vaisnavite forms. Moreover, their numerical presence is not to be discounted: Briggs (1973, 4) reports that, according to the Indian Census of 1911, more than 170,000 yogis were recorded in the Rajasthan Agency alone.

Most critically Naths are known as masters of "showy" supernatural powers (A. Gold 1992, 144). Tantric spiritual proficiency has always focused on the acquisition of supernatural faculties, ideally for the attainment of spiritual awareness. Yet those unable to seek spiritual perfection because of their remaining ties to the material world were often thought to practice acts that, in the mundane world, had results that were identified as magical, whether an exorcism or even a compelling of benevolent gods. Although not specifically Tantric themselves, the Nath yogis are thought to intermix Tantra and other practices that demonstrate a preoccupation with sex and black magic (that is, magic used for particular selfish reasons and not for the overall social good) (Brooks 1992, xiii). It is through oral traditions that we learn the legacy of these traditions. Ideally magic, or accrued supernatural powers, should not be used for one's own sake (Goudriaan and Gupta 1981, 113), although obviously many did not have such scruples. In the folk world of epics, magic is a manipulation of deliberately cultivated powers, often for selfish or destructive purposes.

The evil powers of the yogis are especially prominent in the episode of Phul Singh Panjabi. An extended translation of the concluding scenes focuses most clearly on the role of the yogis and the goddess, and, as we shall see, on Motini.

The Final Scenes of the Battle of Phul Singh Panjabi

Raja Nal, his best friend Mansukh Gujar, and Motini have sought to free his parents from the jail of the cruel Phul Singh Panjabi. Although the parents are eventually released from jail, the battle continues to rage. Nal is abducted by Sarvati's aunt Chando but then freed by a friendly magician from Tamilnadu. He returns to Kampilgarh where he finds Motini. They ready their army for another battle, and Phul Singh again goes to his daughter.

spoken: Sarvati says, "Father, it is not easy to gain our ends now. You must call my guru from Bengal."

Sarvati calls the Baba Jalandhar [one of the better-known Nath yogis]. And the baba comes, bringing fourteen hundred disciples with him.

sung: Baba comes near to Motini.
Baba faces Motini,
Motini hurls a vir to attack him,
And Baba throws one back at her. . . .
spoken: Motini loses her thirteen vir in this way.
sung: And Jalandhar has the power of fourteen vir.
Jalandhar throws another.

Eventually Jalandhar defeats Motini, turns her into a parrot, puts her in a cage, and leaves for his forest ashram.

spoken: Raja Nal does not know where his queen has gone, in which world.
sung: Nal and Mansukh are both crying,
Brothers, they are weeping bitterly.

Meanwhile Motini is with the Baba in Paramkuti.

spoken: Baba says, "You fool. I shall marry you. You have to marry me."
Now Motini thinks, "Oh god, what trick should I play so I can be rid of this difficulty? How can I get my husband? Baba does not accept any of my requests, and he has fourteen hundred pupils! He sits so comfortably." So she said, "Baba, I have a pain in my rib, much too much pain. If you can cure the pain, you can marry me immediately."
So Babaji orders his fourteen hundred disciples to find a doctor or *vaid* (traditional healer) somewhere. They reply, "We live in the forest. Where can we find doctors or vaids?" . . . [meanwhile, what does Nal do?]

spoken: He says, "Look, mother has come."
She replies, "Yes, I have."
He says, "Tell me, where is my Rani Motini?" . . .
She fits magic goggles over the eyes of Nal and says, "My son, look in all four directions to find our queen." When Nal turns his glance, he sees Motini, captured by the fourteen hundred babas. Motini is holding her rib and lying down, pretending to be ill. And she is saying, "Oh God, what should I do?" And Baba Jalandhar is sitting, taking her pulse.

Nal leaves on his horse and flies to Bengal, where he ties his horse at the edge of the forest. And he reaches Paramkuti.

spoken: Suddenly Nal calls out in a loud voice. "To cure ruined eyes, to cure broken teeth, to cure fever. If anyone is suffering from fever, I can treat that as well."
The pupils say, "Guruji, there is a vaid wandering nearby."
"Call him quickly," replies the guru. "My whole plan is failing. There is pain in the queen's stomach. Be quick."
The pupils run to Nal and say, "Come and see our patient."
He replies, "Sure, sure. I shall check. Come with me."
When he is brought to Jalandhar, they say, "See, he is the vaid, Guru Maharaj."

Motini tells Raja Nal to demand knowledge of the fourteenth vir as payment for his treatment: he is to write it down and give it to her. Every time the Baba rebels against a demand, she calls out, "My pain is worse," and the Baba relents. Eventually she learns the fourteenth vir.

spoken: "How are you?" And she would reply, "Sir, I am a bit better day by day. I shall be cured in a few days. I think we can marry then."
The Guruji then asks, "Should I sow barley seed in the Ganges?" . . .
Eventually she responds, "Come on, we have to feast today anyway. I can marry you tomorrow."
As the preparations for a feast proceed, and they are served, Motini says, "My lord husband, go from here quickly! You should leave at once. I will join you somehow. But you go and find your horse."

So Nal leaves and Motini turns into a bird (kite). The fourteen hundred pupils change into hawks and fly after her.

sung: The queen flies hastily.
As a kite, she flies.
And the fourteen hundred come as hawks,
Hoping to pass her,
And take her from the front. . . .
Motini cannot defeat them,
And suddenly falls in the water.

spoken: There is a tank. She transforms herself into a fish and falls into the water. . . . They are changed into herons and start to search from one side. Now Motini is surrounded on one side. So what does she do? She changes herself into a leech. An Oil Presser has come to water his bullock. Suddenly the leech goes into the stomach of the bullock. They continue to search, while she reaches the house of the Oil Presser. When they have searched the tank from side to side, they ask, "Now what has happened?" Then they look (magically) and say, "Maharaj, she has entered the stomach of a bullock."
He says, "Come on. I can cut open the stomach of the bullock. . . ."

spoken: The Oil Presser replies, "My bullock is very weak." They say to sell it nevertheless. . . . So she comes out of the stomach of the bullock in its shit. She rolls on the ground, changes into a kite, and flies into the sky.

sung: Motini is going toward heaven,
And nine hundred Aughars (Aghori is a Tantric sect) are after her.
All the babas are chasing her.
The bride will live no longer. . . .
Then Motini looks around,
As she reaches a city.
The daughter of Raja Cittrakatu, Chitra Reka, is standing on the roof,
Drying her hair.
Motini transforms herself into a necklace worth nine lakhs (*naulakh hār*)
And falls around the daughter's neck. . . .

spoken: She says, "Daughter, do not think that I am a necklace. I am Rani Motini, but I have been caught by the troubles of jugglers. Fourteen hundred Aughars of Paramkuti are after me. But please save my life. Right now, he is devising a plan. So please, don't hand the necklace to anyone."

The Acrobats demand the necklace worth nine lakhs, but the daughter refuses, despite her father's demands.

spoken: So the king goes back to Jalandhar. Jalandhar says, "My lord, your reputation is destroyed because your daughter will not give you the necklace worth nine lakhs. So do one of two things: either give us the necklace or cut out your tongue."

	So the king says, "I shall go again. I shall force her to give me the necklace: it will either break or the neck will break."
	Now Motini says, "Dear, you can't save me now. But listen to my words, Sister. Your father will surely get the necklace this time. But listen, please do not give it to the hand of others. Then you will not save me. Throw it on the stones."
	"Okay," replies the daughter.
sung:	When the father comes to his daughter, The daughter asks to give the necklace before the babas. Holding her wrist, he brings his daughter . . . To give the *darsan* (sight, vision) of the babas. The babas look around, As the father also looks (literally, "spreads his glance") The daughter takes off the necklace, And forcefully throws it on the ground.
spoken:	As she throws it on the ground, it spreads out like fire, pearl by pearl, and those pearls are destroyed.
sung:	And all fourteen hundred pupils become cocks, And all fourteen hundred pupils become cocks, And are picking up the pearls one by one, Motini, looking around, [thinks] "I can't live any longer."
spoken:	The pearl that is Motini is caught in the crack of a drain. Those pupils of Jalandhar pass over her, picking at the pearls. Now Motini is after them.
sung:	And when she sees Jalandhar—
spoken:	What does Motini do?
sung:	She rolls herself, And with the power of fourteen vir, She catches the baba. And Motini kills the baba. She kills some pupils and rebukes others, She destroys Bengal. She wins the fight with Jalandhar, The wife of Nal, Motini, leaves there. . . . And Motini comes to Kampilagarh.

When Motini reaches Raja Nal's parents, Pratham insists on taking his life, as he has been dishonored. Rani Manjha commits sati.

In this section the role of the yogis is as crucial as that of the goddess Kali with whose devotee they side. Further complicating an understanding of this episode is that two distinct sects of yogis are conflated into one. Jalandhar is a noted Nath yogi, but, in the later portions of the battle, Motini fights with yogis identified as Aughar (literally, "not terrible"), referring to those who are members of the Aghori sect of ascetics, one of the most radical of the yogic sects whose severe austerities are the extreme opposite of mainstream Hindu observance. Aghoris are known to inhabit cremation grounds, and are thought to worship Kali and eat corpses, carry skulls as bowls, and observe Tantric sexual practices. By associating Jalandhar with the Aughar yogis, the singers identify those with whom Motini battles as the least acceptable of all yogis, those on the outmost fringe of society. Writing in the nineteenth century, Denzil Ibbetson described the Aughar in these terms: he is found "wandering about the streets stark naked leading a jackal by a string, smeared with blood and human ordure, and carrying the same substances in a skull with which to bespatter him who refused them alms" (1916, 228).

The negative view of yogis in *Dhola* is further supported by the considerable skepticism about yogis in general in Hindu society. The singer Ram Swarup Dhimar once told me,

> When you see a baba in ochre robes, you cry "Baba, Sita Ram." But ninety out of a hundred babas are ones who were dacoits (robbers), or murderers. When they could not be safe [in their regular lives], they changed themselves into babas. Many babas wander to escape their [regular] lives. When people do not have any work, they start to beg. They beg from anyone and support themselves. Nowadays, there are many professional babas.

Writing about gurus, Kirin Narayan comments on a guru who tells stories of false gurus, "implying that deception by the false Gurus was well established in Hindu practice" (1989, 143). Hence it is not surprising that the yogis featured in *Dhola* are thought to be tricksters and work for the wrong side of the battle, especially since they are also noted as devotees of Kali. *Dhola* succeeds in its message affirming Durga precisely by linking the two sets of yogis with Kali. The Nath yogis are associated with the hated Rajput kingdoms, where they served as counselors to the king (especially in Jodhpur and Marwar) (D. Gold 1992; White 2001).[8] The Aghoris are the most marginal of groups, a group linked to Kali through their habitation of cremation grounds.

There is no simple, straightforward way to understand the roles of the goddess and the yogis in *Dhola.* What is clear is that Kali and the yogis stand in opposition to Durga and the heroes of the epic, especially Raja Nal and his first wife, Motini. No doubt Kali is thought to represent the less moral aspects of society and the elements of Tantra traditions, as well as ritual practices that are considered less acceptable by mainstream Hinduism. But the Nath yogis are often thought to be devotees of the goddesses, including (especially) Hinglaj Devi who here is on the side of Durga and Nal, although it is worth noting that the Bhairav who stalks Vaishno Devi, forcing her into her cave, is said to be a Nath disciple of Gorakhnath, so that *Dhola* is not unique in setting up an opposition of a motherly goddess against the Naths. Further, it is through the spiritual practices of the yogis that the enemy goddesses are sometimes understood to be able to acquire the magic that aids them in their battles, confrontations that shift from sword to magic.

A more mundane explanation of the role of the yogis is possible. Remember that *Dhola* is about an upstart king who seeks recognition in the eyes of the prominent Rajput kingdoms. Many of these kingdoms obtained additional help for their battles from the Nath yogis who served in their courts, where the yogis had the reputation of being able to wield magical powers (D. Gold 1992). I have found no evidence that the Jat kingdoms in the areas where *Dhola* is sung cultivated Nath yogis for their powers. Rather, the physical powers the Jats emulated were those of their patron deity Lakshman, brother of Ram (Sehegal 1971; K. Natwar Singh, personal communication). Further, frequent mention is made of their service to the Vaishnava traditions of the Braj area. It is not implausible that *Dhola* represents a subconscious move to deny the powers of the yogis known for their support of the Rajput kingdoms in favor of the more benevolent and respectable goddess Durga, to whom many in the area are devoted.

This tale also illustrates the role of women as followers of gurus. In this episode of *Dhola,* none of the men (Nal, Pratham, Mansukh, or Phul Singh Panjabi) has direct access to the yogis' powers. Honoring gurus is clearly women's work, and they reap the rewards. This connection between gurus, especially the Nath yogis, and women is frequently found in the oral traditions about the Naths. For example, Gopi Chand's mother, Manavati, was a disciple of Gorakhnath (A. Gold 1992). In the legend of Guga Pir, Guga's birth is dependent upon his mother's faithful devotion to Gorakhnath, who blesses her with a child. In my years of research in rural north India I have frequently known women who sought out a guru, and less often have I known men to do so. The real world and the world of the epic may not be so distinct.

Dhola also plays on the ever-present folk beliefs about the sexuality of gurus: Motini wins, after all, only because Jalandhar Baba wants to marry her. That yogis are "mere men" and are tempted by women is a frequent theme in folk tales collected in the village where this episode was sung, as well as throughout India.[9] Another folk motif common to the area and present in this episode is false illness, whether the result of love, of indulging oneself (as in food), or because of other factors. Motini's faked illness is a theme well known to rural audiences.

The Puzzle of Motini

Although *Dhola* is unmistakably an epic about the goddess Durga and her ability to restore order, especially when her devotees are attacked by the forces of disorder, forces often aided by Kali and her associates, it is not possible to sort out the roles of the goddess, the yogi, and the demon without examining Motini and the part she plays in *Dhola,* along with the roles of women more generally. In many episodes Motini and Durga work in tandem to achieve their ends, with Motini stepping in where magic is needed, while Durga wields only her sword and her armies of ghosts. The role of Motini, and of females more generally, is explored in the next chapter.

5 Motini, Dumenti, and Other Royal Women

Nal's woman is a force to be reckoned with. She set fire to the gate of the fort and is now holding a sword. (WA 89:15–17)

Whether it is the goddesses Manjha, Motini, Dumenti or other women, females dominate the action in *Dhola,* in contrast to the prevailing norms and scholarly interpretations of north Indian society. The prevailing norms for women, especially of the upper castes and classes, acknowledge that women have some powers, especially in the realm of ritual and religion, although women are also thought to be oppressed and often constrained by the rules of purdah, or seclusion. In north Indian society it is the men who should leave the home and protect the family. Yet, in *Dhola,* the women are powerful, and the men essentially weak and passive, providing a significant contrast to the standard views of rural north Indian women. Hence the women in *Dhola* continually transgress the norms for proper female behavior, whether talking back to their husbands, moving outside the confines of the women's quarters, or using their magic against enemies.

Women in the Braj region, especially those of higher status and caste, are contained within their houses and courtyards where they follow strict rules of purdah. Purdah involves both the seclusion of women, and their silence and covering in public spaces or before older male relatives, thus limiting women's access to power. This seclusion is evident in the opening scenes of many episodes of *Dhola,* when Motini, Dumenti, Manjha, and other queens are found living in the women's "Rang Mahal" in their husband's or father's kingdom, markedly separated from their male kinfolk (a separation marked by the movement of the men to the Rang Mahal to confer with the women). In the human world, these Rang Mahals of the elite women are the "purest," most confined spaces in the landscape. But as the action moves out of the court, so, too, do the women, only to return to purdah at the beginning of a new episode. For lower-caste women different norms apply; the Oil Presser's wife, for example, moves much more freely about the town and countryside, capturing the freedom of movement found among lower-caste women in rural

India even today, thus marking, more blatantly, the contrast with the elite. As the heroines of the epic leave their secluded palaces, they demonstrate religious powers that extend beyond the usual women's practices of *vrats* (fasting) and *pūjās* (worship of a chosen deity), of protecting husband and family through worship of the relevant gods (Wadley 2000).[1] Moreover, these women are argumentative, challenging their men at every turn, as they seek, with the help of the goddess, to restore order to the kingdom of Narvar.

That women are subverting the accepted forms of male dominance in *Dhola* is clear from the very beginning of the first episode, when Manjha challenges her husband, Raja Pratham, with the bet about whether the birds at the lake are crows or geese. She then schemes to make sure that Pratham wins, even though it means that she must spend twelve years scaring crows off the roof: here the paradigm of the virtuous, secluded, and obedient wife is immediately contested and then reinforced. This is a message that continues throughout *Dhola,* as its female characters act to save their men, while at the same time, because they are pativrats, always worshiping their husbands.

Another key female early in the epic is the Sweeper woman who compels Pratham to seek the help of the gods to gain a son. Roaming the streets in the early morning, as mandated by her job as a latrine cleaner, the Sweeper woman sees the "man without progeny" (Pratham) and, having seen a childless man, a highly inauspicious omen,[2] must go without food for the day. Yet Pratham's actions are not enough to gain that son: only Manjha, having been a sati in a previous life, a woman who immolated herself on her husband's funeral pyre, is able to obtain the rice kernel that will yield a son. This is a story driven by women, rich and poor, high caste and low, goddesses, heavenly nymphs, wives, mothers, and daughters. That women propel the narrative is not new to Hindu mythology: after all, in the *Ramayana,* Raja Dasharath's third wife, Kaikeyi, and her servant force Ram into exile. But in *Dhola,* despite the male heroes, the women either instigate action or come to the aid of the heroes in their times of distress. *Dhola* ultimately portrays a world in which women are very powerful, but it is a power that must be directed toward the needs of family and kin. As we shall see, powers directed to selfish ends, whether those of men or women, lead to sorrow and destruction. So while the women in *Dhola* contest and transgress, through their challenges of geography and behavior, the standard norms articulated in both Sanskritic Hindu texts (e.g., Leslie 1989) and village oral traditions (Wadley 1994, chap. 2), they ultimately reinforce the core idea of the woman devoted to her husband and family. I explore these themes in this chapter, beginning with Motini, the heavenly nymph who continually comes to Raja Nal's aid, both before and after she returns to heaven when he marries Dumenti.

Motini: The Daughter of the Demon and the Wife of Nal

Ram Swarup Dhimar told this story (condensed here) to explain Motini's origins:

> A Brahman meets the demon Bhumasur in the forest and tells him how to rid himself of the sins of his previous lives and hence to rid himself of his giant stature: he must raise a virgin girl and give her in *kanyadan* (gift of a virgin in marriage). Since the gift of a virgin is the greatest of all gifts, he would gain merit and be reborn as a better living being in his next life.
>
> Now the demon goes on grazing in the forest but cannot find a virgin. Finally, one night, as he [comes] from grazing in the Dang Forest, he comes upon a group of apsaras from Indra's heaven playing at a pond. Wanting to see the heavenly nymphs, he moves close. Now Motini is six months old, the daughter of Rambha, and is lying in a swing while the apsaras dance. Bhumasar sees the swing and thinks, "there must be a child in that." Coming closer, he sees that her skin is golden-hued, and decides, whether he dies or not, to try to capture that *kanyā* (virgin girl). So a brawl erupts with Raja Indra, king of the gods. Neither can win. Then Indra says, cleverly, "Come, let us gamble with cowry shells. I will place this child as my bet: if you win, you may take her. If I win, I take your head." Even though the dice are Indra's, Bhumasur wins. Then another battle is fought, and Bhumasur wins the water horse, the whip, the *vīj* mantra, a necklace of eighty-four gems, and the seven-edged sword.
>
> Bhumasur takes the child to the forest where his fort is protected by thorn bushes and bamboo. She is educated in the magic arts of Bengal. When she is twelve years old she still has never seen a human.[3]

Motini, born of the heavens, raised by a demon, and married to a king, is never quite goddess, never quite human. As an apsara, she cannot bear children with her human husband. But as a pativrat, a woman who worships her husband, she can protect him by returning to earth from her heavenly abode after she commits suicide at the time of Raja Nal's second marriage. To Raja Nal and his descendents, she is, in fact, a goddess. Yet unlike the goddess who can use her innate powers to meet the needs of her devotees, Motini must rely on the magic that she learned under the tutelage of the demon and later stole from the Nath yogis.

Raja Nal and his kin and helpers continually call upon Motini as they would (and do) on the goddess. When captured in Bengal at the time of his marriage, Nal's nephew, Kishanlal, appeals to Motini in this way:

sung: Has my mausi (mother's sister) Motini deceived me?
Once you came to Bhim Sikil, and drove the Aharapati (the elephant of Indra) from the fields,
Kishanlal cries and his voice reaches heaven,
Motini awakes and speaks to the apsaras,
"Sisters, you can play together happily,
But trouble has come to my Kishanlal,

I am going to Bengal now."
Holding the container of magic,
Motini moves ahead. (WA 85:306–308)

In a more modern style, Matolsingh composed this version of Motini's arrival at Dhola's wedding,

> Mansukh remembers Motini,
> And tears flows from his eyes.
> The Gujar stands there in deep meditation,
> "zoom, zoom," just then arrives Motini sitting in her flying machine (Matolsingh n.d. [c])

At the time of his ritual of consummation of marriage as sung in Karimpur, Dhola himself calls upon Motini,

> spoken: Then he remembers Motini, and he calls out from the mango trees [where he had been turned into a parrot], "Where are you, Rani Motini, help me in this hour of need. You went away from Narvar with folded hands,
> Now keep its honor, keep the honor of Narvar, Rani."

And Motini responds,

> spoken: Oh my brothers, what does she do, the Rani Motini is showing her magic there.
> Motini uses her magical powers (vir), the queen of Navargarh. Navargarh's woman, Motini, who is loved by the living, she uses her spell. Listen to me, she turns him into a dog. (WA 84:233)

Later in the same episode, even Dumenti calls upon Motini for aid:

> spoken: So what does Dumenti tell the bahu [son's wife; more generally, "wife"]: "Oh Santin (first wife), listen, control yourself, get him out of jail. Get him, the brave one, out of the pit. Make your name known. He is sitting in the cage, Oh son [speaking to Motini], listen to me. In the cage, the prince is crying, at least think a little of him. *Betādev* (son who is god, here directed respectfully at Motini), please get him released from the pit." (WA 84:233)

Just after she marries Raja Nal, the wicked Merchant uncles of Raja Nal quickly learn of Motini's powers, for she stops their boat in the ocean after they throw Raja Nal overboard and will not release the boat until Narad instructs the brothers, "Bow your head to this goddess [Motini], and when she blesses you, your ship will move" (WA 94:24). But Raja Nal does not accept his wife's powers until they are proven in the battle against Phul Singh Panjabi. Initially he refuses to acknowledge her dream of the jailing of Raja Pratham and Manjha; then he refuses to allow her to join his army; and finally he cries on the battlefield when his army is turned to stone, and he and Mansukh are blinded at the boundary to Phul Singh's territory. Mansukh speaks first to Nal.

sung: "Nal! I told you again and again,
But you did not heed my words,
Today if Motini were with us,
She could return our eyesight. . . ."
sung: Nal says, "Oh my friend,
Remember the name of the queen,
Perhaps my queen can help us in this bad time."
spoken: Nal says,
sung: "Oh daughter of the demon,
Take care of me,
Oh Motini, daughter of the demon,
Take care of me. . . ."
spoken: Hearing these words, Motini comes to their tents. (WA 85:303–305)

Yet even after Motini restores their sight and proves her powers, Nal denies them. Initially he stands crying, unable to conjure a plan to free his parents. Motini challenges him, and, finally, sighted once again, Nal wants to leave Kampilagarh saying,

spoken: "It doesn't matter if my parents die or something else happens. We came here to free them, not to be blinded. I have no power to free my parents. If we are blinded again, everything will be destroyed. Let us not move ahead."

Motini then removes Sarvati's magic stone that guards the border to Kampilagarh, but Nal still refuses to step across the border. She comments,

spoken: "It is too much trouble, they are very afraid! It is difficult to direct them correctly."

So Motini herself crosses the border to prove that she will not be blinded. Then Raja Nal bravely asserts that he will set fire to Kampilagarh. Motini responds,

spoken: "My lord husband, just now you were ready to return home and now you are ready to set a fire. You don't have the power to free your parents. You should follow my instructions."
Nal responds, "Tell me."
Motini says, "Listen to me." (WA 85:303)

By the end of the episode of Phul Singh Panjabi, Motini's powers are fully accepted, and thereafter Nal can call on her, as well as Durga, when troubles befall him.

Unlike the goddess Durga who can either direct her monkey helper or her ghosts to aid her devotees or act for herself, Motini must battle with magic, marking her as more like the yogis (and hence more on the boundary between human and deity). Her magic seems all the more powerful because she is a pativrat, a wife devoted to her husband. Motini is the only female magician who is clearly married. At one point Motini speaks directly to her status as a pativrat when responding to a call from Nal's kin:

> chant: "Your brother left me, in the middle of my life he deceived me, . . .
> Now I will not deceive you,
> This is the word of a pativrat." (WA 84:233)

When she is attacked by the evil sons of the Merchant on their ship after they have thrown Nal overboard, she responds,

> sung: "I am a woman who has taken the vow of one husband, I am well protected." (Khacherudas 1975, 28)

Throughout Hindu society the goal of being a pativrat is upheld as the highest standard for female behavior. As Draupadi, heroine of the *Mahabharata* and wife to the five Pandavas, proclaims when asked how she has maintained such control of her five husbands, "There is no deity like him—that is, like one's husband—in all the god-filled worlds; when he is pleased, through his grace (*prasadat*), all desires are fulfilled; when angered, he kills" (quoted in Leslie 1989, 280). Implied here is not only devotion to one's husband but also obedience to him. Ever since the time of the Laws of Manu (circa 200 C.E.), Hinduism has made clear the necessity of female obedience: Manu states that a female in her youth should be ruled by her father, in marriage by her husband, and in old age by her son. Being a pativrat protects Dumenti when she is alone in the forest, after Shanidev separates Dumenti and Nal, for Shani cannot touch her, "as he would have the curse of a pativrat." Thus he must find another way to compel her to action (WA 89:12). Similarly Vir Singh is forbidden to touch the sleeping Dumenti when he kidnaps her from the banks of the Ganges.

Pandit Shankar Lal, a singer of *Dhola* on a commercial cassette, provided a story also found in the *Ramayana* to emphasize the powers of the pativrat.

> It is true that the pativrat can control god. Once there was a sati named Ansuya whose husband had left on a trip and she was all alone. Now Brahma, Vishnu, and Madadev's wives all told their husbands that if Ansuya were more of a pativrat than they, it would insult them terribly. The women had three kinds of tantrums: those of kings, those of women, and those of children. So the three gods were pressured by their wives and were forced to go to Sati Ansuya's door, calling "Give us food."
>
> Sati Ansuya saw the three gods standing at her door, and brought flowers and fruits to offer them. But the three gods refused this offering and demanded food. So Sati Ansuya agreed and had them sit inside while she prepared food. Then the gods said that they had one more condition: they will only eat if she feeds them

while naked. Hearing this, Ansuya was terrified and prayed, "If I send them off without food, it will break the dharma of a householder. And if I stand naked before them, it will destroy my pativrat dharma. If I am a true pativrat, these three gods should immediately become small babies. If a mother stands naked before her baby, it is okay." God heard her and saved her pativrat dharma by transforming the three gods into babies. Then Mother Ansuya took off her clothes and started feeding them milk. Then she pulled out a swing, and all three gods went to sleep in the cradle. (Shankar Lal 1987)

The power of the worshipful wife is seen yet again when Shanidev finds Raja Nal and Dumenti in the forest, and thinks, "Who will believe that Nal is in trouble if his wife is still serving him? I must do something so that both are ruined [separately]" (WA 94:27). So anything is possible when one is a pativrat. Motini, as a pativrat who is not deity and not human, is more powerful than most, especially given her magical skills.

Yet despite their devotion to their husbands, Motini and the other women in *Dhola* contest the image of the pativrat while claiming its status, for Motini is anything but an obedient woman. Dumenti, the Oil Presser's wife, and other married women also continually challenge their husbands, although only the higher-caste women are ever referred to as a pativrat. Pativrat status is difficult to attain, perhaps demanding at least a modicum of female obedience denied to women who must earn their livings alongside their husbands in the marketplace and fields. Moreover, as Motini herself says, "Pativrats cannot be bought in the market" (WA 85:303).

Motini's powers are those of magic. Indeed, in one episode, Raja Nal himself says,

sung: If they will fight with swords, I'll do battle with them;
My Motini will fight against [their] magic. (WA 74:109)

Motini only uses her magical powers against those who have ill treated her kin. Further, she responds only to the calls of her husband's family and his retainers (especially Mansukh Gujar), and her powers are only good against the magic of others. This contrasts with the unmarried and wicked female magicians with whom she battles, especially Sarvati, the daughter of Phul Singh Panjabi; Gendwati, the princess in Bengal; and the two Oil Presser girls who kidnap Dhola and Kishanlal. Both Sarvati and Gendwati wish to marry Nal, and the Oil Presser girls seek Dhola and Kishanlal as husbands.[4] All these women are driven by lust, by uncontrolled sexuality, and it is this lack of control that ultimately leads to their downfall as Motini defeats them.

Throughout north Indian oral traditions, the most powerful magic is thought to center in Bengal, also considered to be the home of the most powerful yogis. (It is important to note that *magic* is not the best translation of the term: what we are talking about here is the use of spiritual powers for this-worldly purposes, purposes that are oftentimes selfish or vengeful.) Numerous folk traditions emphasize the difference between the clever wife and the lady magician. In Indian folklore the most wicked lady magicians are those of Bengal, and they are present in *Dhola* as well as other folk epics such as *Gopi Chand* (A. Gold 1995; Hiltebeitel 1999). These lady magicians of Bengal are low caste and completely without morality. They lie to one another and to their leader, and are ultimately saved only by their wifely and motherly roles, when the bread burns or the babies cry causing their husbands to look for them (A. Gold 1995, 60). These lady magicians (and in folk beliefs, also yogis) leave home for power: they are essentially selfish. In *Dhola,* the contrast between the princesses who are magicians and Motini is not so clearly drawn, but careful attention shows that Sarvati is driven by her father's inherent cruelty ("Phul Singh was cruel since birth. And jinn fought with him by day" [WA 85:302–305]), and Gendwati by her selfishness and desire for marriage to Raja Nal. Motini, though she uses the magic of Bengal, learned from both lady magicians, her demon father, and the yogis, is married, and uses her magic as a pativrat for the sake of her affinal family.

Whereas Phul Singh had been cruel since birth, the implication is that Raja Pratham and Raja Nal have been moral. Sarvati is implicated in immorality because she uses her magic for her father's egotistic venture, for his wrongful pride, as well as for her own desire to marry Raja Nal. As a resident of Karimpur (home of the singer Ram Swarup Dhimar) once told me, "When there is pride, there surely will be sin [*pāp*]. Man makes progress until he becomes proud." At one level Sarvati is acting properly, for it is a woman's dharma, her religious duty, to obey and save her male kin. Given the patriarchal family structures of the region, a woman such as Sarvati would have no option but to help her father in whatever way she could. The result here, as in real life, is that Sarvati aids an immoral person. Motini's magic, however, is used wisely, not for her gain as much as for her kin whom the epic considers righteous and moral. The moral weight of the story is in her favor.

As Ann Gold (1995) has shown, women approve of magic when it represents powers acquired properly and used for righteous purposes. As with her status as neither a human nor a deity, Motini's magical powers and lack of obedience place her on the boundary of proper female behavior. She almost steps outside the limits of properness (she does have these powers, after all), but she never transgresses their use. The implication, especially as Motini invokes her pativrat status when aiding her kin, is that magic as a married woman, as a woman whose role it is to protect her affinal family, aligned with devotional practices, is positive magic. Moreover, as we saw above, Raja Nal often calls upon the goddess Durga as a devotee; she in turn directs him to Motini, so that Motini's use of magic is supported by the gods.

Yet in addition to her knowledge of magic and her pativrat status, Motini has another tool to use against her enemies, her sexuality. As we saw in chapter 4, it is her desirability that leads Jalandhar to teach the physician the fourteenth vir that allows her escape.

Sexuality and Desire

Desire, of men for women and women for men, is continually played out in *Dhola.* Raja Nal is repeatedly the object of female desire, whether it is Motini when she first glimpses him in the demon's fort, or Sarvati who falls for the "Nal as acrobat," or the snake daughter of Basukdev who is so enamored of Nal that she takes birth as a human, or Dumenti who rejects the king of the gods for the human Nal. For men, the picture is more complicated: the heroic men (Nal especially) seem driven to seek wives for status and power,[5] while men who are wicked (the Merchant's sons, Jalandhar the yogi, and Vir Singh), like the women, are driven by desire and lust. Whereas the heroes and villains are separated by their appropriate or inappropriate desires, women are left undifferentiated and lustful, and in line with mainstream Hindu thought. In both Brahmanical texts and oral traditions, the sexuality of the wife/mother is not to be demonstrated, although, as Ann Gold (2000) has shown, certain situations and songs allow women to speak of their own sexuality among themselves. But generally a woman is not only forbidden to speak before senior male kin or outsiders, but her clothing and modesty are continuously monitored, involving head covering within the house in front of senior men and visiting women as well as shawls and other enveloping clothing outside. In fact, "wifeliness" does not involve overt sexuality, something kept for the images of the dancing girl. The sexual flirtatious woman is inappropriate in the household.

In *Dhola,* however, female sexuality is shown, under the right circumstances, to give women power. In the "Battle of Phul Singh Panjabi" Motini must use her sexuality twice—first to gain access to the court of Phul Singh Panjabi as a tantalizing Acrobat and, second, to have Jalandhar, the Nath guru, desire her as a wife. This is a sexuality not associated with women in purdah, with proper female modesty. Motini uses her disguise as a lower-caste woman, an Acrobat (see also chapter 6) to develop this blatant female desirability. This is a theme that resonates in other north Indian folk tales. Folk tales from Karimpur (Wadley 1994, 47–49) frequently involve a woman who must win her husband's love, which has been lost for some reason. Most typically the husband marks his dislike of his wife by refusing the food she makes, marking the link between food and sex that is also strong in north Indian folklore. But as a wife, a woman cannot entice her husband, so she takes on the disguise of a dancing girl, sets up camp in a garden (an area outside normal village life), and dallies with her husband who falls in love with the charming dancing girl (whose face he may never have seen because of purdah and his rejection of his wife). Eventually, after returning to the heavily veiled role of wife, she reveals her true identity to her husband, usually through something having to do with food, reversing the initial rejection via food. But the sexuality that recaptures the husband is not that of a wife but of a dancing girl, comparable to the transformation Motini undergoes in becoming an Acrobat. Here is the description of Motini's transformation to a dancing girl cum Nat/acrobat:

spoken: Finally Nal relents and tells Motini to make herself look like a juggler/acrobat.
See! Look at Motini making herself into a juggler.
sung: She has a sandalwood stool put out for a bath.
spoken: Nal says, "She made us bald, and she is using a sandalwood stool for bathing!"
sung: She has a sandalwood stool put out for her bath,
And has the hot water mixed with the cold.
spoken: What happens next?
sung: And the odor of sandalwood infuses her clothes,
And scented oil is rubbed into her hair.
spoken: When the queen is dressed, what happens next?
sung: She is wearing twenty rings on her ten fingers,
Rings that are stamped, "Made in Agra."
She wears bracelets, chains, and anklets,
And a necklace that is flattering to her breasts,
As she looks at her face in the mirror.
The daughter is not yet fully dressed.
The bodice is like a hill, with a dark border,
a design on its edge.
Nothing about Motini is unattractive,
She wears a wonderful necklace,
Prostitutes are found in her dancing party,
And she wears a gold armband.
She has jewels in her ears, while pendants hang from them,
And rouge glows on her cheeks,
The Queen is beautifying herself thus,
She puts a *bindī* [auspicious red dot] on her forehead,
The moon is shamed at seeing her face,
The beautiful daughter of the demon.
The daughter ornaments herself like this—
She puts on rings with chains,
And looks at her face in the mirror.
The daughter is not fully ready even yet.
spoken: What happens next?
sung: Her beautiful round lips are like a peach,
And *pān* [betel nut] has colored them red.

A diamond hangs from her nose,
Satisfy yourself slowly when gazing at the beautiful Motini.
Let some of that juice [*ras,* sexual energy] go to Narvar,
With that, the husband's respect will be safe.[6]
Motini isn't a moment late.
She stands after dressing,
And the queen of the apsaras feels shame.

spoken: Raja Nal says to Motini, "Queen, what have you done? Look at my condition, dogs will bite me on the road, and you—where you go, you will get respect. The two of us are a pair in such different dress. How will we succeed?" (WA 85:302–303)

With these lines, sung to the tune used by women when describing the dressing of a bride (adding another layer of sexual meaning to the song), the singer captures the beautiful and erotic Motini as she prepares to enter the court of the Panjabi. This description of the dancing girl, similar to descriptions of a bride (who, unlike Motini, once dressed, is then enveloped in shawls to be hidden from view) is in sharp contrast to the women in purdah, hidden behind screens and shawls, and unavailable to the male gaze. (Compare figure 5.1 from a nineteenth-century travelogue of India, to figure 5.2, a modern woman from the Braj region in purdah.) After all, for Motini's plot to succeed, she must attract the attention of Phul Singh. And indeed she does. But, in doing so, she puts herself on the stage, in the public eye, singing and dancing, all considered acts of utter shamelessness by the Rajput elite.

In India, as in many cultures, the eroticized female body and the comparable acceptable sexual male body are relegated to a caste status, the former of the lower caste and the latter of the elite.[7] In the rules governing castes the elite male has power over the lower-caste male, and has the right to claim his woman (as indeed happens when Phul Singh Panjabi attempts to enter Motini's tent at night, since her men were thought to be mere Acrobats). It is that potentiality which is developed here, as Motini makes herself as alluring as possible in the hope of attracting her enemy's attention. In her disguise as a low-caste woman, it is appropriate for Phul Singh to desire her. But, as a wife, Motini should not be desired by any male other than her husband. This concern is reflected in the lines, above, "Let some of that juice [*ras,* sexual energy] go to Narvar, / With that, the husband's respect will be safe." Here the singer acknowledges the inappropriateness of Motini's sexuality vis-à-vis her husband's honor as king of Narvar.

Matolsingh captured the concern for unrestrained sexual desire when he said, "Just as the boat of the greedy always sinks, the person who is sexually awakened is always entangled by beauty" (Matolsingh n.d. [c]). And, indeed, sexual desire does lead to entanglement and downfall. In the "Battle of Phul

Figure 5.1. Dancing girl. Nineteenth-century illustration from Louis Rousselet, *India and Its Native Princes: Travels in Central India and in the Presidencies of Bombay and Bengal,* ed. Lieutenant Colonel Buckle (London: Bickers, 1878), 99.

Singh Panjabi," not only does Phul Singh so crave Motini the Acrobat that he forgoes all sensibility, ignores the guidance of his prime minister, and ultimately is defeated, but his defeat is aided by his daughter's equally strong desire for the male Acrobat, Raja Nal. Sarvati has such enormous desire for him that she makes the fatal error of giving Motini half her magical abilities in exchange for a promise of later marriage. Here both king and daughter reverse the

Figure 5.2. Woman in purdah, late 1990s. Photograph by Susan S. Wadley.

acceptable code for desire, that of desiring the higher status, as both desire one who is low and Other.

One of the challenges facing Motini and Dumenti, two women who most regularly claim pativrat status, is dealing with men, other than their husbands, who desire them. When a married woman is desired by a man other than her husband, as Motini is desired by the Merchant's sons and Dumenti by Lakha Banjara after she loses Nal in the forest, she resorts to a ruse long practiced by female anthropologists and other women living in Hindu society: she addresses him as Brother (or Father or other natal relative) and demands that he treat her as a sister (with whom incest prohibitions rule out sexual relations).

It is in a later episode, however, that we find lasciviousness portrayed more fully. In "The Battle with Vir Singh," Raja Nal and Dumenti have gone to bathe in the Ganges at Banaras. A great saint who came there to bathe daily was Raja Vir Singh. Dumenti and the six-month-old Dhola were in a curtained bathing cubicle when the wind blew the curtain, enabling Vir Singh to see Dumenti with her child:

sung: Seeing the laughter of the queen [as she sat with Dhola on her lap],
Vir Singh loses his control . . .
And the image of Dumenti is from that day stuck in his heart . . .
And five heavenly nymphs come from heaven to serve him, . . .
"Tell me the truth, wise one, what is the problem?"
Vir Singh loses his cool,
He says, "If I do not get Nal's queen, I will kill myself with a sword."
And the fairies from heaven go and tell all,
Someone hold the hand of the son,
"Oh! Son, have you lost your brains?"

spoken: The brave fairy then holds his hand and asks him to cool down, "Oh! Raja Vir Singh! I have never seen such a king in my life. You have done nothing but worship the Ganges. What has come to you today, it will destroy you. Your family will be destroyed, so listen to me, do not attach yourself to this queen."

chant: "When there is no life in this world, only water and wind will remain,
Even if the world treats me badly, today I will become engaged to this queen."

spoken: And Vir Singh says, "Without getting this queen, I will not leave. I have left all worship, even if I am sent to hell. I will not leave her, no matter what." (WA 90:18)

So the fairies from heaven (who tell Vir Singh that they are junior to Motini and hence unable to defeat her) kidnap Dumenti and take her to his fort. But Vir Singh is warned not to touch her sleeping body:

spoken: "The goddess of this world will curse you. You will be burnt to ashes." (WA 90:18)

Eventually, as with Jalandhar and Sarvati, Vir Singh's inappropriate sexual desires lead to his downfall. His pride and sexual desires cause him to give up all knowledge of his powers, powers gained through his years of worship at the Ganges, and this ultimately results in his death. Hence *Dhola* has yet another message about order and chaos, and about appropriate boundaries: keep lust under control and do not desire those to whom you have no rights, for disaster is sure to befall you. Notably, however, males and females are equally at fault: Nal is as enticing to Sarvati as Dumenti is to Vir Singh. This message runs counter to the more dominant Hindu ideology that places the blame for sexual desire, and other evils, onto women, while at the same time, and in a contradictory fashion, extolling women's virtues as pativrat and the producers of sons.

Women's Nature

Writers of Hindu texts and composers of oral ones agree that the nature of the female is ambivalent. Ram Swarup Dhimar expresses his issues with female sexuality in discussing good and bad omens, often used as markers in the singing of *Dhola* for disasters that await the heroes. Omens that one sees at the beginning of a journey are taken seriously: I have been stopped from leaving Karimpur and sent back into the house on some excuse when one of the women, gathered to bid me farewell, has seen a bad omen as I was to depart. The ubiquitous overfilled trucks that fill the Indian highways are painted with good omens in an attempt to ensure the safety of truck and driver. Omens focus our attention on the natures of males and females, and on what is good and bad about each. Female omens focus on reproduction, both of the family through offspring and of the household through prosperity. First, the bad omens: a woman with her head uncovered or a female cobra because "women and female cobras are alike." Women with uncovered heads are not following the dictates of female purdah and are hence shameful and inauspicious. Although Hindu goddesses are often shown with disheveled locks, a woman's hair should be bound, for unbound hair marks a woman lacking control, whether control of herself or control by men: widows and prostitutes are also portrayed with unbound hair.[8] A crazy woman with her head uncovered and scratching at lice is particularly inauspicious: here the loose hair of the woman and the lice indicate an unclean house and a lack of bathing and proper hygiene, all insults against the gods and symbols of the lack of prosperity in the woman's household and her potentially destructive powers because of a lack of sexual control. A widow carrying an empty pitcher is truly ominous, for she portends a lack of both human and household reproduction. Particularly menacing are omens related to the lack of marks on a woman's body denoting her favorable marital status. In rural north India four body ornaments are crucial to marking the marital state. One is glass bangles; at her marriage a woman dons glass bangles, removing them only at her husband's death, when she ritually breaks them, never to wear glass bangles again. A second ornament are toe rings, the counterpart in north India of the wedding ring, which the husband puts on the bride's toes during the marriage ceremony. Third is the bindi, or forehead mark, now often made of plastic and "pasted" on the center of the bride's forehead, also not to be removed unless a woman is widowed. And the fourth adornment is the sindur, a line of red vermilion in the parting of the wife's hair. Especially bad omens for women are a broken bangle, a toe ring that slips off the toe, or a bindi that falls off the forehead: these are all portents of the husband's death and the woman's impending widowhood. In fact, in Matolsingh's performance of Motini's marriage, Motini realizes that the wicked uncles have committed a crime against her husband when her bindi keeps falling off her forehead (WA 89:6).

Good female omens also derive from the fertility and reproductive powers of the female, whether reproductive of humans or of household prosperity. These include a cow with a male calf (the cow symbolizing the female); a Gujar woman (milkmaid or shepherd) with a brass pitcher full of milk; a woman with a child in her lap; a pregnant woman; and a Sweeper taking her pigs to the fields to graze. Ram Swarup described that, although a woman can be Lakshmi, the goddess of prosperity, and a pativrat, the caste (jati) of a woman and a sadhu are the same, implying that both have enormous destructive powers (and also that both fight with magic, something householder men do not do). Indeed, seeing a baba on the road is more inauspicious than any of the bad omens named above regarding women. Still, women should not be insulted, for every person alive, after all, is born of a woman: life depends on women, and women have given birth to great men like Prahlad (a boy who worshiped god against the evil desires of his father and aunt). But we cannot know what is in a woman's stomach, that is, her thoughts and very nature, for women keep their true nature hidden whereas men are open about everything (WA 84:240). Finally, women should know their place, as Manjha acknowledges upon seeing Pratham at Raja Nal's sacred thread ceremony:

> "In matters of the raj (kingdom), women cannot be consulted . . .
> I am governed; he is the king. He knows justice for us." (Matolsingh n.d. [c])

Mothers and Daughters

If a woman's nature is potentially destructive, a mother's nature is not. It is motherhood, after all, that compels the menfolk to bring the lady magicians out of the jungle. Mother and son are linked by the mother's milk. Writing about Rajasthani hero stories, Lindsey Harlan quotes a Rajput who commented, "It's the mother's job to tell the son to kill, to die, to fight in battle," for the son's heroic deeds will "make the mother's milk resplendent." Or, as one Rajput nobleman put it, mothers would say, "you've suckled my breast, now fight" (Harlan 2003, 104–105). The message in *Dhola* is less straightforward, for mothers such as Dumenti often try to stop their sons from setting out on adventures that may lead to battle (usually signaled by bad omens). It is more likely that the son will invoke his mother's milk as a sign of strength, as when Raja Nal says, before he leaves to recover the missing cowry shells needed to free his Merchant grandfather, "You give me the strength of your milk, Mother, for I am not going to stop now" (Matolsingh n.d. [b]). And in this epic of confused identities, a mother's milk is more commonly used as a sign of recognition than as a battle cry.

The scene that most clearly articulates a mother's recognition of her son is Nal's return to Dakshinpur after marrying Motini and being thrown into the sea by his Merchant uncles. Nal returns in the disguise of a Pandit (transformed by the flower given to him by Basukdev's daughter). He claims to be her son, but in his disguise Manjha cannot recognize him. She cries out,

> spoken: "You are tricking me. You are not my son. What is your name? If you were my son, then you would touch the milk in my breast."
> So he puts his mouth to her breast, and says, "Look, I am twelve years old! I don't drink milk from your breast. Your body is all dry and nothing will come out of it."
> Manjha responds, "If you are my son, there will be milk, even if not enough to fill a pitcher . . ."
>
> sung: And Nal calls out to Durga . . .
> And such was the blessing of Behmata,
> That streams of milk came from the mother,
> Streams of milk came from Manjha,
> And fell into Nal's mouth. And the mother of Nal is happy,
> And she embraces her son. (WA 89:21)

In a similar scene Dumenti, about to be kidnapped by Vir Singh at the Ganges, begs the infant Dhola, "Oh my son, drink my milk. . . . If I survive, we will meet again" (WA 90:18). Milk also pours from Dumenti's breast in a Rajasthani version of the Nala story through a wooden breast plate (Harlan n.d.).

But whereas wives support their husbands, and mothers empower their sons, daughters bring sorrow to their parents, especially around marriage. As Motini is torn between her demon father and Raja Nal, the poet comments: "Now she is thinking about one and then the other. In one direction is the father and in the other the husband. After the husband comes, everyone has to leave the house of the father" (Matolsingh n.d. [b])—and, by implication, become a pativrat whose primary devotion is to her husband. Budh Singh himself laments having to deliver his daughter Maru into an "alien's hand," that is, to the unknown upstart servant of the Oil Presser. At issue here is the complex question of hypergamous marriage.

Among Rajput royal families, giving daughters in marriage signals intimacy between the two families and marks their mutual alliance. In *Dhola,* as in other epics (e.g., *Alha, Pritvīrājārasau*) of north India, there is an emphasis on marriage as a mark of alliances, reflecting the importance of alliance politics in medieval India (Kolff 1990, 92). Historically marriage alliances were used to confer Rajput status. Writing on the chronicles of western Rajasthan, Norman Zeigler quotes from a history of Mevar, "[give us your daughter and] make us Rajputs [*mhamn Rajput karo*]" (from the Naisī re Khyāt II:333; quoted in Zeigler 1973, 51). In giving a daughter, a man acknowledges the husband as his equal or better: it is the acknowledgment of this equality or superiority that Raja Nal seeks from Budh Singh. In this way, women become pawns in a game of negotiation and alliance building.

In high-caste Hindu households, a daughter is the greatest gift to be given to another (the kanyadan, or gift of a virgin), but she must be given into a family with higher status than that of her natal family in what is known as an *anuloma* marriage, or "the direction the hair grows—with the grain." Hence taking a daughter from another family is a visible sign to all of one's higher status, and giving a daughter is a mark of one's lower status. It is this problematic that drives both Bhim Sen to seek Indra for Dumenti and for Budh Singh to attempt to stop Maru's marriage to the unknown Dhola. Bhim Sen desires a god for his daughter, to cement his own alliance with the gods, but also because his daughter is so beautiful and talented. Dumenti's mother repeats incessantly the advantages of marrying Indra over a human: "If you go to the kingdom of the gods, you will become a divine queen. You will move about in flying machines, and, moreover, the name of Samudsikul will be famous throughout the heavens" (WA 94:19–20).

For Dumenti to overturn her father's choice of a marriage partner is also an attack on the patriarchal family, for by denying his wishes she subverts his power (see Doniger 1999, 308). She may also bring enormous dishonor. When Dumenti, alone and wearing rags, returns to her father's house after losing Nal in the forest, her father rages:

> "Today, Daughter, you have turned my honor (literally *pagṛī*, turban) worth millions into ashes. Oh, human beings are like worms that live in grain. . . . that is why you have come alone from your affinal home to your natal home." (WA 94:27)

When Raja Nal is thought dead (by everyone but Dumenti) and she agrees to a second svayambar, her father rejoices, for this time he might succeed in getting the alliance he so desires, only to have Dumenti, for a second time, identify her human husband and subvert her father's desire for a divine alliance.

But it is the obverse alliance, and the potential meaning embedded therein, that drives the "Battle of Bhamartal." Here Raja Nal, a man in rags living with the Oil Pressers, somehow manages to defeat Budh Singh at dice. In a cliché common in Indian folk traditions, the bet involves their unborn children:

whoever has a son will marry the daughter born to the other. Budh loses and must marry his daughter, not yet born, to Raja Nal's son, also not yet born. But Budh Singh refuses to acknowledge Raja Nal as an equal and sets before him various conditions that eventually lead him into battle with the Bhils (a tribal group of Rajasthan) and with demons of the forest. Only when he has defeated these adversaries does he prove himself equal to Budh Singh, and the marriage is allowed to go forth.

Raja Nal is under the same imperative: he does not want his queen to give birth to a daughter, for then he would have to marry her to Budh Singh and acknowledge that he is beneath him. As Dumenti begins her labor in the oil press, Raja Nal says to her,

spoken: "Queen, may you have a son,
And I'll have a name in the world.
If you have a daughter in your womb,
Then I'll kill her in the oil press. I'll not keep her, I'll destroy the seed."
The queen's sobs burst from her chest,
And she said, "How can I change my fate? . . . How can I console my heart? How do I know if I'll have a son or daughter?"
And Nal replies, "Oh Queen, bear a son."

Later Nal adds,

spoken: "If a daughter is born from your womb, then I'll behead both of you. And if a son is born, we'll have a name in this country. We have a score to even with Budh, and if Budh has a daughter, then I'll forcibly marry her and take her away."

At midnight the two children were born: Dhola to Raja Nal and Maru to Budh Singh.

sung: And Budh has Maru,
And a shadow falls on Kanauj,[9] . . .
In Bans Bareilly, sadness is everywhere,
All pleasure is dirtied, rubbed in the mud;
Through coercion the kingdom is being given away.

Meanwhile, Behmata, as the midwife to Dumenti, has gone through the city putting a *satiyā*, an auspicious design marking the birth of a male child, on every door. When Budh hears about this, he wonders which sister fucker put the satiya on the doors when a daughter had been born. Instead of readying their musical instruments for the birth or the marriage celebrations (both requiring music), they ready their swords. Meanwhile, Raja Nal and the Oil Presser immediately write a letter to confirm the engagement, saying that they will marry the girl immediately and bring her up themselves. When Budh hears this, he and his wife, Queen Saroja, lament their circumstances, and his wife says,

spoken: "Oh Husband, look at her to your heart's content,
Then I'll tie the daughter to my stomach and jump off some cliff.
I'll keep her unmarried for her whole life,
But I'll not marry her into the house of an Oil Presser!"

Then his ministers say to Budh,

spoken: "You have given your daughter to a foreigner, and you'll get to know it the day that the entire Oil Presser family stands on your doorstep" [the first part of the marriage ceremony at the bride's house is called *dvār* (literally, door), when the first gifts from the dowry are made to the groom's family]. (WA 85:305)

Budh then asks for a gift of 350 maund of newly pressed oil in order to finalize the marriage. The Oil Presser is convinced that all is over, but Raja Nal orders a tank built in the king's outer courtyard and a pipe built to connect it to the oil press. By morning, the tank overflows with 350 maund of newly pressed oil. Eventually, after Motini and Durga arrive, Raja Nal instructs Dumenti to "fill your pot with truth and pour it into the oil press, / Worship this till morning while quickly turning the press" (WA 85:305).

When Budh Singh realizes that the Oil Pressers have, in fact, fulfilled their obligation of filling the tank, he demands that Nal collect sugar cane from the jungle where he will have to fight the demons living there. Nal accepts the challenge and eventually, after fighting both the Bhils and the demons, returns with the sugar cane. (The singers say that this occurred on Deothan, the day that falls in the Hindu month of Kartik [sometime in November] when the gods are awakened after their four-month sleep that begins in the early monsoon, and the first sugar cane for the year is harvested and worshiped.) Aided by the Bhils and demons, he brought loads of sugar cane and piled the bags in front of every house, so that they blocked the doors and the men would trip over them when getting up at night to urinate.

Eventually Raja Nal is recognized. He says to Raja Budh,

sung: Get your daughter married.
I have not come here to stay forever,
My problems are now over, I'll leave the oil press.
Tomorrow I'll return to my own country.
And Nal says, "Now my problems are over.
Oh Raja Budh, tomorrow I will leave." . . .
And [Raja Budh] takes his daughter in his arms,
Dressed, she comes to him,
And Budh performs the gift of the virgin. (WA 90:19)

In *Dhola,* with its origins in the Jat areas of Braj, this emphasis on alliance politics and status gained through marriage is more poignant, as the epic proclaims the right of the he-who-is-thought-low (albeit also he-who-won-battles) to the hand of the daughter of he-who-is-thought-high. In fact, Nal's hypogamous marriage to Motini, the heavenly nymph, is a reminder of the potential disasters befalling those who "go against the hair" and marry a woman of higher status (Donniger 1999, 186). Motini herself points to the potential problems when she acknowledges that she cannot bear children for this mere human but makes Raja Nal swear, in any case, that he will marry her and her alone.

Interestingly, although *Dhola* singers continually "think" through the issues of marriage and alliances by playing with ideas of the social order that challenge the norms of hypergamous marriage, ultimately they back away from these transgressions: Motini returns to heaven and Raja Nal marries a human; Budh Singh's fears of marrying Maru to a lowly Oil Presser are allayed by Raja Nal's prowess in battle, a marked demonstration of his warrior status. Only Dumenti perseveres in challenging the system by rejecting her parents' demands that she marry the godly Indra and choosing, instead, the human, but equal, Raja Nal.

The Puzzle of Motini Revisited

Motini has many identities: the apsara learned in the magical arts of Bengal, the pativrat of a human; the sati returned to her heavenly abode from whence she can aid her one-time kin; the sexual being who relishes the disguise of an Acrobat; the wife who chastises her husband for his cowardliness; the woman unable to bear children. She is a woman firmly on the boundaries between human and goddess and between woman as benevolent and woman as destroyer, a condition sometimes referred to as the split identity of the Hindu female. Although Motini challenges the everyday norms for women, she never fully transgresses them: she always supports her husband, whereas Raja Nal abandons her. Even as a woman without progeny, she aids her husband in founding a lineage, as any proper wife should do.

Unquestionably *Dhola* celebrates female powers, powers denied to women in everyday life. Repeatedly we find beliefs across India that counter restrictions found in the everyday lives of women, women who believe in their ability to maintain a moral order, to restore harmony, to support kin and community. Marine Carrin and Harald Tambs-Lyche (1993) point to the sorcery attributed to women in tribal groups and the association of the goddess and Rajput women in Rajasthan: in both groups women are attributed powers in the supernatural realm, powers denied them in real life, and, also in both, women are thought to use these powers when marital rules are violated. Likewise, in the south Indian epic *Cilappatikaram,* a woman maintains the moral order when her husband flaunts it. Despite her independence and the use of her powers often against her husband's will, Motini is always tied to her husband, and ultimately she submits to familial demands. One message of *Dhola* may be that it is acceptable to be a powerful female, so long as that female uses her powers appropriately. This may be a crucial message in an epic devoted to the goddess, especially the goddess Durga who (usually) stays within the boundaries of rightful action. At one level *Dhola* tells us how to live on earth and use our (female) powers appropriately.

One must also wonder, or at least I do, about this male, lower-caste epic as a site for extolling the powers of women. Women do not sing *Dhola* and are not likely to hear it sung. Yet, unlike most epics, this one extols the powers of wives and of women in general. In a Bengali version of the Gopi Chand epic, Gopi Chand's father states, "You are but the wife of my house, / but I am the master of that house. / If I accept wisdom from a housewife / How can I call her guru and take the dust off her feet" (Kanika Sircar; quoted in A. Gold 1992, 66), thus refusing to acknowledge the divine powers of his domestically powerless wife. Raja Nal, albeit with initial reluctance, accedes to the use of his wife's power, in fact demands it, as he stands tearful and blind at the battlefield where his parents are captured. In later episodes, after he marries Dumenti, he must again call upon this first wife Motini for victory in his battles, for Dumenti's more human birth and rearing have not given her the magical powers necessary for battle. When I asked singers of *Dhola* their views of Motini and Dumenti, they always praised Motini for her action and Dumenti for her devotion. This opposition, too, is part of the cultural knowledge of the rural males who sing *Dhola* even today. Moreover, as we shall see in the next chapter, lower-caste women do not normally adhere to the norms of conduct mandated for the rich and powerful. Whether an Oil Presser's wife or a female Bangle Seller, or indeed the Jat women who regularly work in the fields alongside their husbands, women display powers and participate in social life in ways not always discussed in the Hindu textual traditions or the scholarly literature. By looking through the lens of caste, the varied and complex roles of women in Hindu society come into greater focus. Hence, as the singers comment on their society by playing with caste identities as they sing *Dhola,* they further comment on women and their roles.

6 Oil Pressers, Acrobats, and Other Castes

Raja Nal to the Oil Presser whom he meets when in the forest covered with the sores of a leper: "How can we fit together? I belong to the caste of Chhatri (Warrior/Kshatriya) and you are an Oil Presser by caste. What about the problem of food?" (WA 84:243)

Dhola is performed primarily in the multi-caste farming communities of rural north India, and its performances capture the essence of key social relationships in such communities. Rural villages often contain as many as twenty distinct endogamous caste groups, each living in a specified portion of the village, and with its own caste culture, behaviors that are transmitted from generation to generation, perhaps only through oral learning. Each stereotyped in particular ways (e.g., Merchants, or Banyas, are fat and greedy), caste cultures are reflected in dress codes, in jewelry, in the style of a man's turban, in the likelihood of a child receiving formal schooling, in rules for appropriate female behavior and for marriage, as well as male occupation. Caste culture is also manifested in rituals, as the annual cycle of ritual activity changes as one moves from caste to caste. And it can be reflected (and enacted) in the actual performance of rituals that all groups share, for the details of the same rituals vary by caste (not unlike the ways in which the Irish and the Italians might differ in how they celebrate Christmas or a wedding). Each caste is also linked to a particular occupation.[1]

The social and geographic separation of castes sets up relatively impenetrable social and physical boundaries. *Dhola* singers construct their epic story building upon these core ideas about individual castes, especially using ideas based on occupations, particularly as related to the social geography of north India, to advance their story. Thus it is not surprising that when Kishanlal and Dhola have been kidnapped, it is a Potter they meet on the road who can point them in the direction the boys were taken. Potters, after all, wander the roads and byways looking for cow dung to fuel their kilns, as well as loading their donkeys with their wares and traveling from village to village, town to town, to sell their pots: thus they should be on the road. Farmers, in contrast, stereotypically never leave their village and fields. Using what are believed to be the everyday behaviors and characteristics of a few key representative castes (castes that seem chosen to fit the story line), the *Dhola* singers creatively advance their story, sometimes with hero and heroine (Nal and Motini) being given or taking on the disguise of a different caste and sometimes inserting characters of particular castes. Acting as different castes allows both hero and heroine to cross social and physical boundaries that would otherwise be impossible. Focusing on ideas of social order, bodily difference, and geography, the singers think through and comment on the nature of caste, on issues of birth versus achievement, and on status more generally.

Caste in Hindu Society

In singing women's songs of abuse of the groom and his kinsmen at Nal's marriage to Motini, Behmata says, insultingly, "I do not know your caste, Oh Banvari (one of the forest)" (Matolsingh n.d. [b]). To be of the forest, to be out of the caste system, puts one outside society. In India a person knows how to react to and behave toward another person on the basis of their *jati* (caste). One's jati is a status that is awarded at birth when one's fate is written by the goddess Behmata. This fate is based on one's prior merits and demerits as they were tallied by the Yama, god of death and the accountant who determines one's next birth place. Without caste, one is almost a nonperson, and, in fact, those excommunicated from their caste because of breaking rules of marriage or purity find themselves outside society, unable to interact with others, comparable to Raja Nal's banishment from society as a leper and mad man. When Raja Nal's caste is not known, or is in question, those around him are at a loss as to how to interact with him. Aside from gender, caste is the most salient identity one can have in Hindu India. In many instances caste overrides gender because the proper behavior of both men and women changes by caste.

The chapbook *Dhola* by Gajadharsinh Varma contains a story that illustrates the essence of caste:

> Once there was a swan and a crow who were faithful friends. One day a king invited the swan to a feast, and the crow begged to go also. The swan agreed, but said, "Friend, I can take you only if you do one thing: don't caw because the king has called only those of my caste of birds." So they dressed the crow beautifully and the two traveled to the feast where the king greeted them respectfully and asked them to sit in their caste line. [At feasts in rural India each caste is placed in a separate line of seated feasters. The highest castes are then fed first.] But the crow instead started flying around eating the leftover food, because that is what crows do. (Varma n.d.)

This story shows that one cannot hide one's caste, for its habits are a part of one's nature. It is exactly this message, found in the first chapter of Gajadhar's

Dhola, the episode in which Rani Manjha becomes pregnant with Raja Nal, that permeates *Dhola.* By implication, it is suggested that Raja Nal's true identity cannot hidden, and that the true caste identity of a person cannot be transformed. One's core caste habits remain no matter how one dresses or attempts to transform oneself, for one's caste habits are a part of one's nature, ordained in a co-joined physical body and moral code at birth. Raja Nal cannot hide his Warrior status, although it is continuously contested, nor can the Oil Presser or the Potter or the Acrobat hide his. Gajadhar's metaphoric story, seemingly inserted with little cause, in fact summarizes one major message of *Dhola.*

Postcolonial scholars have questioned the salience of caste as a category in precolonial times, while also critiquing the spiritual understandings of caste of Louis Dumont (1980) and the monist views of Marriott and Inden (1987). What *Dhola* highlights most importantly is that caste "has always been political" (Dirks 2001, 13), and that this political orientation of caste is far more salient than the religious understandings promulgated by generations of Euro-American scholars, from Abbe Dubois to Marriott. As one category of marking identity, one that in *Dhola* we see as fundamentally political, caste has been and remains, albeit in a different political stance, crucial to understanding social relationships in India. Gajadhar's story of the crow captures the essence of caste: with its biological (the crow), moral (what one can eat), and cultural (how to dress and comport oneself) components, caste is crucial to marking the identity of the person.

Hindu notions of personhood, most scholars would agree, are based on a unity of the biological and the cultural. The Hindu person is not merely a biological being in cultural garb but a particular biological being joined with a caste-specific (and gender-specific) set of cultural behaviors and a given moral code (see Marriott and Inden 1987). For those trained in European thought, there is a fundamental belief in a split between nature and nurture, whatever emphasis we may place on one or the other at any time. But to the Hindu, much of what Western thought attributes to nurture (morality, aggressiveness, spirituality) is thought to be inextricably tied into an individual's very biology. For the Hindu, his or her core being is both biological *and* cultural.[2] Each individual is born with a certain biological substance that is encoded with a given set of cultural norms and expectations. This biological/cultural "person" is highly mutable: contact with impure substances can alter the purity of the body as well as how the person must then act. Eating "hot" foods can make the person more aggressive, despite an original quality of personhood that was passive,[3] but the essence of that person remains unchanged and he or she could not be as aggressive as one whose birthright is to be aggressive. This principle is articulated as "the righteous duty of a given person of a stated social status in a particular stage of life." In popular practice, it is more clearly captured in the notion of a caste dharma. Crucial here is the Hindi term *jati,* usually translated as caste. Jati is etymologically related to the Latin *genus.* Those born into a given jati share in both bodily substance (especially levels of purity or the ability to digest certain kinds of foods—or even inauspiciousness) and also moral code, a set of rules for right action *specific to that particular jati.* Hence humans should not share genetic substance across jati lines, as this mixes two kinds of humans. And each jati has rules (albeit culturally defined and continuously changing) for right conduct—for example, whether to eat meat or to drink liquor or even to plough a field. Individuals cannot change from one jati, or caste, to another, for their original personhoods are immutable: they cannot discard the body/moral code to which they are born, although certainly eating, bathing, and other daily activities constantly change the very mutable Hindu body within the limits of bodily substance and morality awarded at birth.

Jatis, the everyday categories of ranking used in rural India, are closely related to but distinct from the four varna, or broad social groupings, of classical Hinduism (in rank order: Brahman, Kshatriya, Vaishya, and Shudra, while outcaste or untouchable, *acchut,* groups such as the Sweepers are outside the varna system). In an ideal world each jati would belong to one of the four varna or the untouchable category. In fact, these identifications are highly contested and widely variable and fluid, so that a caste can claim a Kshatriya status but acceptance of that claim, both historically and now, depends on the approval of higher-caste groups.[4] Furthermore, varna and jati are not the same: for one thing, there are hundreds of jatis in South Asia but only four varna.

Raja Nal's defining quality of human-ness is played out as he is transformed into varying social groups representative of the multi-caste communities of the farming region where *Dhola* is sung. But ultimately Nal cannot be everything, encompass all humanity, because Hinduism mandates that humans be divided by caste. Nevertheless, Nal begins to understand what it means to be human, because each of his imposed identities allows him to see the world as Other, to see the world from the standpoint of those who are not kings. Feminist scholars have recently learned what Nal learned: that one's view of the world depends on where one is standing. Dorothy E. Smith writes that there is a "mode of experience that is distinctive to women and in important ways an experience that has marked us off from men" (1989, 34). Hence a female's view of the social order differs from a male's, while a black female's view differs from a white female's, and a lower-class female's view from a higher-class female's. I would argue that each caste group has a similar mode of experience that is different from other caste groups, an experience that is captured in part in *Dhola.* While Raja Nal is identified as an Oil Presser, he sees the world from that standpoint. Yet especially when working in the oil press, Raja Nal is torn between the world he currently inhabits as a poor, badly clothed laborer and the world to which he thinks he belongs as a king.

As we explore Raja Nal's various identities and disguises, as well as those of supporting actors, I shall highlight those episodes and identities that reveal the most about this tension between biology and culture, between birthright and achievement. *Dhola* does provide a challenge to the core principles of Hinduism, despite its ultimate affirmation of those principles when Raja Nal is acknowledged as a "true kshatriya," accepted (albeit reluctantly) by the kings of the Rajput kingdoms.

Raja Nal in the Oil Press of Raghu

Raja Nal has three major caste-linked disguises: his childhood as a Merchant, his transformation into an Acrobat in order to defeat Phul Singh Panjabi, and his exile as an Oil Presser. It is the episodes involving the Oil Presser that highlight most clearly issues of ascription and achievement in the social order of Hindu society. Scholars are now aware that the ranking systems of the Rajputs, based on lineage and genealogy, were both relatively late constructions (post–sixteenth century) and were also glorified by James Tod in the *Annals of Rajasthan* (1971), to the extent that they are now taken as historically true. But as several have argued (Zeigler 1973; Chattopadhyaya 1976; Kolff 1995), being a Rajput was initially based on one's ability to conquer others and create marriage alliances. Kolff (1995) reads the oral epic *Alha,* popular in the Braj region but also to the east and south, as well as the Rajasthani epics of *Pabuji* and *Devnarayan,* as epics of battles and marriage alliances, that is, of marking one's success as a warrior *through* the respect gained when a more recognized king will marry his daughter into your family. As we saw in the previous chapter, marriage alliances are a major theme in *Dhola.* But Nal's time with the Oil Presser in the kingdom of Marwar clearly articulates the issues involved in gaining recognition from established regimes.

Telīs, or Oil Pressers, were found in every market and many villages of India, driving their blind-folded ox around their oil press.[5] To say that someone is the ox of a teli (*telī kā bail*) implies that he slaves for nothing (Crooke 1896, 375). Telis were also thought to be clever businessmen, with the potential of becoming wealthy (no doubt by cheating their customers). But no matter what their wealth, they were still lowly Oil Pressers, as seen in this proverb recorded by William Crooke (1896, 375): "What comparison is there between a real gentleman and a Teli upstart even if he be made of money?" This idea is reaffirmed in *Dhola* when the king invites the newly rich Oil Presser to court and his eyes become red. The singer Ram Swarup Dhimar comments, "Because he had the power of the newly rich, he could not control himself" (WA 84: 243). Recall that Shanidev, the god sent by Indra to persecute Nal, loses his powers when in the presence of mustard seed and oil; thus by placing Nal in the oil press, Nal is protected from Shanidev and can activate his own considerable powers. By allying him with a low-caste Oil Presser, the system of ascribing status through lineage and genealogy can be challenged. The upstart "poor man" can indeed become king. Further, the Teli woman is envisioned as powerful and strong, a cliché also reiterated in the episode of *Dhola* described in the next section.

The Battle of Bhamartal

After the second svayambar, Raja Nal and Dumenti again depart for the forest because, since god has given them twelve years of trouble, staying with a relative would only bring disaster to the relative as well. So Nal and Dumenti set out in the month of Chait (March–April, when the dry heat increases daily); the hot ground burns the queen's feet, and flies swarm around them because of the open sores from Nal's leprosy.[6] An Oil Presser is passing through the forest to another village to sell his oil. Now this Oil Presser is very weak, because his wife is very strong! He would often leave to sell oil without eating, as his wife would beat him when he asked for bread in the mornings. "He was in trouble," said the singer Ram Swarup Dhimar. Raja Nal greets the Oil Presser who "peers at him from his small eyes."[7] Nal asks for a few drops of oil for his leprosy, but the Oil Presser refuses, saying that his wife would beat him and not give him food even if he is only a few drops short (i.e., does not have sufficient payment for the oil). Finally, the Oil Presser agrees to give Raja Nal a bit of oil, knowing that he will be beaten upon his return home. And he moves on to the next village where he had not sold any oil for more than four years. Suddenly customers flock to him, and he discovers that no matter how much oil he sells his container never runs dry.

When he returns home he ties his earnings in a cloth, puts his full pot of oil on a cot, and goes to find his wife, who is visiting in another neighborhood. (Note here that the woman is out visiting, movement denied to high-caste women: a high-caste man would never find his wife absent as she is never allowed to leave the home.) His wife returns home from a different direction and finds the oil jar still filled with oil: she curses him, saying, "That lazy bastard did not sell a single drop of oil today!" Then she sees the mustard seed and thinks that he must have robbed someone. When she sees the money tied in a towel, she thinks he has started gambling. When the Oil Presser finally returns, his wife is waiting at the door, a heavy kettle in her hand: she is ready to break his head. She accuses him of gambling, but he says, "Sethani, I met a holy man in the forest. He blessed me after I gave him a bit of oil."

spoken: Then the wife becomes angrier, "You don't look after your life."
He asks, "Why do you say that?"
And she replies, "You found a saint like this in the forest and you did not bring him home! If we both serve him, we would no longer be poor."

And without letting her husband eat, she sends him back to the forest to find Raja Nal and Dumenti.

The Teli hurries back to the forest, where he is thankful to find the old leper. He begs them to return with him to his house, saying that his wife has not given him food or water. Raja Nal replies,

spoken: "What caste do you belong to?" The Oil Presser replies, "I am well known as a Teli."
And Raja Nal says, "How can we fit together? I am a Chhatri by caste and you are an Oil Presser. There will be problems with food. How will we be able to arrange food? We cannot live together."

[Here Raja Nal is referring to the pervasive issue of the exchange of food between individuals of different castes. In essence, food that is *kacā* (not cooked in milk or clarified butter) cannot be exchanged outside a family, and food that is *pakkā* (cooked in milk or clarified butter) can be exchanged between castes of similar ranking. The low-caste Oil Presser, a Shudra by varna, and the high-caste Raja Nal, a Kshatriya by varna, cannot exchange even pakka foodstuffs, for the higher-caste Nal cannot take pakka food from someone as low as an Oil Presser.]

Then Raja Nal again refuses to join the Oil Presser, saying that the Oil Presser's poverty will be made even worse: "If you take me with you, everything will be destroyed because Shukra and Shanichar are in me." But the Oil Presser responds,

chant: "Babaji, you come with me. If Shanichar [literally, Saturday, the day of Shani: here the singer errs and means Shanidev, the god Shani] comes into my *kulbārā* [oil press], I'll have him pressed in the press."

The gods Shanidev and Shukra realize that once Nal enters the oil press they will lose him, so they transform themselves into policemen and try to take Nal away from the Oil Presser. But the Oil Presser's wife beats them off with her iron pan. As soon as Nal enters the oil press, he can remember everything—about all three worlds. Most important, he remembers the mantras that he had obtained from Motini's father. Using the *bīj* mantra, Nal is able to press all the mustard seed for the year in one night. Very quickly the

Oil Presser Raghu becomes rich. He soon owns 360 villages and an equal number of oil presses. He has an army of 1,500 soldiers, canon, and elephants and builds a fort called Amba Khas in place of his home. His name is changed to the more high-class Raghunandan. "Now the Oil Presser is like a king."

Meanwhile, Raja Budh Singh of Marwar is afraid that the Oil Presser is richer than he, and Raja Budh Singh feels that he must recognize the upstart Oil Presser. As an excuse for meeting the Oil Presser, he calls all the 52 kings to Marwar for a feast in honor of his son, and also invites the Oil Presser, for he is as rich as any of them is, as well as the families of all 360 oil pressers. "It was done because he [Raghunandan] had become wealthy [*paise se baṛcukāthā*]. Because he had gained respect [*kadar,* merit or worth] in the fort. This work [invitations] was done according to the respect [that one had earned]."

Nal cries when he thinks of his one-time wealth and the insult of an Oil Presser being invited to the king's feast, but he himself, a fellow caste-mate, left uninvited because he is a poor servant. (Later, he says that his lack of invitation was a "matter of caste.") As the Oil Presser and his army are set to depart, Nal cries again. The Oil Presser climbs off his howdah and wraps his arms around Nal, saying, "This is because of you. You should go to the party, either on an elephant or a horse or in a carriage." But Nal refuses, saying that no invitation has come for him.

The Oil Presser goes to court where he is seated on a stool in the midst of the fifty-two kings, who sit (below him) on the floor. Apparently, however, the fifty-two kings do not know that the one so honored is an Oil Presser. When one of Budh Singh's relatives complains about the honor shown the Oil Presser, Budh replies, "Keep silent, you sister fucker. This is Sethji [an honorific for a rich man]. Tell me, who has all the money? Tell me! If we proclaim that he is an Oil Presser, we shall lose all our honor." But the Oil Presser's identity is revealed when the dancing girls sing the songs honoring those who give them money (songs that name the giver, as in *Dhola;* see chapter 3), and the fifty-two kings leave, saying that they have not come to sell their honor.

Meanwhile, Nal takes the Oil Presser's bullocks to Bhamartal to give them water. Angry at his treatment, he destroys the pond, making the bullocks stir up the mud and defecate in it. But the 900 guards awake and attack. Nal again weaps uncontrollably. But bravery returns as he remembers Durga, and then he kills the 900 guards of Budh Singh, wraps a steel bar around the necks of the last two, and returns to the oil press. As the epic singer reminds us in a line more reminiscent of the Rajput hero than the heroes of *Dhola,* "The Brave are born to die in battle, while the timid one dies a thousand times. The Brave one must fight and die in battle, caring not where his lifeless body falls."

When the one survivor of the battle tells Budh Singh what has happened, he and the fifty-two kings rush to the pond. No one can open the steel bar around the necks of the two soldiers. The best wrestlers in the kingdom are called, but none can open it. Eventually they seek out the servant of the Oil Presser, for it was he who bent it originally. The Oil Presser begs Nal to ask Budh Singh's pardon for destroying his army and his pond, saying,

> "Son, tie your hands together and put a piece of dub grass in your mouth [signs of begging pardon and humility] and ask for the king's pardon. Then you will get charity in the form of your life."

But these words pierce Nal's chest "like a bullet," and he responds,

> "A dutiful son dies because of a word, but an undutiful son doesn't die even from a bullet. . . . I am not timid, I am a chattri. I shall kill him [Budh Singh] before the full assembly."

The fifty-two kings laugh as Nal staggers to the pond, for he is weak from lack of food. Nal agrees to do as the Oil Presser asks, saying that he [Nal] is his servant, not the servant of the Thakurs. Then Nal faces a dilemma.

> "If I open the [iron bar] with my hands, my head will bow to the kings of fifty-two countries. I should not bend my head to them because I am their enemy. Why should I bow my head before my foe?" So he decides to open it by kicking with his foot . . . he kicks the bar and it breaks into eleven pieces.

Then the king chastises the Oil Presser for keeping such a brave strong man as his servant, pressing seeds. The Oil Presser responds that he knew nothing of this baba who had fallen on hard times, did not know of his talents.

That night, sitting hungry in the oil press, Nal sings the *dīpakrāg* (the "lamp" melody), causing all the lamps in the city to light at midnight. The Brahman Pandits tell Budh Singh that only Nal knows the dipak rag. So Budh Singh demands to see Raja Nal and sets up a test to uncover his identity; the aim is to kill a fish at 450 paces. No one but Raja Nal can shoot an arrow that can kill a fish at that distance. All the kings attempt the task but fail, so the messenger (*khojā,* a barber cum messenger who proclaims the news like the town crier of medieval Europe) shouts that the earth is empty of brave men and that all are impotent.[8]

> sung: Hail the childless one. . . . This land has become impotent,
> And in this world, all the kings are dead,
> And, Brother, all the queens are barren. (WA 90:2)

Budh Singh says that if it is proclaimed that we are impotent, then the honor of Marwar will be destroyed and no one will marry our sons and daughters. But Budh refuses to call the Oil Presser's servant because he has been insulted by him, so the messenger again says that the kingdom is impotent. Eventually Nal is called and, with the help of Durga whose monkey helper sits on Nal's arrow, kills the fish at 450 paces. But the kings push Nal into a ditch, and each claims that his own arrow killed the fish.[9] The messenger then returns to the Oil Presser's house and tells him what happened. The Oil Presser becomes red with anger, saying, "I didn't come here to live as a slave, nor do I ask for land." And he calls the other Oil Pressers to take their revenge on Budh. They leap on their horses without bothering to saddle them. Arriving at Phul Bagh, the Oil Presser jumps into the ditch and catches Nal in his arms, embracing him with love. Here Nal faces another dilemma.

> The quarrel is with Thakurs. Friendship with small people [literally, "lower people"] and cheap weapons never helps at these times. These are Oil Pressers by caste. If I say that I have been injured, they will start a fight. The Thakurs all have swords, and the Oil Pressers will be killed immediately. They have no power. And then I would have to kill people of my own caste. . . . My brothers will be killed: I must do justice to myself.

So he responds that, yes, he has been pushed, but he is unhurt.

Then Nal goes on to shoot his arrow from 750 paces, and then have it returned to him. The fifty-two kings want to cheat, but they are tricked by Nal and so they cannot. He kills the fish at 750 paces, and the shouting of "impotency" ends.

But Budh still wants revenge, thinking that his kingdom has been taken over by Oil Pressers. So he thinks of another trick to dishonor the Oil Presser and his servant. He invites Raghu to play dice with him, but the Oil Presser claims that he cannot play as he is a mere Oil Presser. But Budh Singh persists. For three days they play for fun. But on the fourth day Budh Singh suggests they play for real. On the first three rounds, the Oil Presser wins. Feeling proud, he bids more and more heavily, until he loses everything: his wealth, his 360 bullocks, his oil presses. Then Budh pushes him off the throne, saying, "Sister fucker, you can no longer sit on the throne. I was furious when you were sitting on the throne with me, you low-caste man [jati *kamīn*]." Budh Singh tells the Oil Presser that if he values his life he must be gone by sunrise; if not, he and his family will be killed.

> spoken: So why has the Oil Presser lost the game? It is a fruit of his sins. And the Oil Presser comes out of the court weeping. . . . [H]e has sought to smoke the water pipe, but instead of smoke got water [proverb]. . . . Nal looks out and sees the Oil Presser coming toward the press. Nal wastes no words. He catches the wrist of the Oil Presser and then takes him in his arms. The king of Narvar talks with his master. And the Oil Presser weeps, his heart broken with sorrow. "Son, there is no life in the world anymore."

Raghu tells Nal that he has no work, that he should leave.

spoken: Nal is perplexed. He is very confused, and asks what the problem is. The Oil Presser replies, "See the cleverness of the Thakur. He asked me to sit on the throne."
Nal replies, "I am a Thakur, too. If we do not act in this way, then how will the power of a lord endure? And you are involved in a difficulty with a very powerful person."

Raghu then relates that he has lost everything and that they will all be killed if they do not leave by dawn. Nal responds,

spoken: "Sister fucker, wait a minute. First you gamble, and now you are trying to run away from here. Wait a bit."
The Oil Presser replies, "Son, as the rosy dawn spreads, we will be hung. There is no way we can escape."
Nal answers, "I earned all this with hard work. Now you have lost it all gambling. Oh Oil Presser, you lost all our wealth in gambling and you dare to show your face to me. You should play one more time with friendly dice."
The Oil Presser responds, "But I do not have anything left except my life, my wife Ganga Telin, and my daughter. I have nothing left: how can I play now?"
Nal responds, "No, you have much wealth . . . enough to play with the king. Go and bet your Ganga Telin on the round. If you had wealth, the king would not play, but if you bid your Telin, he will quickly grab the cowry shells and won't stop for any reason. But tell me, whose cowry shells were you using?"

Nal then gives him Motini's sixteen cowry shells and instructs him to say to himself, as he throws them, "If these are the true got of Nal, [I shall win]."

spoken: The Oil Presser then runs back to the king, and says,
"I am an Oil Presser and you are a Thakur. You have won my bullocks and my oil presses. You should also win my Telin. Your queen will not be able to do this oil pressing work. She is royalty. She will not be able to press oil. You should win my Ganga Telin, so she can do the oil pressing for you."[10]

Budh Singh agrees and invites the Oil Presser to play once again. As Budh Singh loses more and more heavily, he becomes mad (literally, hot). He stakes his whole kingdom. But on that throw, the Oil Presser speaks Nal's name aloud. Budh Singh grabs his wrist and snatches the cowry shells away, saying he will return them only to their true owner. The Oil Presser returns to Nal, and exclaims,

spoken: "The pumpkin doesn't fit in the mouth of a goat. Those who are poor don't have the knowledge to work and don't have the knowledge to keep their wealth. I said your name out loud and the king caught my wrist, asking me whose name I was calling."
To this, Dumenti interjects, "My husband, I have been telling you:

> friendship with the lower castes and blunt weapons are useless in times of trouble."

Eventually Nal returns to Budh Singh's court and they agree to a game, betting their unborn children. The one who loses must give up a daughter, a clear sign of defeat in Rajput kingdoms. Nal defeats Budh, but before he can marry his son Dhola to Maru, he has to undergo one more test, that of fetching sugarcane for the wedding pavilion from Lakhiyaban. Budh still refuses to accept that Nal is his equal or his superior. Nal wins against the Bhils and the demons, and Dhola and Maru are married, although both Nal and Budh put up barriers to their actual meeting as adults, for anyone who seeks Maru's hand will be crushed by the gate to the fort.

Throughout this episode Nal's right to claim kingship and his servitude to Raghu and metonymic status as an Oil Presser work against each other. To the Rajputs of the fifty-two kingdoms, he has no right to claim kingship. His several feats of prowess are continually disregarded, and Nal himself repeatedly questions whether he should be loyal to the Thakurs or to those of the lower castes with whom he associates. The pattern seen earlier also continues: Nal breaking into tears when faced with battle, only to "remember Durga" and, with her help, going on to prevail against the kings allied against him.

Through the figures of the Oil Presser and Nal, we learn of the intrigues against upstarts, against those who have the audacity to claim a status equal to that of the fifty-two kings. Through trickery and cheating, the Rajputs attempt to destroy those who gain wealth and stand against them. And indeed Nal is torn between justice to the "lower castes" and justice to his own people, the Thakurs. From his standpoint as an Oil Presser's servant he does not hesitate to embrace Raghu or to lie about his injuries to save Raghu's life. But he also claims the right of those who rule to lie in order to salvage their rule, in order to prevent those seeking to claim a throne from actually claiming it. In so doing he depicts a universal image, highlighting that image with the loyalty and status intrinsic to the Hindu world.

Nal and Motini as Acrobats

When Raja Nal and Motini take on the identities of Acrobats in order to gain access to the kingdom of Phul Singh Panjabi, they are faced with the challenge of hiding their Kshatriya identities, as revealed in their natural bodies and behaviors. In India, where it is believed that bodies vary by caste, male and female bodies are constructed as stylized caste bodies. As with gender identities, caste identities develop through the stylized repetition of acts over time. Following Judith Butler, caste identities are "a performative accomplishment" (1997, 402). By repeating acts that constitute caste identities, the social audience and the actors themselves come to believe in the performance. As we shall see in the transformation of Nal and Motini into Acrobats, the body becomes a practical locus of control, a surface onto which rules and hierarchies can be inscribed.

In Hindu India these caste bodies are marked by their clothing, how they dress. Nirud Chaudhuri notes that "like language or other features of life which distinguish one human group from another, it [clothes] is part of the national personality, it is one expression among others of a distinctive culture. Therefore no one can change his clothes until there has been, in part or whole, a transfer of cultural allegiance" (1976, 73). In India, as elsewhere, the clash between different styles of clothing is symbolic of a wider conflict regarding cultural and social norms and values (Cohn 1989). Clothes are thought to be "a thing which can transmit spirit and substances" (Bayly 1986, 286). In southern India a higher-caste Nayar man who took off his shirt was said to "take off his caste," for the lower castes are not permitted to wear clothing on the upper parts of their bodies. In Rajasthan the Rajputs do not permit the Jats to wear certain kinds of clothing. As we shall see below, clothing allied with particular kinds of behavior is critical to the transformation into Acrobats of Nal, Mansukh, and Motini.

Although Raja Nal and Mansukh also become Acrobats, it is Motini who chooses the disguise and propels the action, her husband reluctantly following along with her plan. At issue is the need to enter the court of the Panjabi, a goal they surely cannot achieve in their royal garb (figure 6.1), which marks them as the enemy. Acrobats, as entertainers beloved by village folk and court alike, move freely across the countryside, into villages and onto verandahs, setting up tents or building huts for sleeping, and performing wherever they are called (figure 6.2). Sir Denzil Ibbetson describes the Acrobat in this way, "In addition to practicing acrobatic feats and conjuring of a low class . . . [t]hey often practice surgery and physic in a small way, and are not free from suspicion of sorcery" (1916, 285). He goes on to add that they are "to be divided into two main classes, those whose males only perform as acrobats and those whose women, called Kabutri, perform and prostitute themselves. . . . They marry mostly by circumambulation (*pherā*) and burn their dead" (285). Other authors find some Nat groups that bury their dead (a less "Hinduized" custom) or use other marriage rituals than the circumambulation demanded in mainstream Hindu rituals, marking these groups as low and unacceptable to normal village society, where, in any case, they do not live, given their roles as wandering entertainers.

It is these characteristics of Acrobats that find their way into not only British gazetteers but also the imaginations of rural poets. Motini's choice is apt, for

Figure 6.1. A Jat Landlord of the nineteenth century. From Louis Rousselet, *India and Its Native Princes: Travels in Central India and in the Presidencies of Bombay and Bengal,* ed. Lieutenant Colonel Buckle (London: Bickers, 1878), 298.

it not only allows her and her retinue access to the fort of Phul Singh Panjabi[11] but it also provides her with a disguise that can legitimately be used to entice the wicked king. Essential to this disguise is a change in appearance for male and female, although it is a disguise that ultimately does not fully hide Raja Nal's Kshatriya status, for his red eye remains as a mark throughout.

The dual transformations of Nal and Motini introduce us to the Acrobat. When Motini suggests becoming Acrobats, Nal immediately rejects the idea.

sung: (Motini says) "My husband, you of Narvar,
You should become an Acrobat now."
As he hears the word *Acrobat,*
The king replies with rage.

spoken: Nal says, "Are you mad? We are the sons of warriors. Have we come here to be an Acrobat or to fight?"[12]

Motini goes on to convince Nal of the need to be an Acrobat. But before Motini transforms Nal into an Acrobat, she must arrange for the proper belongings, so with the help of her demon uncle Somasur she arranges with the Carpenter for four string cots on which to sleep, and then buys ten male water buffalo from the Grain Parcher, sixteen hundred cocks, and five to ten dogs from the Sweepers. From Acrobats themselves she obtains a drum, cymbals, and other instruments. Only with the proper belongings will they be believable Acrobats.

Now she must transform their appearances:

spoken: (Demon uncle says), "You have to become an Acrobat immediately."
Nal replies, "Dear friend, everything is here. Now we will quickly cause a transformation."
Because Nal's parents were imprisoned, both Nal and Mansukh shave their heads. Their heads are cleaned as smooth as the round bottom of a kettle. Their heads are like peeled potatoes. When this is done, Motini says, "Take off your royal garments." So they also take off their clothes and are left in an undershirt and loincloth, wearing a coarse dhoti, and each holding a bamboo stick. Motini looks at the transformed Nal and smiles at the figure of the Acrobat.
Mansukh says, "She has made us ugly, and now she is laughing. But what does it matter?"

With these lines, we have the outward signs of the elite male body removed, literally, as Nal is stripped of his royal garments, his head shaved, and he is left with a loincloth and bamboo stick. Figures 6.1 and 6.2, taken from a nineteenth-century travel book on India, illustrate the transformation that Ram Swarup Dhimar has described orally. The contrast between the heavily robed royal body, with thick hair and long mustache, hand holding a gun or sword, and the almost naked body of the Acrobat, with shaved head and no mustache, holding only a bamboo stick, is striking.

Figure 6.2. Nat acrobats of the nineteenth century. From Louis Rousselet, *India and Its Native Princes: Travels in Central India and in the Presidencies of Bombay and Bengal*, ed. Lieutenant Colonel Buckle (London: Bickers, 1878), 62.

For the Rajputs, the group with which Raja Nal wishes to be associated, the head was considered the root of a man's body, and this root needed to be tended and cared for, particularly through the oiling of one's hair, the donning of elaborate turbans, and the growth of an elaborate mustache. The head, with its luxurious and well-tended growth of hair, symbolized authority and leadership and, more generally, notions of power and virility, the "ability to assert oneself over others and rule" (Zeigler 1973, 78). Furthermore, shaving or cutting off an opponent's hair in battle rituals was a common element expressive of male virility. A modern folk singer comments on the meaning of the loss of a mustache in this time of the Kali Yug in this way, "Oh, the men have shaved their moustaches and their masculinity is gone" (A. Gold 2000, 217). By stripping Nal of his outward royal trappings, especially his hair, Motini leaves him with only the red in the corner of his eye as an outward mark of his identity and manhood. Moreover, with the loss of his hair, he also loses the right to claim his own wife as his own. But given the innate nature of caste habits, Motini cannot strip Raja Nal of his innate aggression and readiness to do battle; and throughout the ensuing scenes, she must continually hold him back from exposing his identity.

Initially Motini instructs Nal,

> sung: Don't lose your temper,
> While we are in Kampilagarh.
> If someone abuses you,
> Don't let it bother you.

Later the townspeople comment, "We have never seen such Acrobats. Their woman is very beautiful. But their eyes are red. They use their bamboo stick to attack very suddenly. Are they good Acrobats?" Here it is clear, despite clothing and a name change, that Nal's essential Kshatriya character cannot be erased. The folk of Kampilagarh, somewhat confused, take note of this.

Meanwhile, as we saw in chapter 5, Motini's outward form is also changed, as she ornaments herself to be as alluring and sexual as possible to become the dancing girl cum prostitute, leaving behind the veils and the associated barriers to movement into public space that constrict royal and high-caste women.

Once they appear as Acrobats, Motini realizes that they must take on the names of Acrobats, too, saying, "Acrobats' names are also different." While there is no tight association between caste and one's given name, some names are more or less prestigious, and variants on the same name can also carry greater prestige, as we saw with the shift in the Oil Presser's name from Raghu to Raghunandan. Likewise, Paras Ram, which is prestigious, can become Pasu, a low-status name. Motini plays with the idea of names: she assigns Mansukh the name Batana (mortar); Raja Nal becomes Silota (pestle); and Motini takes the name Chatani (chutney).

Once they enter the city, their fame and Motini's beauty quickly spread. The king's prime minister sees her in the market and runs off to court, where Phul Singh, on hearing of the Acrobat's beauty, says, "My dear friend, why don't you bring them to our palace?" Phul Singh immediately desires the beautiful Acrobat, because women of the Acrobat caste, along with those of the Sweeper or other lower castes, are thought to be accessible to higher-caste men. Motini herself takes advantage of this female availability: after enticing Phul Singh with her beauty, she arranges to meet him in her tent that night. Completely enamored of his new love, the foolish king does not realize he has been duped, even when he encounters Raja Nal and Mansukh in the tent where he had arranged to meet Motini.

spoken: Now it is eleven or midnight, and the Panjabi reaches the tents. He arrives right at the place where the bald Nal and Mansukh are waiting, wearing only a loincloth and holding their bamboo sticks. The Panjabi moves his hand slowly over Nal at midnight.
What does he say as Nal's hand comes into his? The Panjabi says, putting his hand on Nal, "Which enemy has broken your bangles?"
What does the Panjabi say?

sung: "Oh Chatani, who has broken your bangles?
Oh Chatani, who has broken your bangles?"

spoken: What does Nal say? "The head Acrobat has broken my bangles, he hit my hand with his bamboo." The Panjabi says, "Oh my dear, live in comfort and don't worry. I'll see that you wear bangles all the way to your shoulder." And then he brings his hand to Nal's head. And finds it smooth like a kettle.

sung: "Oh Chatani, who has cut your hair?"

At this point Nal and Mansukh decide to beat the Panjabi, stripping him of his clothes and sending him back to his palace, racing through the streets completely naked. Portrayed here is a series of transgressions that play off both the body and one's status and place, as first Phul Singh Panjabi caresses the bald Nal in the Acrobats' tent and then is chased naked through the streets.

The scene is based on the rules governing castes, whereby elite males have power over lower-caste males, and have the right to claim the women of the lower-caste males (as indeed almost happens here). It is that potentiality that is developed in this episode, perhaps making it possible for all lower-caste male listeners to revel in the fact that the powerful man is beaten, the man who symbolizes all the elite men who, in actuality, regularly harass or rape their women.

Although disguised as Nats while in Kampilagarh, the trio's identity is nevertheless questioned and challenged on various grounds, indicating the range of factors that signifies one's identity in Indian culture. First, the two men are questioned because each has red in the corner of his eyes. Next, their right to bear the goods they carry is questioned, for the poor would not possess a magical horse, shawls of the finest wool, expensive necklaces, and the nose ring worth many lakhs that Motini wears. The three claim that all these items were gifts from Raja Nal, and the king, at least, believes them.

Finally, Phul Singh brings up the subject of food, a clear mark of dominance and superiority in India. He insists on feeding the Acrobats, as would be expected of any good patron, but Nal claims that, if he eats this food, he would never be able to defeat Phul Singh, playing on a recurrent theme in the epic: taking food (or salt) from a man marks friendship, not enmity. Motini arranges for Mansukh and Nal to fight over the food, which leads those in Phul Singh's court to believe that these Acrobats are definitely not Raja Nal and friends, for although a Kshatriya could go without food, he would never fight over it in this way. Phul Singh himself says to his Divan,

> spoken: "They are quarreling over each scrap of bread. Not only are they Acrobats, but their great-grandfathers were also. They have been Acrobats for seven generations.[13] If they were from a royal family, they could go without eating, but would they fight over every scrap of bread?"

Thus the epic singers make use of the dress and behaviors of the Acrobats, enabling Motini to enter the palace where she can wield her magic. As Elizabeth Wilson writes, "a part of the strangeness of dress is that it links the biological body to the social being, and public to private. This makes it uneasy territory since it forces us to recognize that the human body is more than a biological entity. It is an organism in culture, a cultural artifact even, and its own boundaries are unclear. . . . Dress is the frontier between the self and the not self" (1987, 2–3). Raja Nal, in particular, discovers that how he dresses counts enormously, a message also made clear when he became a servant to the Oil Presser.

Motini as Bangle Seller

Motini's other major disguise takes place in "The Marriage of Kishanlal," the episode discussed in chapter 4, in which Chandi's temple is destroyed. As we saw, here the two girls of the Oil Presser caste steal Nal's nephew, Kishanlal, and son, Dhola, in order to marry them. Skilled in the magical arts, they turn Dhola into a parrot and lock him in a cage, while Kishanlal is transformed into an ox and set to pressing oil. To counter their magic, Motini (who ascends from heaven to help Nal) must gain access to their home. She does this by becoming a Manihar, a Bangle Seller.

Bangle Sellers, who sometimes are Muslim, have the job of going from house to house to fit women with new glass bangles. Each bangle is a narrow band of glass, perhaps one-sixteenth of an inch wide. Women normally wear eight to sixteen bangles on each arm, usually obtaining a new set at marriage and at the two major festivals (Divali in the fall and Holi in the spring). As noted earlier, glass bangles are a requisite part of the adornment of an auspiciously married woman and should only be removed at the death of her husband. Bangle Sellers represent another low-ranking caste, and both husband and wife sell bangles. In Karimpur the male Bangle Seller who arrives sets his basket of bangles outside the door to the courtyard of his higher-caste patrons, and the women, some veiled if younger and married, sit outside the courtyard to choose their bangles and have them put on. If the Bangle Seller is female, she is allowed into the courtyard itself, where she squats with her basket, gossiping with the women as they make their choices.

An important part of the Bangle Seller's art is being able to fit the smallest possible bangle over a woman's hand, because if the bangles on her wrist are too loose they will quickly break, itself an inauspicious omen. This is not always an easy task, given the gnarled, work-worn hands of village women. Taking the woman's hand in her own, the Bangle Seller massages it and then squeezes it into the smallest possible circumference before attempting to maneuver the small circles of glass over the thick knuckles without breaking the bangles. It is this scene Motini plays out in her disguise as a Bangle Seller.

Here Nal's magical water horse calls out to Motini, when Nal and the horse find the two boys in the oil press.

sung: And the horse weeps, and cries,
"Oh my sister,
Sister listen carefully,
Kishanlal's situation is bad,
Fastened to the beam of the oil press. . . ."
Hearing these words,
Tears flow from Motini's eyes,
Motini weeps and weeps,
"When will the day be,
When I shall see Kishan?"

[Motini then beautifies herself, in a song similar to that for transforming herself into an Acrobat]

sung: The loving daughter says a mantra,
and makes bangles,
Motini says a mantra,
And quickly makes a basket,
And makes a pair of bangles,
And sticks magic vir on them, . . .

When Motini comes to Kamaru [the village where the boys are kept],
The loving daughter cries, "Bangles, Bangles!"

spoken: What does she say?

sung: "Buy bangles, buy bangles,
I have brought wonderful colored bangles,
Buy some of the most wonderful colored bangles,
My bangles are colored white, yellow, and black!"

spoken: And Motini moves through each lane, searching for the sons.

sung: Eventually reaching the gate of the Oil Presser,
She finds the son hanging in a cage, . . .

sung: And the Telin comes there,
And looks at the bangles.

spoken: Magic is on every gem, but it fools both of them as they look. The Telin asks, "Sister, tell me the price of these bangles." Moving slowly, Motini holds tight to her basket; fooling them she moves inside their gate. "Sister, buy these in a lovely place."

sung: And Motini spreads her array of bangles.

spoken: Both the Telin are very anxious, saying, "Now we are getting married. We can wear as many bangles as we want. We'll never get such bangles in the future."

sung: And Motini sits quietly,
and lifts her *ghunghat* [veil],
The parrot glances around,
"My *mausi*[14] mother has come!"
And Dhola recognizes Motini.
The calf tweaks his ears forward,
Kishanlal recognizes Motini. . . .

spoken: Kishanlal stands still with pride [he stops because Motini is there], eyes covered by baskets. Immediately the Telin lifts a bamboo stick and hits it across the back of both [the calf's] legs. . . . The calf bellows, and Motini feels as if a bullet has passed through her heart. . . .

sung: "Wear bangles up to your elbow,
Give me this old ox."

spoken: Instantly the Telin cries and says, "I'll not wear any." . . .

spoken: She [Motini] sits on the stool and holds the hand of the eldest first. Her hand is very stiff.
Motini says, "Girl, your hand is very stiff, all the bangles will break." She holds the hand under one knee, "Let me soften it so that it is less stiff."

sung: The young woman is very foolish,
Motini sits holding her hand,
And starts to put on bangles,
She pushes a bangle onto her hand,
Breaks ten bangles on the hand,
A broken bangle pierces the skin,
And blood flows.

spoken: The Telin says, "Sister, I am dying. You are pressing my hand very tightly."

Motini replies, "Why do you have such a stiff hand? Why are you crying now?"

sung: . . . What is Motini doing?
Speaks a mantra and throws it,
Turns both into bitches.
Speaks a mantra and throws it,
Kishanlal is transformed from ox to man,
Throws a mantra on the parrot,
And makes the five-year-old Dhola [appear]. (WA 85:306–309)

By manipulating the acceptable behavior of women of different castes, Motini is able to attain access to spaces normally prohibited to high-caste women. Whether as an Acrobat or a Bangle Seller, it is crucial that she mark her caste status by dress and appearance, and also with the tools and behaviors appropriate to the trade. Only then is her disguise believable. But in the process she is also performing, portraying the look and behaviors of the caste. Both the body and the acts that constitute the body are objects of belief, in this case a belief based ultimately in both the Hindu hymn of the first man and the everyday acts that mark caste identities. As various authors remind us, the body is a powerful symbolic medium onto which a vision of social and political life is inscribed (Bordo 1997; Butler 1997). These bodies are impressed with the stamp of prevailing historical forms of selfhood—in this case, "castehood"—that have become increasingly irrelevant in the twenty-first century, with the loss of caste-associated occupations and urban migration, but that were highly salient through at least the 1970s in most of the region where *Dhola* is performed.

Raja Nal as a Merchant

Raja Nal's other key identity is that of the Merchant who raises him. This episode, the second in the epic, immediately articulates issues of caste identity and disguise, recalling, in fact, the story of the swan and the crow that begins this chapter. The Merchant is also fundamental to the story line, for the Merchants are the ones who travel widely, thus enabling our singers to find Manjha and her newborn son in the forest and to travel across the seas to the shore where Motini is found playing with cowry shells.

As described in chapter 2 in the synopsis of the story, Nal is born to Manjha after her banishment to the forest, where she is supposed to have been killed by the Sweeper. There she is found by a passing Merchant who takes Manjha and her newborn son back to his village, Dakshinpur. The sage Narad names the infant for the Merchant, saying, "Your mother wandered in the forest and you were born in a time of difficulty, so therefore your name is Vipati [difficult time or distress]. Your second name is Nal Banvari [Nal of the forest] as you were born in the forest. And your third name is Nal Chhatravedi [Nal under the canopy of kings]." Narad goes on to explain to the Merchant that his grandson is such a brave person that, by age eleven, he will kill demons, thus accounting for the name given only to those illustrious enough to merit a throne and royal umbrella.

Meanwhile, Manjha, too, needs a new name. The Merchant tells his wife that the daughter whom he conceived is called "Kasmati" (flavorful one), while the one given by god and found in the forest is "Basmati" (fragrant one, also a kind of rice), in a word play the audience understands even if the Merchant does not, as Basmati is the queen honored with the rice grain that gives Pratham a son. Of all the residents of Dakshinpur, only Manjha knows Nal's true identity despite his phenomenal abilities. He grows quickly, learns his lessons before the teacher can even teach them, and develops superb horsemanship and hunting skills (abilities for which Merchants are not noted, another instance where the audience knows more than the story's characters). He is, in fact, a most beautiful young man.

The Seths (Merchants) are worried when they see Nal becoming a leader, for this is not the task of Merchants. Nal replies, "But Grandfather, I like playing with swords" (WA 89:9). At one point Manjha says to him,

> spoken: Son, I know you well. You are not a good Merchant. You must be thinking that you are a Merchant, but you are a king. You are wise and have been born with that wisdom. (WA 89:18)

Yet Nal never doubts his Merchant identity. When he meets Behmata, the goddess of fate, at the seashore making twisted circles of rope that mark a marriage, she asks who he is, and he responds:

> sung: Oh Mother, my village is Dakshinpur,
> My name is Raja Nal,
> I belong to the Merchant caste,
> In my house, salt, pepper, and coriander are sold. (WA 84:233)

Later he tells Motini that he is a Merchant, but recognizing the red in his eye that marks a Warrior, she knows that he is indeed a Kshatriya. She also thinks, "If he is the son of a King, he will be able to play the game of dice, but if he is the son of a Merchant he will be busy tallying his accounts."

Merchants are among the most prominent of the Hindu castes, for they are also the primary moneylenders, and most people of any rural community are in their debt. William Crooke (1907, 111) asserts their high-caste status, saying that "they descend from the trading communities of the Aryan community and their appearance indicates their respectable origin. Some of their women are as high-bred in appearance as any in Northern India; but they are generally secluded." Yet the Merchant is not fully trusted, for as a moneylender he often accumulates great wealth. According to one proverb, "The Thug robs the stranger, the Banya his friend" (Crooke 1907, 111). Merchants are also money hungry, as we see when the two wicked uncles cannot understand why Nal has brought a ship of cow dung cakes. They constantly comment on his lack of regard for making money.

In farming communities, where men labor hard, the Merchant sits in his shop, weighing the grain that is brought to him as in-kind payment for the oil or spices he sells. He is often the only corpulent man in the community (as, indeed, was the case in Karimpur). Crooke comments that the Merchant's "sedentary occupation and excessive indulgence in rich food make the men corpulent and unhealthy" (1907, 111), and he is sometimes described as "soft." One *Dhola* singer captures this idea when Motini, while disguised as a soldier in Nal's army on the way to battle Phul Singh Panjabi, is introduced to Nal. Nal comments on the soldier's soft hands, and Mansukh, aware of the disguise, responds, "but he is a Merchant. That is why his hands are soft." Nal accepts this explanation, and the army continues its march.

Banyas, or Merchants, are classified as Vaishya, the third-highest ranking in the broad classificatory system known as varna, with Brahman (Priest) and Kshatriya (Warrior/King) ranking first and second. Many trading castes are vegetarian. Most include at least some literate males, an occupational necessity. Hence Merchants have, among other traits, a caste culture that embraces schooling for boys, the sacred thread ceremony, and vegetarianism. Yet the rituals of Merchants differ from those of other castes, such that Motini refuses to leave the ship bringing her to Dakshinpur after her marriage to Raja Nal because the women who come to greet her are acting "in the banya way." She demands that, instead, Manjha be brought to greet her (WA 94:24).

Here, again, is the preeminent theme of questioning caste. Although *Dhola* carefully inscribes the stereotypical behaviors and spaces associated with each caste, reinforcing for the rural audiences the fixity of caste status, at the same time the epic raises questions of achievement. In so doing, *Dhola* suggests that if you indeed achieve wealth, goods, and an army, then perhaps you do in fact belong to the Chhatri class. Without the wealth Raja Nal is able to obtain for the Oil Presser, wealth that is ultimately recognized as his own, he would never have been able to regain his rightful stature as a raja. Thus *Dhola,* like *Alha* and others, questions the genealogical reckoning of status in north India.

Caste and Supporting Characters

Other caste groups (or caste-like groups) play major supporting, and stereotypical, roles in *Dhola* that also delineate the social order and landscape of rural north India. These roles further articulate the everyday practices of caste in north India, adding to the messages about caste for *Dhola*'s rural audiences. Reserving a discussion of the Kshatriya, or Chhatri, for chapter 7, here I examine the highest- and lowest-caste groups: the Brahman priests and the Sweepers, respectively. In *Dhola* these two castes are used to reverse the accepted hierarchy, so that it is the Brahmans who err while the untouchable Sweepers maintain the moral code. Three other groups—the Mali, or Flower Grower; the Banjara, or Gypsy/Trader; and the Bhil tribals—convey key concepts about the imagined landscape and terrain of *Dhola,* moving us out of the forts and villages of Kings, Acrobats, and Oil Pressers. The Flower Grower is attached to gardens that are thought to exist on the outskirts of forts and villages, while the Banjara and Bhils convey the essential "otherness" of those living in the forests.

Brahmans are often thought to be of the highest rank in Hindu society (and certainly the many texts they themselves compose position them at the top of the ritual hierarchy). Brahmans, as priests, are required for most ceremonies of the life cycle, such as marriages, as well as for worshiping at some Hindu temples. They are also astrologers, who must plot the astrological charts that many find vital in determining marriages, auspicious days, and so on. Thus Brahmans play critical roles in Hindu society, although in *Dhola* their character is challenged. Here the singers of *Dhola* share a wider worldview that questions the Brahman's prescribed high status and moral qualities, for the Brahman is often ridiculed by the larger populace. Writing on the castes in Panjab in the nineteenth century, Ibbetson says, "He has failed to make himself beloved. He is grasping, quarrelsome, and overbearing, inflated with pride in his own descent and contempt for that of others, while he holds himself aloof from the clients whose pockets he preys upon" (1916, 215). The avarice of the Brahman, so crucial to Manjha's banishment which depends on the other hundred queens of Pratham being able to bribe a Brahman to lie about the king's astrological chart, also did not go unnoticed, as this proverb notes: "Mulla [a Muslim religious leader], the Bhat [genealogist], the Brahman [priest], and the Dum [keeper of the cremation ground]: these four castes were not 'born on giving day' " (Ibbetson 1916, 218). The Brahman's potential for a generally bad character is captured in this proverb: "As famine from the desert, so comes 'evil from a brahman' " (Ibbetson 1916, 218). In *Dhola* the Brahman Gangadhar confirms these proverbial stereotypes as he accepts the bribe from the one hundred queens that leads to Manjha's supposed death. Keeper of the Hindu holy books and astrological charts, he lies out of greed. Taking a gold chain worth a lakh of rupees, he goes to Pratham's court and proclaims, "I have calculated the mathematics; there is a son in the uterus of Manjha but he will cause your death. . . . Please have the wife murdered, then you will be free to live" (Varma n.d.). Brahmans return to the story line when Motini demands that the story known as Nal Katha be told before she will marry Pratham. Pandits (learned Brahmans) from around the land arrive at Pratham's court, but none knows this story. Finally, Nal himself, disguised as a Pandit through the trickery of the flower awarded him by the snake daughter of Basukdev, tells the Nal Katha. One result is that Gangadhar and the one hundred queens are put to death.

Whereas the highest of the Hindu castes cheats and lies to gain gold, the lowest, the Sweeper (*Bhangī*), brings about justice. When the Sweepers are sent to the forest with Rani Manjha they leave her alive, taking the eyes of a deer back to Pratham to prove her death. At the telling of the Nal Katha they are not put to death but are rewarded. Similarly it is a Sweeper woman out cleaning the streets who sets the epic in motion when she sees the face of a "man without progeny" and cannot eat that day. This initial tension between evil high and righteous low helps to frame the message about caste found in the rest of the epic.

Finally, there are three groups who take us outside village and fort, and provide insight into the wider landscape of north Indian rural communities. First is the Mali, or Gardener. Here, too, is a caste whose women are sometimes thought to be magicians, as is Rewa, Dhola's second wife, who was actually a Mali by birth. But the Gardener stands for more, as he or she is the guardian of that space which is neither palace, fort or town, or forest. As a space between the chaos of the forest and the order of the fort, the garden is a space that strangers can enter and is also accessible to women. Hence the garden is used by Raja Nal when he does not want to go to war; it is where Raja Nal finds the injured goose that is carrying the invitation to Dumenti's svayambar; where Mansukh finds the bereaved and bedraggled Nal and Dumenti after their exile from Narvar; where Raja Nal and Kishanlal go upon their arrival in Bengal; and where Dhola first meets Maru when he finally learns of his first wife and goes to seek her. This marginal space on the fringes of both wild (forest) and civilized (fort or town) becomes a place where fundamental transitions in the story can occur. Whether it is the goose flying from Indra's heavenly kingdom or Nal and Dumenti seeking refuge after crossing the wilderness when banished from Narvar by Shanidev, the garden is the locale that marks the transition from one habitation to another. Gardeners themselves are portrayed in an ambivalent light. While the wicked Rewa and her kin are magicians, the female Gardener outside the fort of Gendwati in Bengal works to protect the foreign men who have entered her garden, going as far as dressing Kishanlal as a beautiful woman and claiming him as her daughter-in-law. Like their marginal gardens, the Gardeners themselves are marginal.

Dhola provides us with images of two groups of forest dwellers: the Banjaras, who find Dumenti in the forest after she and Raja Nal are separated by Shanidev, and the Bhils, or tribals, whom Raja Nal subdues in his search for black sugarcane. In the Hindu worldview the forest is a dangerous place, not to be entered by a lone woman or an unprotected man. Home to spirits, especially dangerous spirits seeking victims to attack, the forest is seen as a place of unrestrained and dangerous sexuality, a place void of the proper social order.

The Banjaras are contrasted to the Banya Merchants who rescue Manjha when Raja Nal is born. As peddlers and gypsies, the Banjara are wanderers, with "caravans of pack bullocks guarded by savage dogs, their women with free gait, wearing richly embroidered robes and abundant jewelry" (Crooke 1907, 117). Note that the Merchant Lachhiman Seth was traveling through the forest in a cart, while his main business was conducted by sea. The Banjara, who lacks a settled village, is a man of the forest, and "goes into the jungle with his stick in his hand" (Crooke 1907, 117). Not classified as Vaishya, the Banjaras are outcastes and their inappropriate behavior vis-à-vis Dumenti reveals their lower-caste status. As the singer Ram Swarup Dhimar commented, "The Merchant lives in a house. The Banjara has no home" (WA 02:12). The forest, the only home the Banjara knows, is a place of disorder, a place lacking the structure of everyday life. Dumenti (and Manjha) should not have been alone in the forest. Yet Manjha was treated reverently by her Merchant savior, while Dumenti's honor is challenged by her Banjara rescuer. Here the contrast between forest and civilization is reiterated through the associated caste behaviors of those "without a home" and those "with a home."

The Bhils, considered tribals by the British and "other" by the caste Hindus, live either on the edge of the forest or within it, where often they are hunters and gatherers as much as agriculturalists. They play a minor role in the epic when they are seen on the edge of Lakhiyaban, the forest inhabited by demons where Nal must obtain the sugarcane for Dhola's wedding canopy. One storyteller noted Raja Nal's arrival with these words, "There were twelve guards posted on the edge of the state of Bhil Nagar. The Bhils saw him in the sky as he was flying. They took out their arrows from their quiver. They thought to kill him for food." The epic performers are explicit about the fact that the Bhils kill humans and eat them, as in these scenes told by Raghubar Kachi. After Raja Nal is seated on a cot, the residents of Bhil Nagar begin spreading cow dung on their floors (a ritual to purify them) and whitewash their houses, all signs of an impending festival. One young Bhil girl sees the handsome Raja Nal sitting on the cot.

> When she sees Raja Nal, she says, "Oh, who is sitting at my gate. He will soon be cut and his flesh will be cooked."

Then she begins to cry, and Raja Nal asks her why she is crying:

> She replies, "I am crying because I see your handsome form."
> "At my form?"
> "Yes."
> "Why are you weeping at the sight of me?"
> She replies, "You are sitting at my gate now with great respect. But after a while you will be cut up by these people and your flesh will be cooked. Then I shall feel bad."

Raja Nal then calls upon Motini.

> All the Bhils are sharpening their axes. Later they come to Nal to cut him up. Suddenly Motini uses her magic on one side [of Bhil Nagar]. The west side of Bhil Nagar catches fire and starts to burn. When the Bhils see the fire, they all run there to extinguish it. Meanwhile Motini uses more magic to block the water of the Yamuna. So they run here and there. (WA 68:13)

With this brief excursion into the land of the Bhils (which Raja Nal's son, Dhola, repeats later in the epic) *Dhola* affirms one more stereotype from the cast of characters comprising the north Indian world. The Bhils play the role of the almost nonhuman forest dwellers whose behavior is completely antithetical to the values of the epic's peasant audiences, although ultimately Raja Nal brings the Bhils under his control. Lindsey Harlan suggests that defeating the Bhils also demonstrates the north Indians' ability to defeat the Muslims, the more significant enemy (Harlan 2003, 46).

Exploring caste in *Dhola,* then, raises not only issues of everyday behavior and appearance but also aids in mapping the landscape of rural north India, a landscape marked by villages and towns and forts in contrast to gardens and forests. Different social groups have access to different portions of this landscape, and the *Dhola* singers manipulate these issues of access as their heroes and heroines move across the landscape. Given the connections between space and caste in Hindu society, what groups have access to what spaces, and which women in which groups can go where, caste is intimately intertwined with landscape as well as appearance.

Gloria Raheja speaks of the British entextualization of proverbs, of their "speaking of [caste-linked] proverbs as indexes of consensus and of invariant custom" (1999, 147). This practice, she claims, conceals "the everyday rhetorical and discursive strategies in which proverbs, by their very nature, figure . . . as modes of persuasion and contestation rather than agreement" (1999, 147). *Dhola,* as an extended comment on caste, provides exactly the modes of persuasion and contestation that Raheja finds lacking in the writing of the British colonial officers. Through its representations, in body and language and everyday behaviors of selected castes of the Braj region of peasant farmers, we have extended representations of caste identities. Through Raja Nal's own multiple identities, we have a commentary on the nature of caste itself. While Raja Nal never abandons his dream of being a king, he also realizes that being poor is part of being human, and that one can sometimes be devoted to the poor instead of to one's fellow kings. This message is made even clearer when we look more closely at Raja Nal as a human being, a topic explored in chapter 7.

7 Who Is Raja Nal?

> Then as he goes to wake the sleeping Motini, he hears a voice from the sky saying, "Do not wake her unless you are Nal of Narvar." Nal then thinks to himself, "Behmata said that I was named Nal, I can wake her." (WA 84:234)

Initially Raja Nal is a king who does not know he is a king; later he is a king in search of recognition of his right to be a king. Raja Nal's self-identity as Other brings us back to the hierarchies through which cultures "think themselves." As we have traversed the terrain of *Dhola,* we have seen hierarchy inscribed by and on the human body and its clothing. We have seen the relationship of space to social groups, with the palace and its Rang Mahal, "Palace of Color" (or women's quarters) at one extreme and the forest dwellings of the Bhil tribals and demons at the other, with roads, gardens, and villages mapped in-between. We have explored the identities of various caste groups and the relationships of caste to body and space. *Dhola*'s singers thus provide a wide-ranging commentary on the values and norms of the rural communities of the Braj region and, in the process, view the world from the standpoint of those normally disenfranchised by the powerful. Through *Dhola,* the singers question the rightness of caste, and of caste behaviors, especially those that keep the mighty in power. Most profoundly, however, the performers deal with what it means to be human.

While Raja Nal's social status and birthright are continually questioned, one fact is clear: unlike the gods, he is mortal and is subject to the workings of fate, whether reaping the rewards or punishments of his actions in a previous life or indeed in this one. *Dhola* focuses on these dual features of mortality and fate, for they propel much of the story.

Humans are those whose feet are firmly on the ground (Doniger 1999), living amid the dust and mud, fatigued by work, subject to illnesses such as leprosy, thirst, and hunger. These humans, as we saw in chapter 6, come in a multitude of types, the castes of Hindu India, and Raja Nal is required to negotiate his way through these caste hierarchies, starting his life as a Vaishya but forced later to be a more lowly Oil Presser cum Shudra, though all the while claiming to be a Kshatriya. And the pairing of a god and a human cannot produce a human child. With one immortal wife, Motini, he refuses to marry a second, the daughter of Basukdev, only to have her take rebirth as a human (Dumenti). And he leaves his immortal wife for the mortal one in order to accomplish that most human of goals: to guarantee his lineage by having a son.

The Hindu worldview distinguishes many kinds of beings, including gods (deva) and goddesses (devi); damsels of the court of Indra, heavenly nymphs (apsara); demons (*dāne* and *ásura*), usually mortals who have done great penance, achieved enormous power, and then become so egotistic that they use their powers in non-dharmic ways; and mortals or humans (*manās*) who must live a fated life, have not achieved immortality, and must live out their cycles of birth and rebirth. An intermediary between these various beings is Narad, sage of the gods. A *muni,* or divine being, Narad is not only the mediator between various gods and between gods and humans, but he is a tricky soul, as likely to instigate trouble as solve it. Narad appears in *Dhola* mostly as Indra's sidekick, although he intercedes at key points in Raja Nal's life—at his birth, at both svayambars, and to take Nal from the forest to Kashi where Narad instructs Raja Tikam about the "Mad One." We hear enough of Narad's whispered comments to Raja Nal to know that his goal is to defeat the egotistical Indra.[1]

Beginning with Raja Nal's human-ness, I will then turn to his claim to be a Kshatriya, the one caste group that was not examined in chapter 6, using the Rajput ideal as the probable goal of Raja Nal. Being a Kshatriya demands that one be a king, that one govern properly, and that one's people prosper. Nal's time of distress when famine comes to Narvar and he is banished marks the failure of his rule. Finally, I shall return to the concept of fate with which we began our examination of *Dhola,* for it is only after Raja Nal has become labeled the "Mad One," has been totally ostracized from society, and has been made a complete non-person and thus has accepted his fate that he can begin the long journey back to ruling Narvar.

Raja Nal as Human

Raja Nal's humanity is affirmed and reaffirmed throughout the epic (in a fashion of which Lévi-Strauss [1963, 206–230] might approve, just in case we did not get the message the first time), but it is particularly marked on three occasions: at his conception, at his meeting Motini in the fort of her demon father, and at his marriage to Dumenti. Since his basic quality as a human being is one of the core messages of *Dhola*—his taking on various human identities and thus questioning them—let us start with how Nal as human is asserted. In the process we learn what it means to be human.

Nal's humanity is first marked when the gods are forced by Manjha to give

Pratham the boon of a son. Recall the story of Nal's birth: Manjha, a satidevi incarnate, a human woman who has used her *sat,* her virtuous truth-power, to immolate herself on her husband's funeral pyre and hence gained enormous power vis-à-vis the gods, grabs hold of Narad's feet and will not release him. He goes to the deity Dharamraj (literally, the "king of righteous action") to beg release; Dharamraj discovers that Pratham is fated to have no son for seven births. He finally agrees to counter this fate and asks for a volunteer to take birth as a human.

> But Dharamraj could find no solution [to Pratham's fate] and calls together all 330 million gods and goddesses. He asks the gods to save Narad's body, and the gods say, "But aren't you king of the world? We only obey your orders." So Dharamraj decides to send a god to Manjha's womb, but every god refuses with folded hands, saying that humans eat off food and cereal, but we have godly bodies and live off the smell of flowers and travel through the air. Only one god, Nilgagan [god of the sky, without features], remained. Dharamraj says to him, "My son, you are the most obedient. Go and save Narad." Nilgagan replies, "I will go, I am not scared." Then he asks the gods' blessings and receives a boon that no one in the world would be able to beat him in battle. Then the gods push him down and he becomes a grain of rice that is given to Pratham, who was told to mix it with one hundred more grains and give one grain to each queen. (WA 94:24)

So Nal was born as a human, but of a god. His humanity was marked by what energized and punished him (grain and food, not the smell of flowers). Various singers refer to a human as an "insect of grain," that is, one who lives off grain, clearly marking it as a status little better than that of an insect. What is clear is the separation of god and human.

Nal's humanity is again emphasized when he meets Motini in the fort of the demon Bhumasur. Nal is terrified when he enters the demon's fort and (in some versions) finds piles of human bones. As sung by Matolsingh, the line, "Someone here is eating humans daily," repeated again and again, emphasizes Nal's concern and thus his essential human-ness.

Here is the meeting of Nal and Motini as written by Khacherudas and published in Meerut. Note that the developing argument between Nal and Motini is largely based on his being human and her being non-human.

> motini: "From which country have you come, that you have barged into my home?
> A male (*marad*) has no business here, dear: run to save your life.
> I laughed on seeing you because I have never seen a human before.
> I cried on seeing you because my father will not let you live. . . ."
>
> nal: "You are a non-human (*bin manās*) woman, though very beautiful.
> Why are you sitting around this palace? Why are you rotting within yourself?"

motini: "Tell me, who has incited you? You seem a very uncouth human."
. . . .

nal: "Rani, who is your husband?
With whom have your circled the sacred fire? Tell me right now. . . .
Why are you chasing me out of your house? After all I am a human.
Just consider me one more moon among nine million moon-rays."

Then the demon father returns to the palace:

demon: He sees that the rock closing the door has been moved,
(and thinks), "Seems that some human afflicted by sin (*pāp*) has entered the palace."
"Daughter, Daughter," the demon then calls out.

motini: "Father, no human is with me. Do not accuse a virginal woman, or it will bring harm to you. Did you kill a human in the forest, father? I smell something on your mouth." (Khacherudas 1975, 5–7)

Throughout this episode Nal's human quality is repeatedly emphasized, first in his meeting with Motini and then when the demon knows immediately upon entering his fort that a human has been present. In a scene reminiscent of the European tale "Jack and the Beanstalk," he recognizes Nal because of Nal's smell but is unable to find him because Motini has magically transformed him into a bee and put him into a tiny box in her hair. Motini must hide Nal again and again, for every time the demon returns he smells a human in the palace. Thus humans differ from gods, demons, and heavenly nymphs by their smell. They also differ from the gods because as humans they have sinned.

Sin (*pāp*) and merit (*punya*) are accumulated throughout one's lifetime, sometimes singly and sometimes as a member of a family or lineage or clan, and are closely related to concepts of karma, or fate. Karma, derived from the verbal root *kar-* ("to do, to make") is first of all purposeful action, including mental acts such as desire and physical acts such as murder. Because one is constantly acting, one is constantly accumulating karma. Acts that are meritorious are counted as punya, while harmful acts are considered pap. If one's acts are deemed to be pap (*pāp kartā hai*), one accumulates the fruits (*phal*) of that sinful action. Similarly one also obtains the fruits of one's meritorious actions: enormous merit, such as performing sati, can bring rewards to a family for seven generations. I return to the issue of karma below, but note here that the singer defines the human as a person who can sin, and thus as one who is implicated in the cycle of births and rebirths, as well as punishments in this life, in which the gods keep a tally of one's good and bad actions in order to determine one's future.[2]

As this scene continues, Motini's status as a heavenly nymph is contrasted to Nal's humanity when she reminds him that she can bear him no children and also extracts a promise from Nal that he will not leave her for a human wife who can bear children.[3]

Padam Singh, a singer and author of *Dhola* from Mainpuri, a town near the village of Karimpur, writes of the marriage:

Motini: "I will tell you the truth, which is that I cannot give you any offspring.
Listen my husband, and pay attention in your heart.
Oh my husband, you may take many women with the strength of your dagger and your sword,
But oh my husband, do not wear a wedding crown again [after marrying me].
You must hear clearly and pay attention in your heart, oh my husband.
The day you perform a second marriage, my husband, my husband in a million,
Oh dear, on that day this fortunate woman will die."

> Then Nal makes a cow out of cow dung, listen oh Brother, puts both hands on it and makes a promise with Ganges water, saying, "Oh my queen, oh queen, I will not cheat on you." (P. Singh n.d., 20)

Ram Swarup Dhimar captures the same issues in his telling of the story of *Dhola:*

> Motini said, "Husband, great king, I will marry you only if you make certain promises. You will not get any advantages [from marrying me]. Here I have only unhappiness."
> Nal asks her, "How?"
> Motini replies, "First, I am a god's daughter. Your kingdom in Narvar will be destroyed because I cannot carry a child in my womb, even if you want one. Your lineage will be destroyed. [But] if you marry a human being, you will have children and your throne will survive."
> Nal responds, "Oh, if only you had told me earlier! You are useless now."
> Motini replies, "And you have destroyed everything that I have [that is, my home and my family]." (WA 94:27)

Eventually Nal and Motini agree on the marriage; in this version, too, Nal swears on a cow made of dung and sprinkled with Ganges water, saying, "I have tied this marriage crown with you, Queen. Now I will never marry anyone else." Motini then agrees to marry him.

In a poignant moment as the demon father of Motini is dying, Ram Swarup returns us once again to Nal's human body:

demon: "Daughter, you have wronged me greatly [by trying to kill me]."
motini: "Father, I have wronged you only today, you have wronged me a little every day for a long time."
demon: "How have I wronged you? Tell me."
motini: "Can you see who is standing next to me? Who this is? He is a human being. And do you remember? I asked you a long time ago to get

me a bridegroom, and you brought a *bargad* tree. Now see, he is my bridegroom."

demon: "Oh child, how was I to know? Why didn't you ask me earlier [for a groom]?"

motini: "When I asked you, you brought me a tree!" (WA 94:27)

Nal's essential quality of being human surfaces again when he marries Dumenti, breaking his promise to Motini, who leaves earth and returns to heaven. As David Shulman notes, when a human marries an immortal, it usually leads to "tragic consequences" (1994). Wendy Doniger (1999, 188) suggests that marriage to a goddess (or celestial courtesan) can bring death: in Raja Nal's case, it is not death per se but the death of his lineage that he reacts against. But in breaking his contract with Motini never to marry again, he brings upon himself her curse that he "wander as a beggar," setting up his exile with Dumenti. The asymmetry of Nal's marriage to Motini goes against the most fundamental of Hindu rules for marriage, specifically that the man must be "higher," more powerful, than the woman. Raja Nal has no hope of being more powerful than Motini, whose powers are demonstrated throughout *Dhola.*[4] But he is more powerful than his second wife, the human Dumenti.

For his second marriage we have scenes reminiscent of the Nalopakhyana of the *Mahabharata.* Indra demands that Dumenti marry a god, namely himself, and Dumenti insists on marrying the human Nal. Recall, too, that in *Dhola,* when marrying Dumenti, Nal is marrying the human incarnation of the daughter of Basukdev, the snake king. When Nal meets the snake king's daughter in Patal Lok, the world of the snakes, after he is thrown into the sea by his fictive merchant uncles, he rejects her, saying that he already has one non-human wife and could not marry another. So Basukdev's daughter takes birth as a human, as the daughter of Raja Bhim. When the goose carrying the invitation to the svayambar lies wounded in Nal's garden and delivers the invitation to Nal (in some versions, through an accident, whereas in others the goose is directed to Nal by Dumenti herself), we are, in fact, only seeing a fated story play out. Yet, at the svayambar, Dumenti must choose Nal from among the many Nals the gods create in order to trick her into choosing one of them (particularly Indra).

Ram Swarup Dhimar's version offers several scenes not found in the renditions of others. Therefore I quote his version at length, for it captures both Nal's humanity and the delightful twists of this oral performance.

From Dumenti's Marriage

Raja Bhim refuses to marry his daughter to Nal, who has arrived at his court in torn and tattered clothing, accompanied only by Mansukh and his magical water horse. Bhim wants to fight Nal, saying that the twelve thousand gods would need merely to throw a pinch of dust in order to bury Nal's army completely. But Nal wants to do battle, and suddenly Raja Bhim finds himself trembling.

> Raja Bhim says, "Oh fated one (*bhāgyavān*), where does your fierce power come from?"
> Nal responds, "I was born with my umbilical cord cut.
> I was born with my umbilical cord cut.
> And my mother fed me the milk of a tigress."

On hearing this, Raja Bhim becomes troubled. Then Raja Nal enters the fort at Samudsikul:

> Indra says, "Who is this sister fucker? Where did he come from? Riding such a miserable horse, striding straight in. Why the hell doesn't someone stop him?" He says to Narad, "Why doesn't someone stop him?"
> Narad Muni says, "It is better Maharaj, if you stop him."
> Indra says, "You do it."
> So Narad tries to explain that Nal has come with an invitation. "You are a bridegroom. He is a bridegroom. There is only this difference: you were called by Raja Bhim, and he was called by Dumenti."
> Now Indra becomes worried, thinking, "When I have twelve thousand gods on my side, what is this human going to do to defeat the gods?"

Later Nal, Mansukh, and the horse enter the court, a wedding procession of three when Indra has twelve thousand gods with him. But Indra is again frightened that he will lose, and begs Narad,

> "Make sure that this wedding really takes place. On no account must Dumenti slip past unmarried [to me]."
> Narad responds [perhaps not convincingly], "Lord, you cannot force her. She is also Maha Lakshmi herself."

Then, after it has been arranged to have Dumenti choose from the two turbans, Rani Kamalada speaks to her daughter in the palace:

> "My daughter, you were born with sixteen auspicious marks on your body. A girl with sixteen auspicious marks: that is why these twelve thousand gods have come here today to take you. If you go to the kingdom of the gods, you will become a divine queen. You will move about by flying and, moreover, the name of Samudsikul will be famous throughout the heavens. And we will regularly see the gods. Therefore, Daughter, have the right knowledge of this."
> Dumenti replies, "Parents, this is what I understand. You like the gods. I like someone else." And she begins to get ready.

As Dumenti rides into the court on her bejeweled elephant, she gives Nal a secret sign that today the promise of Patal Lok will be confirmed. But as she looks at the throne with the two turbans, one covered with jewels and the other dirty and stained with turmeric, she is momentarily confused.

> Dumenti then takes Nal's turban to her heart.
> The daughter picks up the turban of Nal, she picks up his. And she throws Indra's turban to the floor.
> So Indra instantly leaps to the platform. When he alights on the platform, he immediately grabs the turban at Dumenti's feet and puts it back on the throne. [He shouts angrily,] "If you knew you wanted to marry a human, then what was the point of calling the gods here in the first place? She must have cheated me. Otherwise, how could she choose a man's turban over a god's? . . . The gods are more beautiful (than humans)."
> Narad replies, "But the gods' beauty is visible only to the gods. If you ask this daughter, she will not see it."

After Dumenti chooses the turmeric-stained turban of Nal, Narad consoles the tearful Indra.

> "Maharaj, this does not suit you. He is a mere mortal. Are you going to let him get the better of you? Trick him, cheat him, we have been doing thus throughout the ages. It is our way, and we will continue to cheat in that way, we gods. Your standing among the gods will rise if you do so." (WA 94:19–20)

Indra then insists that Dumenti garland her chosen husband, with the ensuing scene, found in most versions of the Nala and Damyanti story, of the gods' taking on Nal's appearance and Dumenti having to choose the human among them by noting that his garland is wilted, that his feet touch the earth, that he perspires, and that he has a shadow.

As we saw in chapter 5, when Dumenti returns to her natal home, after she and Nal are separated in the forest, her father once again refers to Nal's human-ness. These key lines are worth repeating here:

> Daughter, you have turned my honor [literally, *pagri,* or turban] worth millions into ashes. Oh, human beings are like worms that live in grain. Look, you married a human being in spite of me, that is why you have come alone from your affinal home to your natal home. (WA 94:27)

Thus, through these repeated reminders of Nal's humanity, it is clear to all that Nal is a human. Like an insect, he lives off grain. His beauty is not comparable to the gods, nor are his clothes, even those of a king, as marvelous. He smells and perspires. And he sins and is subject to fate, a "fated-one." The issue of his being human is doubled when Raja Nal rejects his heavenly wife, Motini, and Dumenti rejects her equally heavenly suitor Indra. These acts firmly reiterate Nal's essential human character. Whatever challenges Nal faces as the story of *Dhola* proceeds, he is rooted in his humanity.

Raja Nal, the Warrior

Raja Nal, hero of *Dhola,* seeks to be recognized by the kings of the fifty-two forts, a clear reference to acceptance by the Rajput rulers in what is now the state of Rajasthan. To succeed in this effort he must defeat his enemies and, as we saw, marry his son to one of their daughters. The title "Rajput" was continuously contested: as noted by Richard Fox, this title was "a status title which local groups assumed as part of their claim to social positions or higher rank on a regional level. The title required of its claimants an ideological and minimal behavioral commitment to a life style defined as Rajput" (1971, 16). Hence Raja Nal needs only to act as a Rajput hero in order to successfully claim a seat among the kings of the fifty-two forts. But in this he is unsuccessful for he displays few attributes of a Rajput hero, as defined by scholars such as Lindsey Harlan (1992; 2003), Karine Schomer (1989), and Norman Zeigler (1973). Before turning to Raja Nal's behavior on the battlefield, let us first examine the key components of the Rajput ethic.

From British times on, the Rajputs have been seen by various outsiders as the embodiment of martial and masculine virtue (Harlan 2003, 2–4). James Tod (1971, 57) claimed that the Rajputs have a vigor and boldness not found in other Indian males, characteristics that were revealed through their bloody deeds. Various writers concur that the essence of the Rajput ethic is a commitment to valor without regard for the consequences: what is most important is that the hero stand in battle. His bravery in battle, with or without victory, is more crucial than the victory itself (Rudolph and Rudolph 1984, 42). The true hero is he who dies in battle, his head cut off (a self-sacrifice to the goddess) but battling on nevertheless, until he reaches the boundary of his village. Death in battle was itself seen as salvation (Harlan 2003).

A medieval Rajasthani text reads thus: "You bind a turban on your head. You take up a weapon in your hand. You have assumed/possessed the body of a Rajput. There is only one opportunity to die" (from the Naisī re khyāt I:75; quoted in Zeigler 1973, 67). Zeigler goes on to list the attributes of the Rajput: great warrior, victorious in battle, dies in battle, has great strength and power. If the warrior is successful, recitation of his valorous acts gains him fame and renown. Further, the Rajput is the giver of gifts, grain, and protection to all those who rely on him (Zeigler 1973, 69).

In discussing *Alha,* an epic associated with the Rajput rulers of Kanauj, Karine Schomer (1989, 150) lists the components of rajputi, or Rajput honor: never turn back in time of war, never strike the first blow, never strike a woman, never achieve one's goals by stealth or treachery, never leave a wrong unavenged, do not fear omens, retain loyalty to those whose salt you have eaten, prize your reputation more than your life, and always help a woman who asks. While Raja Nal adheres carefully to some aspects of this ethic (particularly retaining loyalty to those whose salt one has eaten), he does not die in battle—indeed, none of our heroes die in battle. And this in itself is perhaps the strongest indication possible that *Dhola* is not a story that derives from the Rajput traditions.[5] To the contrary, Raja Nal is fearful of war, he demands to turn back when losing a battle, he would quite happily have left his parents in prison, he is shaken by bad omens, and he applauds Budh Singh's treachery with the Oil Presser. Finally, unlike the true Rajput hero who dies alone, singled out from the herd of goats that are the potential sacrifices to the goddess, Raja Nal and his family mimic the way that the gods associated with Vaishnavism leave the earth: like Ram and Lakshman in the *Ramayana,* they end their time on earth by submerging themselves in water, in this case in a rising lake.

It is Raja Nal's bravery that is most contested. Let us first look at Nal's questionable behavior in the battle with Phul Singh Panjabi. When Nal's parents go to bathe in the Ganges and are captured by Phul Singh Panjabi, Nal does not believe Motini's dream of their capture and refuses to go to save them. Then a Brahman who saw the battle returns from the Ganges and reports that the army has been turned to stone. Nal still refuses to move, saying, "Rani, it is nothing. I shall not take a single step out of Narvar." Motini replies, by insulting his lineage and questioning his identity:

sung: "Husband, I did not think you so very weak,
Or perhaps your mother committed a sin,
Who knows who came from her womb in the forest,
Husband, you stay in the palace,
I will fight against the Panjabis." (WA 85:302–304)

That women insult their men when bravery is called for occurs in Rajput stories as well. Ann Gold tells of an occasion in which the hero is insulted as a way to motivate him:

> Hari Rani said, "Wear my bangles, and give me your sword, and sit secure in the circle of these four walls; and don't ever call yourself a Rajput." (A. Gold 1994, 35)

Lindsey Harlan tells a story, supposedly true, in which the identity of the Rajput family where it took place is concealed:

> This story is about Rana Maha, Rao Sahab of Bathera. A *rao* . . . came back from war: he was frightened. He told a maidservant to get a coal for smoking a pipe. His wife said to the maidservant, "Don't take an iron thing for the coal, take a wooden thing. He's frightened of swords, so don't take an iron thing." He was so ashamed, he committed suicide. (Harlan 2003, 73–74)

Later in the battle with Phul Singh Panjabi, Nal and Mansukh are blinded when they attempt to enter the battleground at the Ganges, and Nal immediately gives up the fight:

chant: Nal says, "Oh god,
The royal throne is gone,
I will no longer live in the palace,
A bad time has come,
Fate has opposed us from all sides.
sung: How can we release my parents from prison? We have been made blind."

It is Mansukh who suggests that they call Motini, who will be able to aid them in freeing Nal's parents (and Motini is there, in the army, in disguise); she comes quickly to their aid, lifting the magic that had made them blind. After Motini restores their sight, Nal once again shows his cowardice when, on starting back to Narvar, he says,

spoken: "It doesn't matter if my parents die . . . we have come here to free my parents, not to become blind. I do not have enough power to free my parents. If we are blinded again, all will be ruined. Let us return." (WA 85:302–304)

Eventually, after finding his parents in jail, Nal is captured by Chando, the sister of Phul Singh's wife, whose magic can initially counter Motini's. Her first act is to capture Nal, lock him in a cage as a parrot, and then (in manly form?) tie a kerchief around his neck that makes him lose his senses. In this state he acts as her female servant, the ultimate insult to a warrior, until he is freed by a Tamil woman he meets at the well where he has gone to draw water (a woman's job). The Tamil woman finds him an oddity, dressed like a warrior, carrying a sword, but drawing water. When she removes the kerchief, he regains his memory, " 'Where is my army? Where are my mother and father? And where is my queen?' Nal was angry, and suddenly tears flowed from his eyes" (WA 85:305). Except in situations of bhakti, devotion to the gods, it is highly inappropriate for a Hindu male to cry, especially a warrior. And Rajput heroes never cry.[6] The Tamil woman gives Nal a magic potion to turn Chando into a mare, and then Nal and Motini again proceed to wage war against Phul Singh.

Throughout this episode Nal acts in a manner inappropriate to a Kshatriya: he refuses to go to war, tries to run from the battlefield, and weeps when he should be fighting a battle. Nal's behavior is not that of the Rajput hero, who delights in the blood of war and will sacrifice his life, home, and livelihood in order to protect family honor. If I am correct that this Braj version of *Dhola* is a metaphoric statement on Jat rule, the continual questioning of Nal's identity and warrior behavior throughout the first section of *Dhola* makes sense.

Before he can claim to be equal to the "kings of the fifty-two forts," he must be able to win battles. He does, but only because of the women at his side. Motini and Durga win the battles, and Nal weeps, as a lower-caste coward might, on the sidelines.[7]

Particularly problematic are Raja Nal's frequent feminine behaviors. The heroic Rajput abjured anything that might be considered feminine (Zeigler 1973, 81), but, as we saw above, Raja Nal, without his knowledge, is even transformed into a female. (His nephew Kishanlal is also transformed by the gardener into a woman disguised as a daughter-in-law.) At still other times the singers use various strategies to mark Nal's femininity. In "The Marriage of Kishanlal," when Raja Nal's army is ready to march to battle, Mansukh seeks Nal out, only to find him lingering in a woman's garden. Not only is he lingering in a place as culturally remote as possible from battle, amid the flowers of a woman's garden, but to mark this femaleness even further the singer describes his actions to the melody of malhar, a woman's song of longing for her lover and natal family.

spoken:	And in what fashion does Nal leave there?
sung (malhar):	Oh, slowly, slowly Nal goes from the garden, Oh, slowly, slowly Nal goes from the garden, O, Brother, Nal is very sad at heart. The King of Narvar, Brother, goes from the garden. Oh, seeing him come, Oh Brother, the Gujar [Mansukh] said, . . . King of Narvar, Oh Brother, fix your mind on the forest. (WA 74:109)

Through the song genre and the words themselves, Raja Nal is feminized, something highly inappropriate for a Rajput.

Raja Nal cries in another crucial scene, when he is alone in the forest, separated from Dumenti. Lost and wandering, he comes across the snake with its head pinned to the ground by the arrow of Ajaypal, Nal's maternal grandfather. The snake shows Nal his own *kal,* or life force and threatens to kill him, and Raja Nal cries.

spoken:	The snake then says, "You are not the real Nal. Nal would have laughed at seeing his kal and you are crying. I'll not bite such a coward." (WA 94:27)

When the daughter of Raja Viran has Nal thrown into the dried-up well for refusing to marry her, he cries for three months, until he finally remembers Basukdev and seeks Basuk's help. Yet at other times Raja Nal speaks out against cowards, even saying about his own son, "If he [my son] is a coward, then let him die. Cowards must die" (WA 90:10).

Raja Nal continually struggles with his own bravery. When fighting the battle of Bhamartal, Raja Nal takes the Oil Presser's bullocks to Bhamartal to give them water. Angry at the way he is being treated, he destroys the pond, making the bullocks stir up the mud and defecate in it. But the nine hundred guards of Budh Singh awake and attack. Nal again weeps uncontrollably. Remembering Durga, filled with bravery, he then kills the nine hundred guards, wraps a steel bar around the necks of the last two, and returns to the oil press. As the epic singer reminds us, in a line more reminiscent of Rajput heroes than the heroes of *Dhola,* "the Brave are born to die in battle, while the timid one dies a thousand times. The Brave one must fight and die in battle, caring not where his lifeless body falls" (WA 84:244).

Finally, Raja Nal's bravery is sometimes used to identify him: when Motini and Nal are alone in the demon's fort, Motini suggests,

> sung: "Husband, take me secretly,
> Husband, otherwise it will be very difficult. . . ."
> spoken: Nal responded, "I will not steal you." . . .
> Motini answered, "Do not worry. I was just testing if you were a king, for a king will not steal but will fight and take what is his." (WA 89:19)

And yet later, when Nal wants to go home, Motini taunts him,

> spoken: "I thought you were some great brave man. Now you seem like a Merchant. . . ." (WA 89:19)

Critically, it was only because of the Rajputs' brave and valiant deeds and heroic acts on the battlefield that the maintenance of order was possible (Zeigler 1973, 68). It is precisely Raja Nal's loss of the possibility of being a warrior that throws his kingdom into disorder, and it is his regaining of his powers as a warrior, albeit not a Rajput warrior, that allows order to be restored. But before turning to the time of distress and the nature of the chaos that descends on Narvar and Raja Nal, let us briefly examine the role of the dice game in reversing Raja Nal's misfortunes.

The Dice Game

In contrast to the role of the dice game in various episodes of the *Mahabharata* and other Indian traditions where dicing sets off events that bring disorder and chaos to the heroic losers (such as the Pandavas in the court of the Kauravas or Nala himself in the Nalopakhyana; see Handelman and Shulman 1997), in *Dhola* dicing is used as a device to reestablish Raja Nal's identity, to move him not into chaos but toward order. In this sense *Dhola* presents a fundamental reversal of the dominant textual traditions.

Recall that in the *Mahabharata,* it is the dicing game between the heads of the Pandava and the Kuru clans that sets up the Pandavas' loss, the disrobing of Draupadi, and the banishment of the Pandavas from their kingdom. Here the dice game takes place among cousins, or equals. In the Nalopakhyana, Raja Nala makes the fatal error of not washing the tip of his big toe, which allows the god Kali (angry at not having won Damayanti at the svayambar) to enter him and take possession of his body, leading to his loss at dice and ultimately to his banishment from his kingdom. The exile in *Dhola* is not related to dicing and is clearly caused by Indra, with his helpers Shanidev and Shukra, although Motini's curse as a result of Nal's second marriage certainly has a role in his banishment. Rather, in *Dhola* the dice games work to eliminate disorder. Nal plays three critical dice games—the first with Motini in the fort of the demon; the second with Raja Basuk in the underworld of Patal Lok, after Nal is thrown overboard by the wicked sons of Lachchaman Seth; and the third with Budh Singh, when Nal wins the right to marry his son, Dhola, to Budh's daughter Maru. Nal wins at dice both because of his Kshatriya status and his use of the magical cowry shells that he won from Motini.

When Nal meets Motini in the fort of the demon, he refuses to play dice with her, saying that he is not a Kshatriya and hence doesn't know how to play. Here he plays on the idea that dicing is a game of kings, not a game to be played safely or well by lower castes. But Motini, on seeing the red in his eye and realizing he is indeed a Kshatriya, although he himself does not know it, convinces him to try anyway.

With this scene, Raja Nal's first exile with his mother draws to a close, as the dice game identifies him as a Warrior, not a Merchant, and sets up his marriage to Motini. The second dice game takes place in Patal Lok, where Raja Nal meets Basukdev, King of the Snakes. This game seems less charged than the other two, as Nal's identity does not depend on it, although he does beat Basukdev, who becomes his ally (in some versions of later episodes Raja Nal is able to call upon the snakes to wreak havoc on his enemies). The third dice game has a similar function: as we saw earlier, the Oil Presser and Budh Singh play dice, with Budh badly defeating the Oil Presser who, "because he is [of a] lower caste did not know how to play dice." Then with the help of Raja Nal, the Oil Presser returns to Budh's court and defeats him repeatedly. Finally, Budh realizes that there are extraordinary powers behind the Oil Presser's victory and invites his servant, Raja Nal, to play dice with him. It is in this game that Raja Nal wins Budh's daughter for his unborn son, Dhola, and begins his own reacceptance (still several battles away!) into society.

Hence the dice game in *Dhola* is used to mark a turn toward righteousness, toward the reversal of the disorder wrought by those, whether human or divine, who brought injustice to Raja Nal and turned his kingdom into a barren land and his life into one without kin or friends.

The Time of Distress

The portion of *Dhola* in which Nal and Dumenti are exiled from Narvar begins with an episode entitled, "Nal's Time of Distress" (aukha). Structurally this episode is the center of the epic, since the liminal state imposed on Nal during his time of distress is central to his reemergence into the world as a king, with wife, family, and friends. Ram Swarup Dhimar claimed that it was very difficult to sing this episode since the issues dealt with were heavy and so, unlike other episodes, it was not fun to perform.[8] It is a period in which the moral order of Narvar is upset by the divine injustice of Raja Indra wrought with the help of Shanidev. While the distress (aukha) is directly attributed to Indra and Shanidev, we must not forget that Motini cursed Nal with a life of penury and without a kingdom when he insisted on marrying Dumenti, although we know, too, that this marriage was fated by Behmata, the goddess of fate, when she sat at the seashore and made two marriages for Nal. At yet another level, *Dhola* can be read more broadly as a time of distress, for indeed injustices, both human and divine, permeate the epic. Manjha is banished, through the actions of the one hundred queens of Raja Pratham; Phul Singh Panjabi unfairly attacks Pratham at the Ganges; Indra's own ego leads to his getting Shanidev's help in bringing ruin to Narvar; Raja Nal's own brother, Pushkar, refuses to send a marriage procession for his nephew's wedding; and so on. Here I explore the disorder and upset wrought especially in this time of distress, for this theme is central, both linearly and conceptually, to the epic as a whole.

For initial insight into this theme, I turn once again to Norman Zeigler's analysis of the moral codes of the Rajput kingdoms based on the textual traditions of the bards and chroniclers. According to Zeigler, during the middle period of Rajasthani history, the kingdoms of the true Kshatriya Rajas were lost and the Rajputs, or sons of the kings (*rāj putrā*), were forced to wander in search of new lands where they could establish their kingdoms. This period was marked by distress and confusion (*vikhau*), not unlike that in the seventeenth century when Jats rose to power at the decline of Mughal rule. During such periods there is a mixing of castes and resultant disorder. Zeigler describes one event that is reminiscent of Raja Nal's birth and upbringing. The story concerns the Sisodiyas, a clan that ruled in Mewar in southern Rajasthan from the eighth century C.E. on. The king established his rule, but he had no son. Upon appeal to the god Suryaji, he was promised a son, but only if the king and queen made a pilgrimage to Anbai Devi. On the pilgrimage the king is killed, and the queen camps in a village of Brahmans. Begged not to commit sati when pregnant, she gives birth to a son and then again readies herself for sati. As she reaches the pyre, she hands the infant to the Brahman, who cries out, "What should I do with the son of a Rajput? Tomorrow this boy would play at the hunt and kill animals. . . . In his company, I would become unrighteous and immoral (*adharm*)." (Naisī re khyāt I:1–2; quoted in Zeigler 1973, 115). This boy went on to found the Sisodiya clan. Other stories tell of boys who are raised, as was Raja Nal, without knowledge of their origins, only later to be recognized as a Rajput. Another story ends with these lines,

> In the face of all these thieves, not even a dried-up bone has a chance of survival in our village. We have constant thought of bringing a Rajput [warrior] from some distance away in order to man a watch-post. By our good fortune, however, a great Rajput, the son of a great house, has come and is sitting hungry in our homes. We should certainly keep him and put him to work. (Naisī re khyāt I:9; quoted in Zeigler 1973, 117)

There is one significant difference between the disorder (vikhau) thought to be affecting the Rajput kingdoms and the distress (aukha) brought upon Raja Nal. Vikhau was thought to be recurring, caused by improper actions and not fulfilling one's dharma. Although these demerits are thought to affect descendents, they are discussed in terms of their effects on an individual's current life. But, in *Dhola,* Indra wrongs Raja Nal without an error in his dharmic duties (although there is Motini's ever present curse). But there is also the continual persistence of fate: as I discuss below, it is Raja Nal's fate, his demerits from this and previous lives, that he must come to terms with before he can regain his kingdom and restore order.[9] What these stories of supposed Rajput refugees illustrate, however, is that the tale of Raja Nal and his banishment, his time as an Oil Presser, and his eventually regaining his throne is not a story that would have been thought irregular or unusual in the wider area ruled at times by Rajputs.

What were the effects of this divinely caused disorder, this aukha? While the Rajput chronicles talk of a mixing of castes and a confusion of their order, of kings who were refugees, without land or power, *Dhola* is more specific in its delineation of the effects of disorder. This becomes most evident by following Raja Nal on his journey into exile.

Initially he loses his wealth, his power, and his kingdom. There is severe drought in Narvar, and his people begin to die of starvation. Even the leaves in the Mali's garden dry up. With no money, not even a horse to ride, Raja Nal and Dumenti steal away in the night. First they go to Mansukh Gujar's kingdom, but there the food is contaminated and the hook swallows the necklace worth nine lakhs of rupees. Then they go to Nal's sister's place, but she refuses to help. On the outskirts of a village they see a woman feeding her child, and when the woman goes for food the child dies in their care. On a commercial cassette recording of this episode, the singer Pandit Shankar Lal repeats the following line numerous times: "In times of distress, all your close friends and relatives desert you" (Shankar Lal 1987). A poor woman in Karimpur once told me that the poor have no friends, for friends are only for those who have something to give in return.

This idea is reinforced by various singers. One wrote: "Tulsidas write the truth. The person to whom Ram gives great sorrow, he takes away his intellect first, so that his mind cannot function" (C. Singh 1966). When Raja Nal is in trouble, Ram Swarup Dhimar frequently sings this refrain:

sung:	In distress comes misfortune, in adversity comes calamity,
	In distress comes misfortune, in adversity comes calamity,
	Then brothers and relatives don't speak to you,
	And descendents turn their backs.
spoken:	What does Behmata say?
sung:	When destruction comes to man,
	First lightning falls on the brain,
	One's own mother is like a lion,
	One's own father seems like Yamraj. (WA 84:237)

In the battle at Bhamartal, Nal's sword turns into a snake when he goes to fetch it for the battle. At that point Raja Nal comments, "Everyone has deserted me; my weapons at least should not desert me!" (Shankar Lal 1987).

Thus chaos descends: family and friends desert the refugee, and Raja Nal becomes a king without a kingdom. Eventually he even loses his wife, when Shanidev and Shukra realize that no one will accept that he is truly miserable if his wife is still with him: "Oh, who would say that Nal is cursed by aukha when the king and queen are still living together?" (WA 84:236). Moreover, castes become mixed together, as Raja Nal turns horse trainer and Oil Presser. With Shanidev in charge, Nal also loses his gods, for he has lost the ability to cry out to Durga as well as his knowledge of the mantras that might aid him. (In fact, except for Nal's and Dumenti's one night in a temple, he is able to call only upon Basukdev from the time he leaves Narvar until he reaches the safety of the Oil Presser's house. Notably, however, the sage Narad keeps track of him and even takes him to Raja Tikam in Kashi before the second svayambar, after which he loses his senses and intelligence.) While journeying out of the forest, a woman asks him where he is from, and Raja Nal responds, "There is no village I belong to. I have nothing" (WA 84:236). With all this gone, with no intelligence, no friends or relatives, no food or clothing, no shelter, no honor left of any kind, Raja Nal, now called the "Mad One," ends up sitting on a dung heap.

Nal as Madman

Nal's encounter with the agony of poverty and with the bodily destruction that afflicts him when he becomes a leper lead him to be marked as a madman and to lose all sense of himself and the world. As David Shulman (1994) has commented on Nala in the Nalopakhyana, it is Nala's suffering, his madness, that allows him to see the world as other and hence to begin to understand the meaning of human identity. In *Dhola* this message is writ large, for Nal suffers mightily and views the world through a variety of lenses. He also begins to understand the meaning of human identity, and most critical to this newfound understanding is his transformation into a leper and a madman. Once he becomes a man without contact with other humans, Nal is no longer concerned with his kingly status.

After their food is destroyed in Mansukh's palace, after a son dies in Dumenti's care, after the hook swallows the necklace, Nal and Dumenti finally give up any hope of relying on family and friends, and they retreat to the forest to avoid bringing further disasters on their loved ones. There, too, hunger awaits, for the fish jump from the frying pan back into the lake, and birds fly away with Nal's clothing, after which Dumenti shares half her sari with him. Then Nal departs to find water but, led astray by Shanidev, wanders deep into the forest where he comes upon a snake whose head has been pinned to the ground by an arrow. The king who shot him has started a fire to finish him off, but, upon seeing Nal, the snake cries out, "Oh brother Nal, only you can save me." By now Nal's brain is already addled by Shanidev, and he answers, "But who will save me?" The snake then reminds him that he knows the water mantra; Nal recites it, and the fire is extinguished. The curse placed on Nal by Motini when he married Dumenti, that he would become a leper and beg for alms, again returns to haunt him. The snake bites him, and he awakens to find his body covered with festering wounds, pus dripping everywhere. He makes his way to the sacred pond where, upon bathing, his senses and intellect are immediately restored. But upon emerging from the pond, his sores are twice as angry and his mind is further destroyed. And thus the servants at the pond hail him, "Oh lunatic leper" (*pāgul koriyā*).

Eventually the sage Narad takes Nal to Kashipur, where he arranges for Nal to work for Raja Tikam. Naming him Bavariya, the "Mad One," Narad tells Raja Tikam that his new servant requires a wage of only one *ser* (slightly less than one kilo) of barley a day.[10] No one should talk to him, for it is said that he kills twelve thousand people every six months. Tikam thinks, "But, counting me, we are exactly twelve thousand!" Only if Tikam needs to travel quickly should he call upon Bavariya. So Bavariya is left alone, his body black and oozing pus. Considered crazy, barred from human interaction because he is banned from speaking, Bavariya is truly an outcaste, the non-person Motini had cursed him to be.

Meanwhile, Dumenti asks her father to "find that crazy one" (WA 84:237). Dumenti writes a message to the one kingdom that has not yet received an invitation to the second svayambar.

When Tikam finally receives the invitation to Dumenti's second svayambar, Nal quickly proves the veracity of his name. Tikam calls Bavariya to ready his chariot and horses. And this follows:

> spoken: When Bavariya heard of the need to leave and learned of the entire situation, the only thought that came to his mind was that my Rani has sent out an invitation for a svayambar, and all these other men are unnecessarily giving up their lives for it. Some are dressing in elaborate clothes, some are bathing, some are quickly making sandalwood paste. Some say that they will take her forcibly, while others say that if she dies, they will die also. Everyone is thinking only of themselves.

When Tikam tells Bavariya that the svayambar is in five days, Bavariya curses him:

> spoken: "Oh sister fucker, why are you fretting today? Oh we can start on that very day and return also that day."
> Tikam responds, "That is why you are known by the name of Bavariya! You are absolutely crazy!" (WA 84:237)

The Mad One then searched through Tikam's stables for appropriate horses, rejecting all but the most decrepit.[11]

After meandering about for several days, the Mad One returns from his morning ablutions at about 10:00 A.M. (very late in a country where people rise at 4:00 or 5:00 A.M.) and finds a Grain Parcher's two horses that are nearly dead. They do not eat; their coats are bad; their skin is visible; children sit around chasing birds off them. It seems they will die any minute. Finally, Bavariya buys the horses. Bavariya says, "Master, you take one, and I'll take the other." So they begin to pull the horses, but the horses' hooves buckle immediately, and they cannot move in either direction. So Bavariya drags one and Tikam the other. Then Bavariya decides that both horses should be massaged. Tikam agrees to massage one, for he thinks that the six months are about up and perhaps Bavariya will become angry and kill them all. Finally, Tikam sits in the chariot, hanging on for dear life. Bavariya hits the horses, and they fall down. For an hour the horses lie motionless, as if dead. Then Bavariya tries to get them to their feet, staining his clothes with blood in the process. The same happens to Tikam. He massages the horses again while Bavariya finds a kilo of good grass, and he and Tikam feed the grass to the horses by hand.

Finally, they actually depart. Tikam sits like a lord in a chariot, and Bavariya speaks the bij mantra into the ears of the half-dead horses. As he speaks the bij mantra, the horses' ears point up and they fly into the sky. Tikam cannot decide if his servant is a man, a god, or a demon! Tikam, himself a great gambler, challenges Bavariya to count the leaves on a tree. Bavariya stops the horses and learns the secrets of gambling, although the epic singers attribute his later success against Raja Budh Singh as resulting from Motini's cowry shells and not the expertise he learned from Tikam. Tikam never learns how to drive the horses. They go on.

The horses cover nine hundred kos (perhaps five hundred miles) and reach the border of Bhim's kingdom in only one and a half hours. Everyone is gathered at the court when Bavariya drives his pair of bloody horses right to the spot where Indra is sitting. He leads them right onto Indra's gorgeous carpets, because Indra is his foe and has destroyed him. Now Narad Muni arrives, for Bavariya, acting out of anger, would have driven the horses right over Indra. Indra says,

chant: "Leper, you are acting wrongly.
Do you not feel shame (*sharam*)?
You have rubbed my honor (*ijjat*) in the mud."

Other kings comment on the servant Nal's black complexion, while still others note that only these two arrived, without an army. Meanwhile, Indra calls Bavariya names. Bavariya responds,

sung: "I have not come here to live and I am not asking for a kingdom.
Today I shall sit here on the carpet, tomorrow I will be gone.
If you continue to talk, I will come over and kick your crown.
spoken: Indra Maharaj, if you speak a single word more, I will have these horses climb on your head."
At the same time, Narad Muni says, "Oh Brother Leper, keep your chariot to one side."

Narad then tells Nal that no one will take his queen, and that he, Narad, will help him, even though he is part of Indra's retinue. Bavariya places his blanket on a dung heap, while Tikam sits on a rich carpet.

spoken: Bavariya thinks, "Either one should live or die, or someone can take his queen with him. It is out of my power." Raja Nal sits there without a care and, looking around, says,
chant: "What will be is powerful (*honi ho balwan*),
And what is in one's fate cannot be changed (*aur karamgati ṭare na ṭare*)." (WA 84:239)

When everyone is ready for the svayambar, Dumenti asks her father to see who arrived in just one and a half hours. Bhim greets each king: it took some a year to arrive, some six months. Finally, he reaches Tikam who tells him to ask the servant. When Raja Nal tells Bhim that he came nine hundred kos in one and a half hours, Bhim comments sarcastically, "What healthy horses!" And he says, "See those horses that have arrived in one and a half hours!" Then he reports back to Dumenti, who gets ready for the svayambar, only to have second thoughts.

Dumenti has a further request, and asks,

spoken: "Father, extinguish all the fires in the city. Then give each king two sticks and cow dung cakes and ten kilos of flour. Order them to cook without fire and then to eat it."

None of the kings can start a fire (even those who went to the city to obtain fire, only to learn that all the fires in the city had already been extinguished). Tikam is hungry, and the Mad One says, "Eat quickly."

Raja Tikam says, "Who can cook? Give me uncooked food."

But the Mad One replies, "Give me the flour. I will cook for myself."

Raja Tikam tells him that he is mad, but Nal takes all the cow dung and sticks and mixes the flour. Everyone thinks he is totally mad: why is he making dough when there is no fire? Then, when the dough is ready, he says the fire [*agni*] mantra and lights the fire. Dumenti, watching, knows that her husband is there. But Indra is furious: he pours two jugs of water on Nal's hearth. He swears at the Mad One, calling him a clever Nat [Acrobat, a caste, as noted above, known for its possible abilities at sorcery]. Nal replies, "I am not an Acrobat; I am hungry and so I am cooking." Then he lights all the fires in the court.

But when Dumenti comes into the court, she cannot find Raja Nal, for his body has been transformed by the leprosy. Finally, with the help of the goddess, she finds Raja Nal and places the garland on him. Again Indra is furious and insists she redo it. Now Indra makes fifteen hundred lepers, all resembling Nal! But since the true Raja Nal has a shadow, Dumenti is again able to garland her beloved.

Dumenti's words, when seeking her husband, in the note she sends to the one kingdom that had not yet received an invitation to the second svayambar, summarize the essence of the epic's message about being human, especially when combined with the statement Nal makes while sitting on his dung pile. Speaking as a wife (and metaphorically as a deity, for the wife is the Lakshmi of the house), Dumenti says,

"Oh exalted one who is like Shiva; please maintain our dignity,
Let me be the one filled with petty weaknesses; you remain as deep and calm as the ocean.
Oh exalted one who is like Shiva; please maintain our dignity,
Let me be the one filled with petty weaknesses; you remain as deep and calm as the ocean.

I am like a poor person now; please make sure that I do not lose my husband,
They have given it the name svayambar; when you look at the letter, don't just sit there. I will wait for you till four o'clock."

A short time later, as we saw above, Nal, sitting on a dung heap behind the kings who are gathered for the svayambar, says,

"What will be is powerful,
And what is in one's fate cannot be changed."

In Dumenti's first two lines, she calls upon Nal's marriage bonds and dignity, saying that she should be burdened with the world's pettiness, bestowing on Nal the gift of equanimity. She concludes with a prayerful hope of regaining her husband. Raja Nal, alias Bavariya, the Mad One, indeed seems to have achieved equanimity in his six months of having been in a liminal, almost non-human state. He reflects solely on the workings of fate: whatever has befallen him, and whatever lies ahead, is the workings of fate and cannot be undone or changed. He has learned that, as a human, fate rules all.

Fate, Time, and Being Human

In framing the story of Nala and Damyanti in the *Mahabharata,* Bṛhadasva says, "Reflecting always on the impermanence of man's riches, be serene in their coming and going, and do not worry" (Van Buitenen 1975, 364). This is the same message captured by Raja Nal in the lines above. He might also add: "reflect on the nature of one's identity and its impermanence," a message made more forcefully, perhaps, in *Dhola,* where a frequent line reads, "When there is no life in the world, only air and water will remain."[12] When combined with the couplet "Time is all powerful, Man is not powerful" (WA 84:237), *Dhola* provides a potent message about the ultimate nature of life, this play of fate that brings Nal into the world.

Karma in Hindu philosophical writings is based on theories of transmigration. Many believe that one's actions, one's karma (remembering that the root of karma is *kar,* "to do") in a previous life completely define one's karma, one's fate in this life. In this view, the gods and their representatives tally up one's merits and demerits, and fix one's future in immutable "headwriting" (lines on one's forehead that contain one's fate, as defined by karma). In the most extreme interpretation, what is written is unchangeable. This view is also thought to remove the possibility of placing full moral responsibility on any one individual, for it is actions in previous lives that lead one to illness or fortune in this life. At some level, one is not responsible for one's actions in this life. In *Dhola,* too, some singers see fate as fully controlling. As Matolsingh (n.d. [b], 2) wrote, "No one can do anything with regard to fate." Another singer claims, "It is not your fault, it is the fault of fate" (WA 74:109). Pandit Shankar Lal (1987) said, "Fate is all powerful. Because of fate, Raja Nal has to live like a beggar." When Dumenti is found by the Banjaras, whose leader then tries to force her into marriage, their camp begins to burn. Narad muni appears in the guise of a Brahman priest, and the Banjara complains, "Panditji Maharaj, our camp is burning." And Narad responds, "Son, you must have committed some sin."

Note, however, that these singers are not clear as to whether this fate is from a previous life or this one. The epic narrative is itself ambiguous. In the episode where Behmata sits at the seashore making marriage rings to toss into the ocean, she is the goddess of fate, and proclaims that Raja Nal will have two wives. But Nal's distress, his aukha, comes when he does marry a second time (even though that marriage was fated), and Motini curses him with becoming a leper and a beggar. Was Nal only acting out his fate, and was even Motini's curse preordained? Curses (*strap*) appear to be a form of fate that can affect one in this life and also be carried into the next (as in the case of the four daughters of Raja Pratham who cursed him with being childless in his next seven lives).

Contrary to the rigidity of some understandings of fate as occurring in one's previous lives, many Hindus, and all those whom I know in the Braj region, believe that their actions in their current life do count toward good or bad fortune *in this life.* Bhakti as a religious system based on devotion to the gods is, at least for its rural audiences, a system in which devotion to the gods pays off in this lifetime. Writing about rural peasants near Delhi in the 1960s, Oscar Lewis also notes that these Jats insist that the results of one's actions are realized in this life, and not in another (1965, 253). Many local religious texts clearly state that if one has misfortune one can perform a meritorious act such as bathing in the Ganges, and the misfortune could possibly disappear. Or an individual can perform rituals such as vrats (fasts) and pujas that will convince the gods to alter that person's life fortunes (Wadley 1983). The most common phrase ending a vrat katha, a ritual story associated with a fast, is this: "and through the telling of this story [itself a form of devotion], all one's sorrows will be removed." Further, many vrat katha narratives tell of a fated act, such as the death of a son at the age of twelve, an act that is altered because of devotion to the gods in this life. One such vrat katha, that of the Monday worship of Shiva, explicitly states that the god must alter his devotee's preordained fate because of the latter's extreme devotion (Wadley 1975, chap. 3). Other vrat kathas emphasize the immediacy of one's sins (as when a child dies) and the removal of the error once the appropriate deity is worshiped (Wadley 1983). It is also apparent, however, that regardless of whether an individual believes that prior or current actions determine one's fate, fate is seen as determining one's life.

Dhola is performed in a region with a dominant and pervasive bhakti tradition of worshiping the Vaishnavite gods Krishna and, to a lesser extent, Ram. Worshiped with love and devotion, Durga and other gods and goddesses of the bhakti tradition are believed to be able to overcome one's preordained fate. The Jat rulers of the area manifest this bhakti tradition in both their worship of Lakshman, the brother of Ram and their tutelary deity, and, marking their Vaishnavite traditions, their vegetarianism. In *Dhola,* rural singers emphasize not a Vaishnavite devotion to Krishna but rather a devotion to the goddess (although a related version by the poet Todarmal [1975] focuses on Krishna, and not Durga). In blatant opposition to the Rajputs to the west, this Durga is both "not-Kali" and a vegetarian, displaying clear ties to the vegetarianism of the Jat rulers and the Vaishnava elites of the area. It is this Durga, and her counterpart Motini, who can counter the fate of Raja Nal and his kin. Yet, as noted above, Durga is all but absent from the episodes concerning Nal's banishment: it is precisely these episodes that focus on fate. The absence of the goddess and the concurrent emphasis on fate imply that unless one accepts the fruits of one's actions, and one's essential humanity, even the gods are useless.

The message of *Dhola* is not just about accepting one's fate; it is also about the nature of life. As Ram Swarup Dhimar, our primary guide to *Dhola,* said in one episode, "When there is death, why should one fear? Everyone will die one day. When life is for duty, why sorrow unnecessarily? . . . Do noble deeds with body, soul, mind, and wealth. Life may go, but noble deeds remain forever" (WA 85:307). Again and again the singers inform their audiences, "Time is all powerful. Man is not powerful" and "When there is no life in the world, only air and water will remain." Fate may control this life, but ultimately life itself is nothing but the deeds one does, and air and water.

Raja Nal is the quintessential human, of any race. Unquestionably he battles for what he believes in, but he makes the most fundamental of human errors: he seeks a wife who will give him progeny, displaying, after all, the most basic human drive, which is to procreate. Raja Nal exhibits another feature of humans more generally in his multiple identities. Stuart Hall (1997) has addressed the issue of identity, especially the matters of subjectivity and a "unitary I." As Hall notes, personhood is comprised of many individual identities, something Raja Nal clearly exemplifies: he is Merchant, King, Oil Presser, Acrobat, the Mad One, and, eventually, only air and water. In the web of meanings *Dhola* weaves, in its very ideology, the only identity that ultimately counts is being human and having one's future in the hands of fate. In time, the Other finally becomes oneself.

In the end Raja Nal has only himself to rely on. Even his goddess cannot penetrate the barriers created by Shanidev, who indirectly, and for the wrong reasons, is acting out Motini's curse. Yet in his willingness to meet whatever may come his way, Raja Nal epitomizes the human being, for life essentially means to accept the fruits of one's deeds and thus to accept one's fate. And, as the singers continually remind us, all life returns eventually to air and water. Until one truly accepts that one has no control over one's life, until one sits "without care" on a dung heap, nothing, not even the goddess, can provide any solace.

Appendix 1
List of Characters

Bharamal, husband of Taro, who is the sister of Maru
Bhil "tribals"
Brahman Pandit (Gangadhar), astrologer to Raja Nal
Chandi, a goddess, often ferocious and associated with Kali
Chando, the mausi (mother's sister) of Sarvati, daughter of Phul Singh Panjabi
Chandrakala, bride-to-be of Raja Nal's nephew Kishanlal
Chudaman, the leader of the demons inhabiting Lakhiyaban. After he kills a calf, he is entombed in the gate to the fort of Raja Budh Singh
Dharamraj, a god (literally, "the king of righteous behavior")
Dhola, son of Raja Nal and Dumenti who is married to Maru, daughter of Budh Singh
Dumenti, the daughter of Basukdev, reborn as the daughter of Raja Bhim
Durga, the goddess to whom Raja Nal is devoted
Gendwati, the magician daughter of Raja Karampal of Bengal who seeks to marry Raja Nal
Hariyal, a daughter of jinns, in love with Raja Nal
Indra, king of the gods, he is Raja Nal's enemy; he is also egotistic
Jalandhar, the leader of the Nath yogis with whom Motini battles
Kachua Dev, the tortoise deity on whose back Raja Nal falls when thrown into the sea
Kali, a powerful Hindu goddess, here associated with Phul Singh Panjabi
Kishanlal, Raja Nal's nephew, son of his cousin-brother Pushkar
Lachhiman Seth, a Merchant (Banya) by caste, he rescues Manjha and Raja Nal from the forest where Raja Nal is born and takes them to his home
Lakha Banjara, a gypsy who finds Dumenti alone in the forest after she and Nal are separated by Shanidev; when he threatens Dumenti's honor, his camp is burned by the goddess
Maru, daughter of Raja Budh Singh, she is married to Dhola while an infant; when she matures, she seeks her husband Dhola
Narad, Heavenly sage and adviser to the gods
Nilgagan, the god who takes birth as Raja Nal, never to be defeated in battle
Pareba of Mundnagar, sister of the Rewa, Dhola's second wife and daughter of Raja Mal
Pavan, the flying camel that came in Maru's dowry; it returns daily to Marwar to graze, returning to Narvar every night
Phul Singh Panjabi, the king who battles with Raja Pratham and then Raja Nal over the right to bathe first at the Ganges River
Pushkar Sultan, cousin-brother of Raja Nal
Raghu (later renamed Raghunandan), the Oil Presser who takes in Raja Nal and Dumenti; Raja Nal's abilities make Raghu very wealthy and a threat to the king Budh Singh
Raja Bhim of Samudsikal, father of Dumenti

Raja Budh Singh of Marwar (or Pingul), father of Maru and enemy of Raja Nal
Raja Chandrapal of Shankaldeep, Kishanlal's future father-in-law
Raja Mal of Malwa, a Gardener by caste, and father of Dhola's second wife Rewa
Raja Pratham of Narvar, husband of Manjha and father of Raja Nal
Raja Tikam of Kashipur, the kingdom where Raja Nal resides as the "Mad One"
Raja Ved Singh of Vityagarh, he battles Dhola
Raja Vir Singh, a very religious man and the king who lusts after Dumenti as she nurses her babe on the banks of the Ganges
Rani Kamla, wife of Raja Bhim, mother of Dumenti
Rani Manjha, most beloved of Raja Pratham's 101 wives and mother of Raja Nal
Rewa, daughter of Raja Mal and the second wife of Dhola
Sarvati, the daughter of Phul Singh Panjabi and a magician in her own right
Shanidev, the god worshiped on Saturday, known to be allergic to oil seed
Shukra, the god worshiped on Friday, often a helpmate of Shanidev
Sweepers, outcastes given the most impure and inauspicious jobs
Taro, the sister of Maru whose husband instigates more tests for Dhola and his father
Virmati, daughter of Ved Singh, she desires to marry in the lineage of Raja Nal

Appendix 2
Oral Performances

From the Wadley Collection (WA), archived at the Archive for Traditional Music, Indiana University, and the Archive and Research Center for Ethnomusicology, American Institute of Indian Studies, New Delhi.

Singers/Storytellers

Ram Swarup Dhimar (see chapter 3) (Watercarrier) is a resident of Karimpur, Mainpuri District, Uttar Pradesh. He learned *Dhola* as a young boy and has no education. He usually sings with one dholak (drum) player and one cimta (steel tongs) player. He used to have a "company" of some ten members and performed in a folk opera style, and now he farms for a living. He was in his late sixties in 2002.

Raghubar Kachi (Farmer) is a renowned storyteller in Karimpur who does not sing *Dhola.* He told portions of the *Dhola* story at various times, including in 2002 for this book. He was in his early sixties in 2002, has two years of schooling, and reads minimally. He earned his living by farming.

Ram Swarup Kachi (Farmer) was a blind performer in Karimpur. He performed *Dhola* and other traditions, with a dholak player and cimta player. He was in his twenties in the 1980s and died in the 1990s.

Mata Din Garariya (Shepherd) was a sometime resident of Karimpur who performed *Dhola* professionally at times. He was in his thirties in the 1980s.

Pandit Shankar Lal was a Brahman living in a village on the outskirts of Aligarh. He recorded *Dhola* for Brij Cassettes in 1987. He was probably sixty-plus years old when the author met him at his home in 1989.

Matolsingh Gujar (see chapter 2) (Shepherd) is from the village Dhamari, Bharatpur District, Rajasthan. Matol was a renowned *Dhola* singer called to Jodhpur by Komal Kothari to work with this author. He wrote a major edition of *Dhola.* His troupe consisted of Harman Gujar (aged thirty-eight) on cikara, Chote Gujar (aged forty-five) on *manjīrā,* and Pandit Lakshman Prasad (aged thirty-two and crippled) on dholak. Matol died in 1992, at just over sixty years of age.

Manjulal and Nanhe Lal Kachi are from Farrukhabad District, Uttar Pradesh, and performed in Karimpur, at the request of the author, with a dholak player (Pyare Lal). They were in their late forties in 1989 and were illiterate small landowners. Nanhe Lal has since died.

Mangtu Lal Chamar was a blind performer in his fifties or sixties who performed for the Jats in his Jat-dominated village (Jahlaka) in Harayana. He also played the double-flute. He learned *Dhola* in his late teens, after he was blinded by smallpox.

Ram Swarup Dhanuk (Midwife caste) was from the village Himmatpur, Mainpuri District, Uttar Pradesh. He heard that *Dhola* was being performed in Karimpur and showed up. He was in his sixties in 1990.

Table 1. Oral Performances Consulted in This Analysis

Tape #	Singer	Episode	Where Sung or Told	Date
68:9	Davinder Pandey	Sumeri from Dhola	Karimpur	1968
68:11	Raghubar Kachi	Story of Dhola	Karimpur	1968
68:12	Ram Swarup Dhimar	Lakhiyaban ki larai	Karimpur (as a "company," verandah of Ram Swarup Brahman)	10/12/68
68:13	Raghubar Kachi	Story of Dhola (narrative)	Karimpur	1968
68:19	Raghubar Kachi	Story of Dhola	Karimpur	1969
74:106	Raghubar Kachi	Phul Singh Panjabi	Karimpur	1974
74:109	Ram Swarup Kachi and Ram Swarup Dhimar	Kishanlal ki byah	Karimpur (verandah of Raj Bahadur Pandey)	4/24/75
84:207	Raghubar Kachi	Story of Dhola	Karimpur	4/10/84
84:221	Ram Swarup Dhimar	Interview	Karimpur	4/12/84
84:232	Mata Din Gariya and Ram Swarup Kachi	Dhola ka gauna	Karimpur (verandah of Raj Bahadur Pandey)	4/2/84
84:233	Ram Swarup Dhimar	Motini ka byah	Karimpur (verandah of Raj Bahadur Pandey)	4/7/84
84:234	Ram Swarup Dhimar	Motini ka byah	Karimpur	4/7/84
84:235	Ram Swarup Dhimar	Motini ka byah Nal ka auhka	Karimpur	4/7/84 4/14/84
84:236	Ram Swarup Dhimar	Nal ka aukha	Karimpur	4/14/84
84:237	Ram Swarup Dhimar	Nal ka aukha	Karimpur	4/14/84
84:238	Raghubar Kachi	Story of Dhola (narrative)	Karimpur	4/10/84
84:239	Raghubar Kachi	Story of Dhola (narrative)	Karimpur	4/10/84
84:240	Ram Swarup Dhimar	Interview	Karimpur	4/12/84
84:243	Ram Swarup Dhimar	Bhamartal ki larai	On a rooftop in Mainpuri	5/4/84

84:244	Ram Swarup Dhimar	Bhamartal ki larai	On a rooftop in Mainpuri	5/4/84
84:245	Ram Swarup Dhimar	Bhamartal ki larai	On a rooftop in Mainpuri	5/4/84
84:301	Ram Swarup Dhimar	Interview	Karimpur	7/24/85
85:302	Ram Swarup Dhimar	Phul Singh Panjabi ki larai	Village near Karimpur (verandah)	7/24/85
85:303	Ram Swarup Dhimar	Phul Singh Panjabi ki larai	Village near Karimpur	7/24/85
85:305	Ram Swarup Dhimar	Phul Singh Panjabi ki larai	Village near Karimpur	7/24/85
85:306	Ram Swarup Dhimar	Kishanlal ki byah	Village near Karimpur	7/26/85
85:307	Ram Swarup Dhimar	Kishanlal ki byah	Village near Karimpur	7/26/85
85:308	Ram Swarup Dhimar	Kishanlal ki byah	Village near Karimpur	7/26/85
89:2	Ram Swarup Dhimar	His life story	Karimpur	12/2/89
89:3	Ram Swarup Dhimar	Interview	Karimpur	12/4/89
	Pandit Shankar Lal	Interview	Adda, Village near Aligarh (his courtyard)	12/7/89
89:4	Manganiyars	Dhola-maru	Jodhpur (Rupayan Sansthan)	12./15/89
89:5	Matolsinh	Interview	Jodhpur (House of Komal Kothari)	12/15/89
89:6	Matolsinh	Interview	Jodhpur	12/15/89
89:7	Matolsinh	Manjha ka nikasa	Jodhpur (in a tent behind the house of Komal Kothari by the train tracks)	12/16/89
89:8	Matolsinh	Manjha ka nikasa	Jodhpur	12/16/89
89:9	Matolsinh	Manjha ka nikasa Motini ka vivah	Jodhpur	12/16/89
89:10	Matolsinh	Motini ka vivah	Jodhpur	12/16/89
89:11	Matolsinh	Motini ka vivah	Jodhpur	12/16/89
89:12	Matolsinh	Gohitpur ki larai	Jodhpur	12/17/89
89:13	Matolsinh	Gohitpur ki larai	Jodhpur	12/17/89
89:14	Matolsinh	Gohitpur ki larai Phul Singh Panjabi	Jodhpur	12/17/89 12/18/89
89:15	Matolsinh	Interview	Jodhpur	12/17/89
89:16	Matolsinh	Interview Interview		12/17/89 12/18/89

Table 1. (continued)

Tape #	Singer	Episode	Where Sung or Told	Date
89:17	Matolsinh	Phul Singh Panjabi	Jodhpur	12/18/89
89:18	Manjulal and Nanhelal	Motini ka byah	Karimpur (under the tree near the house of Bela Charan Pandey)	12/22/89
89:19	Manjulal and Nanhelal	Motini ka byah	Karimpur	12/22/89
89:20	Manjulal and Nanhelal	Motini ka byah Nal ka katha	Karimpur	12/22/89
89:21	Manjulal and Nanhelal	Nal ka katha	Karimpur	12/22/89
89:22	Raghubar Kachi Manjulal	Interview Interview	Karimpur	12/22/89
89:23	Manjulal and Nanhelal	Nal ka katha	Karimpur	12/23/89
89:24	Manjulal and Nanhelal	Nal ka katha	Karimpur	12/23/89
89:25	Manjulal and Nanhelal	Nal ka katha Phul Singh Panjabi	Karimpur	12/23/89
89:26	Manjulal and Nanhelal	Phul Singh Panjabi	Karimpur	12/23/89
89:27	Ram Swarup Dhimar	Dumenti ka dusra svayambar	Karimpur (Dharamshala)	12/25/89
89:28	Ram Swarup Dhimar	Dumenti ka dusra svayambar	Karimpur	12/25/89
89:29	Ram Swarup Dhimar	Dumenti ka dusra svayambar	Karimpur	12/25/89
89:30	Ram Swarup Dhimar	Bhamartal ki larai	Karimpur	12/26/89
89:31	Ram Swarup Dhimar	Bhamartal ki larai	Karimpur	12/26/89
89:32	Ram Swarup Dhimar	Bamartal ki larai	Karimpur	12/26/89
89:33	Manju lal Ram Swarup Dhimar	Interview Interview	Karimpur	12/24/89 12/26/89
89:36	Raghubar Kachi	Story of Dhola	Karimpur (room in the house of Umesh Pandey)	12/27/89
89:37	Ram Swarup Dhimar	Lakhiyaban ki larai	Karimpur (Dharamsala)	12/27/89
89:38	Ram Swarup Dhimar	Lakhiyaban ki larai	Karimpur	12/27/89

89:39	Ram Swarup Dhimar	Lakhiyaban ki larai	Karimpur	12/27/89
89:40	Raghubar Kachi	Story of Dhola	Karimpur	12/28/89
90:1	Ram Swarup Dhimar	Bhamartal ki larai	Karimpur (verandah of Umesh Pandey)	12/7/90
90:2	Ram Swarup Dhimar	Bhamartal ki larai	Karimpur	12/7/90
90:3	Ram Swarup Dhimar	Phul bagh ki larai	Karimpur	12/8/90
90:4	Ram Swarup Dhimar	Phul bagh ki larai	Karimpur	12/8/90
90:5	Ram Swarup Dhimar	Lakhiyaban ki larai	Karimpur	12/8/90
90:6	Ram Swarup Dhimar	Lakhiyaban ki larai	Karimpur	12/8/90
90:10	Ram Swarup Dhimar	Lakhiyaban ki larai	Karimpur	12/10/90
90:11	Ram Swarup Dhimar	Dhola ka byah	Karimpur	12/10/90
90:17	Ram Swarup Dhimar	Dhola ka byah	Karimpur	12/12/90
90:18	Ram Swarup Dhimar	Dhola ka byah	Karimpur	12/12/90
90:19	Ram Swarup Dhimar	Dhola ka byah	Karimpur	12/12/90
90:22	Ram Swarup Dhanuk	Motini ka byah	Karimpur	12/13/90
90:23	Ram Swarup Dhanuk	Motini ka byah	Karimpur	12/13/90
90:24	Ram Swarup Dhanuk	Motini ka byah	Karimpur	12/14/90
90:25	Ram Swarup Dhanuk	Motini ka byah	Karimpur	12/14/90
90:26	Paras Ram's wife	Story of Raja Nal	Karimpur (her house)	12/14/90
94:5	Ram Swarup Dhimar	Story of Dhola	Karimpur (verandah of Davendra Pandey)	1/31/94
94:6	Ram Swarup Dhimar	Manjha ka nivas	Karimpur	1/25/94
94:7	Ram Swarup Dhimar	Manjha ka nivas	Karimpur	1/25/94
94:8	Ram Swarup Dhimar	Manjha ka nivas	Karimpur	1/25/94
94:9	Raghubar Kachi	Story of Dhola	Karimpur	1/25/94
94:11	Ram Swarup Dhimar	Motini ka byah	Karimpur (verandah of Davendra Pandey)	1/27/94
94:12	Ram Swarup Dhimar	Motini ka byah	Karimpur	1/27/94

Table 1. (continued)

Tape #	Singer	Episode	Where Sung or Told	Date
94:13	Ram Swarup Dhimar	Motini ka byah	Karimpur	1/28/94
94:14	Ram Swarup Dhimar	Nal ka katha	Karimpur	1/28/94
94:16	Ram Narayan Agrawal	Interview	Braj Kala Kendra, Mathura	2/13/94
94:17	Ram Swarup Dhimar	Nal ki dusri shadi	Karimpur	1/30/94
94:18	Ram Swarup Dhimar	Nal ki dusri shadi	Karimpur	1/30/94
94:19	Ram Swarup Dhimar	Nal ki dusri shadi	Karimpur	1/30/94
94:20	Ram Swarup Dhimar	Story of Dhola	Karimpur	1/31/94
94:22	Ram Swarup Dhimar	Dhola ka byah	Karimpur	2/1/94
94:23	Ram Swarup Dhimar	Dhola ka byah	Karimpur	2/1/94
94:24	Ram Swarup Dhimar	Story of Dhola	Karimpur	2/2/94
94:25	Ram Swarup Dhimar	Story of Dhola	Karimpur	2/2/94
94:26	Ram Swarup Dhimar	Story of Dhola	Karimpur	2/2/94
94:27	Ram Swarup Dhimar	Story of Dhola	Karimpur	2/3/94
94:29	Mangtu Ram	Motini ka byah	Jahlaka, Haryana	February 1994
94:30	Mangtu Ram	Motini ka byah	Jahlaka, Haryana	February 1994
94:31	Mangtu Ram	Motini ka byah	Jahlaka, Haryana	February 1994
95:2	Ram Swarup Dhimar	Narrating story	Karimpur	12/31/94
95:3	Ram Swarup Dhimar	Narrating story	Karimpur	1/1/95
02:2	Raghubar Kachi	Story of Dhola	Karimpur	1/3/02
02:3	Raghubar Kachi	Story of Dhola	Karimpur	1/3/02
02:5	Raghubar Kachi	Story of Dhola	Karimpur	1/4/02
02:6	Ram Swarup Dhimar	Story of Dhola	Karimpur	1/4/02
02:7	Ram Swarup Dhimar	Story of Dhola	Karimpur	1/5/02

02:8	Ram Swarup Dhimar	Story of Dhola	Karimpur	1/6/02
02:9	Ram Swarup Dhimar	Story of Dhola	Karimpur	1/6/02
02:10	Ram Swarup Dhimar	Story of Dhola	Karimpur	1/7/02
02:11	Ram Swarup Dhimar	Story of Dhola	Karimpur	1/7/02
02:12	Ram Swarup Dhimar	Story of Dhola	Karimpur	1/7/02
02:14	Ram Swarup Dhimar	Story of Dhola	Karimpur	1/8/02

Commercial Cassettes

Also consulted were these commercial cassettes, available in the markets and roadside stands in Uttar Pradesh and Rajasthan as well as at the Electronics Market across from Red Fort in Delhi.

Table 2. Commercial Cassettes Consulted in This Analysis

Singer	Title	Date	Produced by	Episode
Pandit Shankar Lal	Dhola Raja Nal	1987	Brij Cassettes Aligarh	Tapes numbered 1–21
Kailash and Laturi	Kampilgarh ki larai (set of 3)	1988a	Dee Cee Electronics Daryaganj, New Delhi	
Kailash and Laturi	Raja Nal ki dusri shadi (set of 3)	1988b	Max Cassettes, New Delhi	
Kailash and Laturi	Panjab ki larai (set of 3)	1989	Dee Cee Electronics Daryaganj, New Delhi	

Glossary of Key Hindi Terms

Adharm	Lacking in righteous duty, acting against the rules of proper conduct
Ādiśakti	The original powers of the universe
Ālhā	An oral epic performed mostly in the state of Uttar Pradesh in north India. It tells of conflicts between the Muslim rulers and local kin. It is also the name of the melody to which the epic is usually sung.
Anuloma	Against the grain, as in marriages that run counter to the normal rules of hypergamy (marriage of the female to a man from a superior group)
Apsāra	Heavenly nymph, a damsel from the court of the gods
Aukhā	Distress, trouble, a time of chaos
Baigi	An exorcist, a spiritual healer
Bali	Offering to the god, a sacrifice
Bārahmāsī	A genre of songs; literally, "of the twelve months"
Bārāt	The bridegroom's marriage procession, usually just his male kin who travel by bullock cart, bus, truck, or cars to the village of the bride where they are hosted for several days
Bhābhī	kinship term for older brother's wife
Bhagavād Gītā	The Hindu text in which the god Krishna entreats the Pandava hero Arjun to fight a just war
Bhāgyavān	"fated one," the one who lives by fate
Bhairon	Male demons, associated with the goddess, (often) as her servants
Bhajan	A religious song, frequently sung as a way to show devotion to the gods
Bhakti	The feeling of love and devotion that a devotee has for his or her chosen deity
Bhangī	A person belonging to the caste group that cleans latrines and streets
Bhenṭ	Sacrifice, offering to the goddess
Bīj mantra	The ritual saying that makes things happen quickly, as when Raja Nal makes the horses fly through the air
Bindī	The auspicious red dot that women put on their foreheads
Cikāṛā	The three-stringed bowed instrument used for singing Dhola
Ḍānk	A ritual that cures those bitten by snakes, performed in the rural areas of western Uttar Pradesh

Dānu Demons

Darśan Sight or vision of the gods/goddesses

Ḍholā The epic story of Raja Nal, his wives Motini and Dumenti, and his son, Dhola

Ḍholak The two-headed folk drum used in north India

Deva Gods

Devī Māhātmyā A Sanskrit text in honor of the goddess, written about the sixth century C.E.

Devī-bhagavata purāṇā A Sanskrit text in honor of the goddess, written about the twelfth century C.E.

Devnārāyaṇ An epic popular in rural Rajasthan, performed in front of a scroll that portrays the epic story

Dharam bhāī Literally, "brother by religion," that is, a fictive kin relationship that is affirmed religiously

Dharamśālā A pilgrim's way station or rest house, often attached to a temple

Dharma Righteous duty

Ḍholā-Mārū A ballad sung in western Rajasthan and Gujarat, considered by some to be one of the earliest Hindi compositions

Dīpak rāg The melody that lights lamps; given to Raja Nal as part of his dowry from Motini

Dohā A metrical form common to Hindi prosody, with two lines of twenty-four metrical syllables

Gālī Songs of abuse, sung by the women of a bride to the groom's wedding party

Gaunā The ritual that marks the consummation of a marriage, traditionally occurring some years after the actual marriage ceremony and after the girl reaches puberty

Ijjat Honor, something to be defended at all costs

Jaldāriyā The flying water horse that Raja Nal finds in the demon Bhumasur's locked room, to be ridden only by Indra or Raja Nal

Jāṭ A caste of agriculturalists found in north India

Jāti Caste, related to the Latin term *genus;* designates a kind of person

Jāṭiyā Belonging to the Jat caste, here referring to workers in a Jat village

Jūrī Two ropes tied together into a ring, used here to symbolize a marriage alliance

Kacā Raw, unrefined, uncooked, unbaked

Kahār A member of the Water Carrier caste

Kamīn The worker in a patron-client relationship

Kanyā Virgin girl

Kanyādān The gift of a virgin girl in marriage

Kar	The verbal root "to do" which is the core of the concept of karma, or fate
Kaulā	A fierce demon, associate of the goddess
Khāppār	The pot in which the goddess in her fierce incarnation collects the blood of those sacrificed or killed
Khyāl	Folk dramas performed with music, typical of Rajasthan
Kos	A distance slightly longer than a kilometer
Kuldevī	The goddess associated with one's lineage
Langur	The monkey-helpers of the goddess
Māhabhārata	The Hindu epic that tells of the war of the Pandavas
Māhavidyās	The ten goddesses associated with Kali
Malhār	A folk song genre usually sung by women in the rainy season; associated with women's love and longing for the natal kin
Manās	Human being
Manihār	A person belonging to the caste of Bangle Sellers
Mārkaṇḍeya *Purāṇa*	One of the older Puranas, and named after the sage Markandeya, this Sanskritic text focuses on Indra, Surya, and Agni
Naiśādhacarita	An early Sanskrit poem that tells the story of Nala and Damayanti up to and including their marriage
Nal purāṇ	The Purana of Nal, linking the story of Nal to other proclaimed Indian histories
Nalopākhyāna	The name given the story of Nala from the *Mahabharata*
Naṭ	The caste of Acrobats
Nauṭankī	A style of rural folk theater
Nihālde	The name of a north Indian ballad and melody
Nirbīj	Literally, "without seed"
Pabūjī	A god worshiped by the camel herders of Rajasthan; a major epic relates his story, and is performed in front of a large scroll that serves as a portable shrine as the itinerant singers move from village to village
Pagṛī	A man's turban
Pakkā	Baked or ripe, a term used to refer to the quality of food as well as to describe fruits or even bricks
Pāp	Sin
Pativrat	A woman who worships her husband, an honorable, auspicious woman
Prakriti	"Nature," the female principle of the universe, that which is not cultured
Pritvīrājā rasau	The story of King Pritvi, popular especially in Rajasthan and Panjab
Pūjā	The Hindu worship ceremony that honors the deities with offerings of food, clothing, cooling substances, and so on
Punya	Merit

Rājā The term for a Hindu king

Rajas One of the three humors in the Hindu Ayurvedic model of the human body, implies passion

Rāmāyaṇā The epic story of the god-hero Ram and his wife Sita

Ras Juice, as in juice of a fruit, but here used as the juice or energy of Motini

Śaktī The female energy that powers the universe

Śakti pithā A site where the dismembered body of the goddess fell to earth, noted for their energy and divine qualities

Sarpānse The gambling game played throughout *Dhola,* involving throws of sixteen cowry shells

Sat Truth, purity

Sati devī A woman who has committed sati, throwing herself on her husband's funeral pyre and igniting it with her truth-force, revered as a goddess

Satiyā The auspicious design, similar to the Aryan cross, or swastika; often put on the doors of houses where a son has been born to denote the happiness and auspiciousness of the birth

Sindūr The red powder used by married women in their hair parting to mark their auspiciousness

Sumerī Remembrance, the opening verses to any performance of *Dhola*

Svāng A folk theater group, especially popular in Panjab

Telī Oil Presser by caste

Vartā Narrative prose, as distinguished from sung verses

Vrat A ritual of fasting and worship, taken as a vow

Notes

Preface

1. Karimpur is a pseudonym given to this community by William and Charlotte Wiser, the first Westerners to study its social life. The literature on this community is extensive (W. Wiser 1933, 1958; Wiser and Wiser 2001; Wadley 1975, 1994). For continuity of referencing I have maintained this pseudonym, though I am fully cognizant of the need to acknowledge the true identities of folk performers. The singers of *Dhola* are, in fact, the only men in the village to whom I refer by their real names: all other names in my writings and those of the Wisers are pseudonyms. I would be happy to reveal the "true" name of Karimpur to anyone who has a valid reason for seeking it out.
2. I am marking occupational designations that designate caste groups with an initial capital letter. Thus Farmer is the caste group whose members may or may not be farmers; farmer is a person who farms. Ram Swarup himself never carried water, nor did his wife. Today he is a farmer by occupation.
3. In order to fully link the episodes I spent ten days in January 2002 working with Ram Swarup Dhimar and with Raghubar Kachi on the missing episodes as well as on the linkages between episodes.

1. Introducing *Dhola*

1. WA refers to the Wadley Collection of Folklore, archived at both the Archive for Traditional Music at Indiana University and the Archive and Research Center for Ethnomusicology, American Institute of Indian Studies, New Delhi. Tapes referenced here are listed in appendix 2 by year and tape number. (Note that the two archives each use their own numbering systems, but with a cross-reference to mine.)
2. An idea captured in the 1950s American popular song by Doris Day, "Que sera, sera."
3. *Alha,* a closely related epic sung in the region, has a similar structure of "battles" (larai) and, like *Dhola,* it is thought to be related to the *Mahabharata.* It is referred to by singers as the "*Mahabharata* of the Kali Yug" (Schomer 1989, 142).
4. Ram Narayan Agrawal, Braj Kala Kendra, Mathura, January 1994.
5. I am following Hindi conventions for transcribing names, except when I refer specifically to a Sanskrit version, hence Nal (Hindi), Nala (Sanskrit),

Dumenti (Hindi dialect), and Damayanti (Sanskrit). The dialects where *Dhola* is sung vary, and I have chosen the spelling most common in Braj. Further toward Kanauj, it became Dumaiti. I am not using diacritics for any personal names found in the epic, nor for commonly recognized gods, goddesses, and places.

6. There is a small Rajput kingdom called Narwar (Navar) near Gwalior in what is now Madhya Pradesh that is said by some, including Tod (1971, 282), to be the place from which Nala, as in the Nala-Damayanti story, comes as well as being the original kingdom of the Amber Kacchwa Rajputs. Later scholars, especially Qanungo (1960), dispute this assertion, saying that Tod fabricated the connection on inappropriate evidence. Ganguli (1983, 55) reports that Rajput bards claim Dhola as the son of the Kacchwas who ruled in Navar, but these are likely to be the same "bards" that sing the epic considered here. I have found no evidence that there is a consistent link between the Nala-Damayanti story and the *Dhola* story west of Bharatpur, aside from the naming of Dhola's father as Nala in some versions of *Dhola-Maru.* Grierson (1890) does indicate, however, a more complicated Nal connection in the Chattisgarh version that he collected. More to the point perhaps, as we shall see below, there is a Jat village in Mathura District called Narvar, and one of the more important Jat clans is called Narvar (Drake-Brockman 1984 [1911]). As the Muslim historian Qanungo said, regarding the search for the factual history of the Rajasthani epic *Padmani,* "it is un-literary to run after the shadows of history in such stories" (1960, 25). I can only hope that the historical connections I am claiming here would not gain his condemnation.
7. For another vision of caste in Indian oral traditions, see Blackburn 2001.
8. The idea of cliché comes from the work of Joseph C. Miller (1980) on African oral traditions in which he develops the idea of the cliché as a highly compressed statement of meaning, often stark and dramatic, that captures the elementary narrative themes of oral history.

2. The Story of *Dhola*

1. Although many have translated the word *hans* as swan, I am using the more accurate translation, goose. Further, illustrations from the nineteenth-century version of *Dhola* portray a bird that far more resembles a goose (or partridge) than a swan. As McGregor (1974) notes, the word *swan* is correct only "by poetic license," and hence I have chosen the more culturally appropriate goose, excepting for "The Battle of Shautiban."
2. Some versions have the one hundred other queens leaving Manjha only one grain of rice in the pot of cooked rice as her portion: this grain, however, is the magic grain that brings a son.
3. In what is now Pakistan, Hinglaj is a noted site of goddess worship. It also has associations with the Nath yogis, which complicates the anti-Nath theme throughout most of the epic (see, especially, chapter 4).

4. Hindus believe that speaking words while submerged in the Ganges River or other holy water spots gives them power. Men who learn curing mantras, for example, cannot use them to cure until they have said them submerged in a holy river and made them powerful.

5. A katha is a religious tale. The story of Nal demanded by Motini is also sometimes called the Nal Purana, linking it to the Hindu scriptures known as the Puranas. Some printed versions of *Dhola* subtitle it Nal Purana.

6. Mansukh is sometimes known as Mansukh Maina.

7. This need seems driven by the impurities that she has gained by living in a lower-caste household, not by any alleged sexual impropriety.

8. Ann Gold (personal communication, 2003) wonders at this colonial intrusion into Hindu etiquette, while I am intrigued by its localization through conventions of husband-wife propriety. Vandana Tivary (personal communication, 2003), a student of mine with an Indian military background, reports that shaking hands is standard in the Indian army unless a lady officer is one of the pairing, in which case hands are sometimes not shaken.

9. Nats are a caste group found throughout north India, whose traditional occupation is performing as acrobats. Even today, they travel from village to village, performing wherever they can arrange an audience.

10. This portion of the epic is enormously funny and engaging, no doubt leading to its popularity among rural audiences.

11. Ann Gold (personal communication, 2003) reports shock at this incident as Jalandhar is the Nath yogi who, in other sources, is the least likely to mess with women.

12. Note the disorder represented in these inauspicious signs.

13. Here we face once again the question of the translation of hans/hansa. See Wadley 1999 for a nineteenth-century illustration in which the bird bears no resemblance to a swan. Whatever the biological bird, it does feast on pearls.

14. This is a play on names, as Phoola (*phūl*) means flower.

15. Here, the singer has condensed eight to nine months into one, as Savan is comparable to July–August, and Chait is the spring harvest month of April–May.

16. Dank is a ritual commonly performed in western Uttar Pradesh to cure snakebite. For more details, see Wadley 1976.

17. Literally *sāle,* that is, the male married to one's sister. Often the epic singer uses the more literal *bahen choud.* In both versions the implication is "sister fucker."

18. This is a frequent bet in Indian folklore and relates to hypergamous marriage rules; that is, the loser must marry his daughter (the lower position)

to the son of the winner. By giving one's daughter, one acknowledges the superiority of the receiving lineage. See also chapter 5.

19. Most older Indian homes do not have toilet facilities, and men, especially, use the lanes and fields as latrines. There is a similar scene in the Gopi Chand epic translated by Ann Gold (1992).

20. See Wadley 1975, 208–213, for more on the ritual of Deothan. Without knowing this connection, I have seen the gods awakened and the sugarcane worshiped on several occasions.

21. My colleague Jishnu Shankar believes that this is a religious allegory, that is, that these men aspired to be shaktas, worshipers in the Gorakhnath Shivite tradition. Note that only the females, representing the power of femininity, have survived the Bengali onslaught.

22. In rural north India dreams can be read as revealing reality, so Maru suspects from her dream that she is married.

23. Matolsingh, the poet/singer most renowned in the Braj area in the 1980s, told me that this episode was the hardest to sing and hence was seldom sung, for it so filled the singer with sorrow that he was overwhelmed. Matol did write a version of it (Matolsingh n.d. [a]).

24. See also A. Gold 1992 for more on magic from Bengal.

25. I am grateful to Vanit Nalwa not only for sharing her family history but also for finding and sending me a copy of the Hindi version of the comic book of Hari Sinh Nalwa.

26. My thanks to Adeesh Sathaye for this reference.

27. From the Wiser Collection of Folklore, song 42 (Archives of the Divinity School, Yale University).

28. I was able to tape such a performance at Rupayan Sansthan in Jodhpur with the gracious aid of Komal Kothari.

29. I must reiterate the interconnections between performance styles and text: neither exists separately, nor did they develop separately, but are inextricably intertwined.

30. The etymology of Jat is unclear. A story popular with Jats themselves alludes to their Shiva ancestry, where they are connected to his hair (jatiya), hence jat.

31. One of these court poets, Somnath, wrote the *Sujan vilas* containing a Braj rendition of the popular stories of King Bhoja. Because the Oil Presser story found in *Dhola* is sometimes associated with King Bhoja (Narayan 1997), I am attempting to obtain a copy of this work.

32. The preceding history of the Jats is based on Dwivedi 1989; Entwistle 1987; Qanungo 1925; and Spear 1951.

33. *Dhola* is also silent on the issue of Muslims and the British. The battle for

honor appears to be a Hindu one, not one to be validated by Muslim emperors or British colonial rulers.

3. *Dhola* as Performed

1. Ram Swarup usually used the term *guru* when talking with me, but when interviewed by the ethnomusicologist Scott Marcus in the mid-1980s, he used the word *ustad.* Ram Swarup has a finely honed sense of linguistic propriety and once told me of the mistakes that low-caste people made linguistically, mistakes that he himself made until one of his gurus "beat" them out of him (his examples were mainly of a shift of the phoneme l to m in lower-caste language, as in *kalsā* going to *kamsā* and *baltī* to *bamtī*).

2. I tried throughout the late 1980s and 1990s to find a company to record. We knew of one in 1991, but the communal riots and curfews associated with Ayodhya prevented us from hiring them.

3. There are several possible, no doubt intersecting, reasons for this style of prose/song, including folk theater traditions and early poetic styles. For example, the poetic forms of the early Rajasthani ballads of *Dhola-Maru,* on which part of this epic is based, are sections marked by different metrical patterns (doha, caupai, or even barah masi), suggesting that the interplay between styles and singing was present from the earliest renditions of the epic (see Vaudville 1962; Williams 1976). These twentieth-century singers preferred to augment the Dhola style with folk songs familiar to their rural audiences and with film tunes that are currently popular.

4. Doha is a common couplet meter found in north Indian literary traditions and is the dominant form in the *Dhola-Maru* song tradition. Each line consists of twenty-four *mātrās,* arranged as 6 + 4 + 3, 6 + 4 + 1. The four quarters (*pada*) are often distinct clauses, as is common in Dhola. Matras are weighted syllables, based on the length of the syllables that make up a line, with short or "light" syllables (usually a short vowel) and long or "heavy" syllables (a long vowel). In Dhola, doha have a distinct cadence and are performed as heightened speech, resembling neither song nor everyday spoken forms as found in varta.

5. All excerpts in this chapter are scheduled to be available on GLOBALSOUND, through the Smithsonian Institution. For a minimal fee, these can be downloaded for listening or use in the classroom. All proceeds go to the original singers or their descendents. This piece is from WA 84:235.

6. These are all omens of impending disaster.

7. Although desert musicians (Mangiyars and Langas) from western Rajasthan were present at Komal's that week, and they themselves sing *Dhola-Maru,* they had little interest in this different musical style, were unfamiliar with the episodes being sung, and seldom joined us as an audience.

8. Personal communication, Deep Chand Booksellers, Hathras.

9. All of Matol's children were educated: his son was studying for his MBBS (medical degree) at his death, and his daughters had MAs. Further, he claimed to have let his daughters choose their own husbands.

10. Each of the troupes and main singers with whom I worked had a different style and aesthetic. One equally divergent from both is that of Manju Lal and Nanhe Lal, Kachis (Farmers) from Farrukhabad District, who had a more jocular style with constant questioning from the second singer. Their audiences laughed a good deal.

11. For those who have read my article in *Oral Epics in India,* this piece takes off where the example there ends (see Wadley 1989).

12. Because this episode was performed at night, I was unable to videotape it.

13. Both Entwistle (1987) and Lutgendorf (personal communication) associate Durga's langur with Hanuman.

14. This is a very clear Hindi phrase (*dhokārī ne marbāy dīo*) which the words "the old woman has killed me today" do not capture, for the full intent is that Behmata has caused someone else (i.e., the demon) to kill Nal.

15. *Nal kī samajh mēn ek bāt āy gāī.* Notably this phrase attributes no agency to Nal: the understanding comes to him but not from his own mind. Note his lack of active agency throughout this section.

16. See Wadley 1992 for a discussion of malhar as a genre of folk music. Here the printed line reads: *iḍiryansiḍiryan lālā ūpar carh gayau jī, aijī koī de de bhamarkalīn mēn pām.* The sung line goes, *are iḍyan diryan lālā ūpar carī gayo, e iṛiyan diṛyan lālā ūpar carī gayo, ejī de de bhamar hambe de de bhavar kalīn bhaiyā pāmro.*

17. Gajadhar's reads:

> Nal kicked the stone and it slipped slightly. Now he could go inside. As he kicked the stone, the demon in the forest cried out. But he entered the palace without any worry and reached the courtyard. Meanwhile, in the forest the demon was afraid. When Nal reached there, he saw the girl sleeping and it started to rain. Nal sat on the edge of the bed, and Motini awoke at once and looked around. (Varma, n.d.)

Ram Swarup's goes thus:

> [Durga says,] "Oh, loving son of Manjha, you must note this stone. The demon will die by your hand: Karta has written it thus. Kick this rock. Kick it. And you will have darshan for your bride." Oh, Nal moved forward; he took Manjha's name, remembered Parvativali. And when he kicked the rock, it moved back three feet. And when he opened it, Durga said, "My loving son, oh, you will meet the lady whom you will marry. Here now the gate is open." And Durga stretched and sped off. Durga disappeared from there and Raja Nal entered the palace. What did he see?
>
> Nal moved forward and saw a wooden bed of gold. Oh on that was sleeping the lovely daughter, resting on silk cloth. She was covered with a beautiful cloth, she was sleeping on a golden cot. So what did Raja Nal say, "Oh, I feel my last time in Danigarh has come. Oh, my boat has come into a whirlpool. Only the one who rides a

peacock can protect me today. Oh virgin daughter of the demon, I have no connection to her. If I wake her, she will turn me to ashes." (WA 84:233)

18. Darvaza is the first ceremony that takes place at the bride's house after the groom's marriage procession arrives.

19. For two other selections demonstrating Matol's oral and written difference, see Wadley 1998.

20. The one exception is a small group of Braj aficionados at the Braj Kala Kendra in Mathura. Interestingly, however, the singer that they knew was Brahman, one of only two Brahman *Dhola* singers of whom I have heard. See also Sharma 1992.

4. The Goddess and the Bhakti Traditions of Braj

1. Lakhiyaban is a forest where Nal had an earlier battle.

2. In Karimpur, khappar is a ritual in which the accumulated sins of the village are collected in a clay pot which is broken in the fields of an adjoining village (thereby releasing the sins in that community). Here khappar refers to both the pot and the ritual. In more traditional ascetic lore, the khappar is the bowl carried by an ascetic, often made of a coconut shell but sometimes from the upper part of a human skull. In this epic context, it refers to a bowl, most probably of the human skull, which the goddess is often portrayed as carrying. I am extremely grateful to Jishnu Shankar for his insights into goddess worship in north India and his careful interrogations (and sometimes revision) of every conclusion presented here.

3. *Bhairon* refers to a male guardian deity found at or near the entrance of many goddess shrines.

4. *Kaulā* are tantric adepts of the Himalayan tradition, here devotees of the goddess.

5. I will be using the term *Tantric* in the sense used by Western scholars of Hindu traditions, that is, as a religious practice or method that advocates reversals of accepted social norms. This is not necessarily the way in which the term is always understood in India, where many belonging to sects, such as the Aghori, considered Tantric by Western scholars, would find the term offensive. This is not to say that these sects do not follow practices that challenge, especially, Brahmanical norms but that they particularly abhor Western scholars' association of Tantric and rituals involving sexual practices.

6. The oldest Vaishno Devi temple in Delhi uncovered by Rohe (1997, 143) is dated 1948.

7. Chandi is sometimes associated with Durga but is more commonly understood as a destructive goddess more closely resembling Kali. Kinsley (1986, 117) says that Chandi is an epithet used for both Durga and Kali. In

Dhola Chandi usually seems to appear in her Kali-associated manifestation, although rarely she is invoked to protect or guide a character such as Dumenti.

8. Closely related to the yogi is the *dānu* (Sanskrit *dānava*), a term often translated unfortunately as demon, for in fact the *rakśāsa, aśura,* or danava of the Hindu tradition is not the evil demon of Christianity. Dane, and other types of so-called demons, obtain their powers through the same austerities by which gurus or yogis obtain theirs. The *Puranas* contain numerous tales in which the dane perform austerities which require that the gods give them immortality (with some restrictions, so that Ravana, for example, can be killed by a not-man/not god). But the *siddhis* performed by those who become dane and those who are or become yogis seem of the same type: they involve intense austerities and concentration of the mind. The difference appears to be that the dane have evil intentions in seeking these powers, whereas the yogis (supposedly) do not. These dane become filled with pride, often leading to their downfall, or are in some other way tricked by the gods into losing their powers. In the villages the line is less clear and the dane are regarded as a caste (*jāti*). Ram Swarup Dhimar says that Bhumasur became a demon because he performed bad deeds for seven lives. As the consequence of his bad deeds, he became a giant and belonged to the demon caste, meaning that he ate meat and drank liquor. What is clear in this epic is that the line differentiating dane and yogi is muddled; the yogis are shown to have bad intentions, and in this episode the danu (Somasur, Motini's uncle) is on the side of righteousness. Even the character of Bhumasur is muddled, for though he eats humans he also lovingly cares for his adopted daughter Motini.

9. The yogi as scoundrel is featured and discussed at length in Narayan 1989.

5. Motini, Dumenti, and Other Royal Women

1. See also the story of Mirabai, wife of a raja who abandoned the court for the temple, and her husband for Krishna (Harlan 1995). Mirabai is not highly thought of by all Rajput women, because she abandoned purdah and the behaviors of a pativrat.

2. We have no evidence as to what visible mark indicates that this man is without progeny, unlike the other omens with which I am familiar, for example, the auspicious omen of a Dhimar (Water Carrier), with a handful of fish, or the inauspicious sign of an Oil Presser in the lane.

3. From an interview with Ram Swarup Dhimar, resident of Karimpur, Uttar Pradesh, in 1984. Tape number unknown. Other singers say that her father was Raja Ananatal and her mother the witch Hadamba, and that she was cursed by Indra, forced from his kingdom, and then found and raised by Bhumasur.

4. The marital status of Sarvati's mausi (mother's sister), Chando, is never stated.

5. In this version of the Nala-Damiyanti story, Nal is not described as infatuated with Dumenti as he is in other renditions, most especially Goswamy 1975.

6. In other words, let Nal partake of some of this blatant sexuality in order to protect the prestige of his kingdom.

7. This issue is enormously complex. As I understand it, in many societies the elite female is not allowed a sexual presence, has her sexuality denied, whereas the lower-class female represents female sexuality (the virgin and the whore, once again). The elite man has acceptable sexuality, whether a Rajput king or James Bond, while the lower-class male, also sexual, is feared (as is the African American in *Birth of a Nation*). So there is a continuum from "asexual" (elite female) to acceptable sexuality (elite male) to somewhat unacceptable sexuality (lower-class female) to feared sexuality (lower-class male).

8. Modern Indian women violate this rule continuously, see Wadley 2003.

9. Here the singer invokes a city in central Uttar Pradesh, not Rajasthan.

6. Oil Pressers, Acrobats, and Other Castes

1. For another Indian epic lodged in a multi-caste community, see Beck 1982.

2. My indebtedness to the work of McKim Marriott and Ronald Inden (especially 1987) should be obvious.

3. An example is given by R. S. Khare (1965), who discusses a group of Uttar Pradesh Brahman males who eat meat precisely because they must become "warrior-like" in order to protect their families. Normally Uttar Pradesh Brahmans do not eat meat (or onions, garlic, or even tomatoes) because it would make them too "hot."

4. A similar notion pervades American notions of racism, where "blackness" is thought by many to imply certain learned behaviors, often denigrated by white society. The recent turmoil over Thomas Jefferson's "black" offspring, several of whom "disappeared" into white society, suggests the complexity of this issue not only for Indians but for Americans, too.

5. Nowadays the stone kohlu and its ox have been replaced by electric mills, and most Oil Pressers have had to seek other ways to make a living.

6. Anyone who has seen flies on a child's pus-filled eyes in India or around a wound of any sort can begin to fathom what Nal and Dumenti were experiencing.

7. All references to the episode of the Oil Presser come from WA 84:243–245, unless otherwise noted.
8. The word used here is *nirbīj* (literally, "without progeny") but is used here as an insult, implying without power, impotent in every way.
9. Doniger (1999) sees episodes such as this as primarily erotic. Here I believe that it is connected to manhood.
10. There are implied sexual connotations here.
11. The heroes of the epic *Alha* (Waterfield 1923) use a similar strategy when they become yogis, also entertainers and holy men who have access to a king's court.
12. All quotations from the Battle of Phul Singh Panjabi are taken from WA 85:303–305.
13. Seven is commonly used as a mark of significant generational depth in various Hindu kin reckonings.
14. *Mausi* means mother's sister, referring here to Motini; she is a "sister" because she is the co-wife of Dumenti.

7. Who Is Raja Nal?

1. This is especially true in the chapbook version attributed to Todarmal (1975). In one episode in a nineteenth-century version of Todarmal's *Dhola,* Indra is forced to be the midwife at the birth of Dhola, whose birth is a clear sign of Indra's defeat by Raja Nal.
2. For more on sin in local folk beliefs, see Wadley and Derr 1989.
3. Read metaphorically, this could also be a comment on the inappropriateness of mixing caste status in marriage, and not merely marriage between heavenly nymphs and humans.
4. We could also say that Raja Nal has no desire to be married a second time to a powerful goddess, and hence his rejection of Basukdev's daughter. Perhaps it was not progeny that he wanted but rather an upper hand.
5. Confirmed by Lindsey Harlan in a personal communication, circa 2002.
6. This point on bhakti comes from Jishnu Shankar. When I queried Lindsey Harlan about whether the heroes there ever cried, I received a one-word answer: "Never!" A Tamil proverb says, "Don't trust a man who cries, and a woman who loves" (Vasudha Narayanan, personal communication, 2002).
7. Many instances throughout the epic link lower castes with cowardice.
8. Humor returns only as the epic shifts back to Nal's regaining his wife. The scene in which Raja Nal, as the Mad One, seeks horses to fly to Samudsikul leaves the audiences howling with laughter.

9. For other stories of Rajput disorder, see Zeigler 1973, chapter 5.

10. According to Zeigler (1973), Rajputs were said to be "grain eaters" (specifically wheat), while members of the lower castes were barley eaters.

11. Bavariya actually caused several of the best horses to die. The stomach of one horse burst when Bavariya put his arms around it.

12. A Jat from a village near Delhi confirmed the depth of this idea in rural Uttar Pradesh, when he told Oscar Lewis, "After death the air in a man mixes with the air; his body turns to earth" (Lewis 1965, 253).

References Cited

Austin, J. L.
1962 *How to Do Things with Words.* Oxford: Clarendon.

Babcock, Barbara A., ed.
1978 *The Reversible World: Symbolic Inversion in Art and Society.* Ithaca, N.Y.: Cornell University Press.

Bakhtin, M. M.
1968 *Rabelais and His World.* Cambridge, Mass.: MIT Press.
1981 *The Dialogic Imagination.* Austin: University of Texas Press.

Barrington Moore, J.
1966 *The Social Origins of Dictatorship and Democracy: Lord and Peasant in the Making of the Modern World.* Boston: Beacon.

Bauman, Richard
1977 *Verbal Art as Performance.* Rowley, Mass.: Newbury House.

Bayly, C. A.
1986 "The Origins of Swadeshi (home industry): Cloth and Indian Society, 1700–1930." In *The Social Life of Things: Commodities in Cultural Perspective,* ed. Arjun Appadurai, 285–322. Cambridge: Cambridge University Press.

Beck, Brenda E. F.
1982 *The Three Twins: The Telling of a South Indian Folk Epic.* Bloomington: Indiana University Press.

Bender, Ernest
1951 *The Nalaraya-davadanticarita (Adventures of King Nala and Davandanti).* New Series. Vol. 40, pt. 4. Philadelphia: American Philosophical Society.

Bingley, A. H.
1978 [1899] *History, Caste, and Culture of Jats and Gujars.* New Delhi: Ess Ess Publications.

Blackburn, Stuart H.
2001 *Moral Fictions: Folktales from Oral Tradition.* Helsinki: Academica Scientiarum Fennica.

Bloch, Maurice
1974 "Symbols, Song, Dance, and Features of Articulation: Is Religion an Extreme Form of Traditional Authority?" *Archive European Sociology* 15:55–81.

Bordo, Susan
1997 "The Body and the Reproduction of Femininity." In *Writing on the Body: Female Embodiment and Feminist Theory,* ed. K. Conboy, N. Medina, and S. Stanbury, 90–112. New York: Columbia University Press.

Briggs, George Weston
1973 *Gorakhnath and the Kanphata Yogis.* Delhi: Motilal Banarsidas.

Brooks, Douglas Renfrew
1992 *Auspicious Wisdom: The Texts and Traditions of Srividya Sakta Tantrism in South India.* Albany: State University of New York Press.

Butler, Judith

1997 Performative Acts and Gender Constitution: An Essay in Phenomenology and Feminist Theory. In *Writing on the Body: Female Embodiment and Feminist Theory,* ed. K. Conboy, N. Medina, and S. Stanbury, 401–418. New York: Columbia University Press.

Carrin, Marine, and Harald Tambs-Lyche

1993 La vengeance des femmes dans ce monde et dans l'autre, quelques exemples de l'Inde. *Cahiers de Litterature Orale* 34:47–74.

Chattopadhyaya, B. D.

1976 Origin of the Rajputs: The Political, Economic, and Social Processes in Early Medieval Rajasthan. *Indian Historical Review* 3, no. 1:59–82.

Chaudhuri, Nirud

1976 *Culture in a Vanity Bag.* Bombay: Jaico.

Coburn, Thomas B.

1984a "Consort of None, Sakti to All: The Vision of the Devi-mahatmya." In *The Divine Consort,* ed. J. S. Hawley and D. M. Wulff, 153–165. Delhi: Motilal Banarsidass.

1984b *Devi-Mahatmya: The Crystallization of the Goddess Tradition.* With a foreword by Daniel H. H. Ingalls. Delhi: Motilal Banarsidass.

1991 *Encountering the Goddess: A Translation of the Devi-Mahatmya and a Study of Its Interpretation.* Albany: State University of New York Press.

Cohn, Bernard S.

1989 "Cloth, Clothes, and Colonialism: India in the Nineteenth Century." In *Cloth and Human Experience,* ed. A. Weiser and J. Schneider, 303–354. Washington, D.C.: Smithsonian Institution Press.

Crooke, William

1896 *The Tribes and Castes of the North-western Provinces and Oudh.* Calcutta: Office of the Superintendent of Government Printing, India.

1907 *Natives of Northern India.* London: Archibald Constable.

Dimock, Edward C.

1966 *The Palace of the Hidden Moon: Erotic Mysticism in the Vaisnavasahajiy—A Cult of Bengal.* Chicago: University of Chicago Press.

Dirks, Nicholas B.

2001 *Castes of Mind: Colonialism and the Making of Modern India.* Princeton, N.J.: Princeton University Press.

Doniger, Wendy

1998 The Immortal Foot: The Ingersoll Lecture on Immortality. *Harvard Divinity Bulletin* 27, no. 213:16–21.

1999 *Splitting the Difference: Gender and Myth in Ancient Greece and India.* Chicago: University of Chicago Press.

2000 *Bedtrick: Tales of Sex and Masquerade.* Chicago: University of Chicago Press.

Drake-Brockman, D. L., ed.

1984 [1911] *Mathura: A Gazetteer.* Allahabad: Superintendent, Government Press, United Provinces.

Dumont, Louis

1980 *Homo Hierarchicus: The Caste System and Its Implications.* Translated by Mark Sainsbury et al. Chicago: University of Chicago Press.

Dwivedi, Girish Chandra
1989 *The Jats: Their Role in the Mughal Empire.* New Delhi: Arnold.
Entwistle, Alan W.
1987 *Braj: Centre of Krishna Pilgrimage.* Groningen: Egbert Forsten.
Erndl, Kathleen M.
1993 *Victory to the Mother: The Hindu Goddess of Northwest India in Myth, Ritual, and Symbol.* New York: Oxford University Press.
Flueckeger, Joyce B., and S. S. Wadley, eds.
n.d. "Understanding Nala." Unpublished manuscript.
Fox, Richard
1971 *Kin, Clan, Raja, Rule: State-Hinterland Relations in Preindustrial India.* Berkeley: University of California Press.
Freeman, R.
n.d. The Performative Context of Nala in Late Medieval Kerala. In "Understanding Nala," ed. J. B. Flueckiger and S. S. Wadley. Unpublished manuscript.
Ganguli, Kalyan Kumar
1983 *Cultural History of Rajasthan.* Delhi: Sundeep Prakashan.
Ghosh, Anindita
1998 Cheap Books, "Bad" Books: Contesting Print-Cultures in Colonial Bengal. *South Asian Research* 18, no. 2:173–194.
Gold, Ann Grodzins
1992 *A Carnival of Parting: The Tales of King Bharthrai and King Gopi Chand as Sung and Told by Mathdu Natisar of Ghatiyali, Rajasthan.* Berkeley: University of California Press.
1994 "Gender, Violence, and Power: Rajasthani Stories of Shkati." In *Women as Subjects: South Asian Histories,* ed. Nita Kumar, 26–48. Charlottesville: University of Virginia Press.
1995 "The 'Jungli Rani' and Other Troubled Wives in Rajasthani Oral Traditions." In *From the Margins of Hindu Marriage: Essays on Gender, Religion, and Culture,* ed. Lindsay Harlan and P. Courtright, 119–136. New York, Oxford University Press.
2000 "From Demon Aunt to Gorgeous Bride: Women Portray Female Power in a North Indian Festival Cycle." In *Invented Identities: The Interplay of Gender, Religion, and Politics in India,* ed. J. Leslie and M. McGee, 203–230. Delhi: Oxford University Press.
Gold, Daniel
1992 "The Rise and Fall of Yogis' Power: Jodhpur, 1803–1842." *Estudios de Asia y Africa* 87, no. 1:9–27.
Goswamy, B. N.
1975 *Pahari Paintings of the Nala-Damayanti Theme in the Collection of Dr. Karan Singh.* New Delhi: National Museum.
Goudriaan, Tarun, and Sanjukta Gupta
1981 *Hindu Tantric and Sakta Literature.* Wiesbaden: Otto Harrassowitz.
Gramsci, Antonio
1971 *Selections from Prison Notebooks.* Edited and translated by Q. Hoare and G. Nowell Smith. New York: International Publishers.

Grierson, George

1890 "A Grammar of the Dialect of Chhattisgarh in the Central Provinces." *Journal of the Royal Asiatic Society of Bengal* 59, no. 2:101–153.

Gupta, Sanjukta

2003 "The Domestication of a Goddess: Caraṇa-tīrtha Kālīghāt, the Mahāpitha of Kālī." In *Encountering Kālī in the Margins, at the Center, in the West,* ed. R. F. McDermott and J. J. Kripal, 60–79. Berkeley: University of California Press.

Haberman, David L.

1994 *Journey through the Twelve Forests: An Encounter with Krishna.* New York: Oxford University Press.

Hall, Stuart, ed.

1997 *Representation: Cultural Representation and Signifying Practices.* Thousand Oaks, Calif.: Sage.

Handelman, Don, and David Shulman

1997 *God Inside Out: Siva's Game of Dice.* New York: Oxford University Press.

Handiqui, K. K., and Narayana Bendaraja

1965 *Naisadhacarita of Sriharsa.* Poona: Deccan College Post-Graduate and Research Institute.

Harlan, Lindsey

1992 *Religion and Rajput Women: The Ethic of Protection in Contemporary Narratives.* Berkeley: University of California Press.

1995 "Abandoning Shame: Mira and the Margins of Marriage." In *From the Margins of Hindu Marriage: Essays on Gender, Religion, and Culture,* ed. L. Harlan and P. Courtright, 204–227. New York, Oxford University Press.

2000 "Battles, Brides, and Sacrifice: Rajput *Kuldevis* in Rajasthan." In *Is the Goddess a Feminist? The Politics of South Asian Goddesses,* ed. A. Hiltebeitel and K. M. Erndl, 69–90. New York: New York University Press.

2003 *The Goddesses' Henchmen: Reflections on Gender in Indian Hero Worship.* New York: Oxford University Press.

n.d. "Nal and Damayanti's Reversals of Fortune: Perspectives on When a Woman Should Know Better." In "Understanding Nala," ed. J. Flueckiger and S. S. Wadley. Unpublished manuscript.

Haynes, Douglas E., and Gyan Prakash, eds.

1992 *Contesting Power: Resistance and Everyday Social Relations in South Asia.* Berkeley: University of California Press.

Hershman, Paul

1977 "Virgin and Mother." In *Symbols and Sentiments: Cross-Cultural Studies in Symbolism,* ed. J. Lewis, 269–292. New York: Academic Press.

Hiltebeitel, Alf

1999 *Rethinking India's Oral and Classical Epics: Draupadi among Rajputs, Muslims, and Dalits.* Chicago: University of Chicago Press.

Hume, Cynthia

1990 *The Text and Temple of the Great Goddess: The Devi-mahatmya and the Vidhyacal Temple of Mirzapur.* Vol. 2. Iowa City: University of Iowa Press.

Ibbetson, Sir Denzil

1916 *Panjab Castes: Being a Reprint of the Chapter on "The Races, Castes, and Tribes of the People" in the Report on the Census of the Panjab Published in 1883 by the Late Sir Denzil Ibbetson, K.C.S.I.* Lahore: Superintendent, Government Printing, Panjab.

Jason, H.

1989 *Types of Indic Oral Tales.* Helsinki: Folklore Fellows Communications 242.

Joon, Ram Sarup

1967 *History of the Jats.* Delhi: N.p.

Keyes, Charles F., and E. Valentine Daniel, eds.

1983 *Karma: An Anthropological Inquiry.* Berkeley: University of California Press.

Khacherudas

1975 *Nal ka byah.* Meerut: Jawahar Book Depot.

Khare, Ravindra S.

1996 "A Case of Anomalous Values in Indian Civilization: Meat-Eating among the Kanya-Kubja Brahmans of Katyayan Gotra." *Journal of Asian Studies* 25:229–240.

Kinsley, David

1986 *Hindu Goddess: Visions of the Divine Feminine in the Hindu Religious Tradition.* Berkeley: University of California Press.

1997 *Tantric Visions of the Divine Feminine: The Ten Mahavidyas.* Berkeley: University of California Press.

Kolff, Dirk H. A.

1990 *Naukar, Rajput, and Sepoy: The Ethnohistory of the Military Labour Market in Hindustan, 1450–1850.* Cambridge: Cambridge University Press.

1995 "The Rajput of Ancient and Medieval North India: A Warrior-Ascetic." In *Folk, Faith, and Feudalism: Rajasthan Studies,* ed. N. K. Singhi and R. Joshi, 257–294. Jaipur: Rawat.

Lapoint, Elwyn C.

1978 "The Epic of Guga: A North Indian Oral Tradition." In *American Studies in the Anthropology of India,* ed. S. Vatuk, 281–308. New Delhi: Manohar.

Leslie, I. Julia

1989 *The Perfect Wife: The Orthodox Hindu Woman according to the Stridharamapaddhati of Tryambakayajvan.* Delhi: Oxford University Press.

Lévi-Strauss, Claude

1963 *Structural Anthropology.* New York: Basic Books.

1966 *Savage Mind.* Chicago: University of Chicago Press.

Lewis, Oscar

1965 *Village Life in Northern India.* Urbana: University of Illinois Press.

Malhotra, Anshu

2002 *Gender, Caste, and Religious Identities: Restructuring Class in Colonial Panjab.* Delhi: Oxford University Press.

Manuel, Peter

1993 *Cassette Culture: Popular Music and Technology in North India.* Chicago: University of Chicago Press.

Marriott, McKim, and Ronald Inden

1987 Social Stratification: Caste. *Encyclopaedia Britannica* 27:348–356. Chicago: Encyclopaedia Britannica.

Matolsingh

n.d. (a). *Dhola: Magadhital.* Hathras: Deepchand.

n.d. (b). *Motini ka byah.* Hathras: Deepchand.
n.d. (c). *Dhola.* Hathras: Deepchand.

McDermott, Rachel Fell, and Jeffrey Kripal, eds.
2003 *Encountering Kali: In the Margins, at the Center, in the West.* Berkeley: University of California Press.

McGregor, Ronald Stuart
1974 *Hindi Literature to the Nineteenth and Early Twentieth Centuries.* Wiesbaden: Otto Harrassowitz.

Miller, Joseph C., ed.
1980 *The African Past Speaks: Essays on Oral Tradition and History.* Folkstone, U.K.: Dawson-Archon.

Nandy, Ashish
1980 *At the Edge of Psychology: Essays in Politics and Culture.* Delhi: Oxford University Press.

Narayan, Kirin
1989 *Storytellers, Saints, and Scoundrels: Folk Narrative in Hindu Religious Teaching.* Philadelphia: University of Pennsylvania Press.
1997 *Mondays on the Dark Night of the Moon.* New York: Oxford University Press.

Padamsinh
1975 *Motini ka byah.* Mainpuri, India: Padamsinh.

Pal, Anant, ed.
1994 *Hari Sinh Nalwa* (Amar Chitra Katha). Bombay: India Book House.

Pargiter, F. E.
1969 *The Markandeya Purana.* Delhi: Indological Book House.

Prasad, Pandit Lakshman
1890 *Dhola Maru Nal ki Sagai.* Agra: N.p.

Qanungo, Kalika Ranjan
1925 *History of the Jats.* Vol. 1: *To the Death of Mizra Najaf Khan, 1782.* Calcutta: M. C. Sarkar.
1960 *Studies in Rajput History.* Delhi: S. Chand.

Raheja, Gloria Goodwin
1999 "The Illusion of Consent: Language, Caste, and Colonial Rule in India." In *Colonial Subjects: Essays in the Practical History of Anthropology,* ed. Peter Pels and Oscar Salemink, 117–152. Ann Arbor: University of Michigan Press.

Raheja, Gloria Goodwin, and Ann Grodzins Gold
1994 *Listen to the Heron's Words.* Berkeley: University of California Press.

Rohe, Mark Edwin
1997 "Where the Sakti Flows: The Pilgrimage and Cult of Vaisno Devi." Ph.D. dissertation, Department of Anthropology, University of Chicago.

Rudolph, Susanne Hoeber, and Lloyd I. Rudolph
1984 *Essays on Rajputana: Reflections on History, Culture, and Administration.* New Delhi: Concept.

Rushdie, Salman
1990 *Haroun and the Sea of Stories.* London: Granta.

Schomer, Karine
1989 Paradigms for the Kali Yuga: The Heroes of the Alha Epic and Their Fate. In *Oral Epics in India,* ed. S. Blackburn et al., 140–154. Berkeley: University of California Press.

Sehegal, K. K.

1971 *Rajasthan District Gazetteers: Bharatpur.* Jaipur: Directorate, District Gazetteers, Government of Rajasthan.

Shulman, David

1994 "On Being Human in the Sanskrit Epic: The Riddle of Nala." *Journal of Indian Philosophy* 22, no. 1:1–29.

Singh, Chauduri Candan

1966 *Damayanti svayambar.* Meerut: Jawahar Book Depot.

Singh, Padam

n.d. *Motini ka Byah.* Mainpuri: Padamsingh Bookseller.

Sircar, R. C.

1973 *The Sakta Pithas.* Delhi: Motilal Banarsidas.

Smith, Dorothy E.

1989 "Sociology Theory: Methods of Writing Patriarchy." In *Feminism and Sociological Theory,* ed. R. A. Wallace, 34–64. Newbury Park, Calif.: Sage.

Smith, J. D.

1989 "Scapegoats of the Gods: The Ideology of the Indian Epics." In *Oral Epics in India,* ed. S. Blackburn et al., 176–196. Berkeley: University of California Press.

Spear, Percival

1951 *Twilight of the Mughuls: Studies in Late Mughul Delhi.* Cambridge: Cambridge University Press.

Stallybrass, Peter, and Allon White

1986 *The Politics and Poetics of Transgression.* Ithaca, N.Y.: Cornell University Press.

Stokes, Maive S. H.

1880 *Indian Fairy Tales.* London: Ellis and White.

Suman, Amba Prasad

1962 *Brajbhasha shabdavali.* Allahabad: Hindustani Ekedemi (Academy).

Tod, James

1971 *Annals and Antiquities of Rajasthan or the Central and Western Rajpoot States of India.* New Delhi: K.M.N. Publishers.

Todarmal

1879 *Nalacaritamtat arthat Dhola Maru.* Mathura: N.p.

1975 *Asli Dhola Maru.* Mathura: Venkateshwar Pustakalaya.

Van Buitenen, J. A. B., trans. and ed.

1975 *The Mahabharata.* Vol. 2: *The Book of the Assembly Hall.* Vol. 3: *The Book of the Forest.* Chicago: University of Chicago Press.

Varma, Gajadarsingh

n.d. *Dhola narbargarh.* Hathras: Srikrishna Press.

Vaudeville, Charlotte

1962 *Les Duha de Dhola Maru, une ancienne ballade du Rajasthan.* Pondicherry: Publications de l'institut Français d'indologie.

1976 "Braj, Lost and Found." *Indo-Iranian Journal* 18:195–213.

1982 "Krishna Gopala, Radha, and the Great Goddess." In *The Divine Consort: Radha and the Goddesses of India,* ed. J. S. Hawley and D. M. Wulff, 1–12. Berkeley: Graduate Theological Union.

Wadley, Susan S.

1975 *Shakti: Power in the Conceptual Structure of Karimpur Religion.* The University of Chicago Studies in Anthropology series in Social, Cultural, and Linguistic Anthropology, no. 2. Chicago: Department of Anthropology, University of Chicago.

1976 "The Spirit 'Rides' or the Spirit 'Comes': Possession in a North Indian Village." In *Rituals, Cults, and Shamanism: The Realm of the Extra-Human,* ed. A. Bharati, 233–251. The Hague: Mouton.

1978 "Texts in Contexts: Oral Traditions and the Study of Religion in Karimpur." In *American Studies in the Anthropology of India,* ed. S. Vatuk, 309–341. New Delhi: American Institute of Indian Studies.

1983 "Vrats: Transformers of Destiny." In *Karma: An Anthropological Inquiry,* ed. C. F. Keyes and E. V. Daniel, 147–162. Berkeley: University of California Press.

1989 "Choosing a Path: Performance Strategies in a North Indian Epic." In *Oral Epics in India,* ed. S. H. Blackburn et al., 75–101. Berkeley: University of California Press.

1992 "Beyond Texts: Tunes and Contexts in Indian Folk Music." In *Texts, Tunes, and Tones: Parameters of Music in Multicultural Perspective,* ed. B. Wade, 71–106. New Delhi: Oxford and IBH Publishing.

1994 *Struggling with Destiny in Karimpur, 1925–1984.* Berkeley, University of California Press.

1999 "A Bhakti Rendition of Nala-Damayanti: Todar Mal's 'Nectar of the Life of Nal.' " *International Journal of Hindu Studies* 3:1–29.

2000 "Hindu Women's Family and Household Rites in a North Indian Village." In *Unspoken Worlds: Women's Religious Lives,* ed. N. Falk and R. Gross, 103–113. Menlo Park: Wadsworth.

2001 "Popular Culture and the North Indian Oral Epic Dhola." *Indian Folklore Research Journal* 1:13–24.

2003 "Clothing the Female Body: Education, Social Change, and Fashion in Rural North India." Paper presented at the workshop "Grounding Gender in the Local Spaces of Globalization," Maxwell School, Syracuse University.

Wadley, Susan S., and Bruce W. Derr

1989 "Eating Sins in Karimpur." *Contributions to Indian Sociology* 23, no. 1:131–148.

Waterfield, William

1923 *The Lay of Alha: A Saga of Rajput Chivalry as Sung by Minstrels of Northern India.* London: Oxford University Press.

Wheelock, Wade T.

1980 "A Taxonomy of the Mantras of the New- and Full-Moon Sacrifice." *History of Religions* 19:349–369.

1982 "The Problem of Ritual Language: From Information to Situation." *Journal of the American Academy of Religion* 50:49–71.

White, David Gordon

1996 *The Alchemical Body: Siddha Traditions in Medieval India.* Chicago: University of Chicago Press.

2001 "Yogis and Political Power among the Nath Siddhas of North India." Paper presented at the Conference on Asceticism and Power in the Asian Context, School of Oriental and African Studies, London.

Williams, Richard

1976 "Dhola-maru ra Duha and the Rise of the Hindi Literary Tradition." Ph.D. dissertation, Department of South Asian Languages and Literatures, University of Chicago.

Wilson, Elizabeth

1987 *Adorned in Dreams: Fashion and Modernity.* London: Virago.

Wiser, William H.

1933 "Social Institutions of a Hindu Village in North India." Ph.D. dissertation, Cornell University.

1958 *The Hindu Jajmani System.* Lucknow: Lucknow Publishing.

Wiser, William, and Charlotte Wiser

2001 *Behind Mud Walls: Seventy-Five Years in a North Indian Village.* Updated and expanded edition, with new chapters by Susan S. Wadley and a foreword by David G. Mandelbaum. Berkeley: University of California Press.

Zeigler, Norman Paul

1973 "Action, Power, and Service in Rajasthani Culture: A Social History of the Rajputs of Middle Period, Rajasthan." Ph.D. dissertation, Department of History, University of Chicago.

Zvelebil, Kamil V.

1987 *Two Tamil Folktales: The Story of King Matanakama; the Story of Peacock Ravana.* Delhi: Motilal Banarsidass.

Index

Page numbers in italics indicate illustrations.

achievement, 3, 7, 61, 143, 146, 165
Acrobats, 24–26, 142–170, *157,* 191; Mansukh and, 154; Motini and, 128–29, 140, 153–60; Nal and, 7, 146, 153–60; women, 154
adharm, 186; defined, 207
adisakti, 108; defined, 207
Aghoris, 116, 117
Agra, 59, 60, 103
Ahirs, 59
Aja, 67
Ajaynagar, 46
Ajaypal, 34, 48, 182
Alha, 56, 63, 71, 136, 146, 165, 179–80, 211n4, 220n11; defined, 207
alha (melody), 71, 75–76, 77
Aligarh, 60
alliance marriages, 136–40, 146
alliance politics, 136–37, 139
Alwar, 60
Amar Chitra Katha, 57, 58
Amba Khas, 149
Amrit Pond, 35
Ananatal, Raja, 218n3
animal sacrifice, 103, 110, 111
Annals of Rajasthan (Tod), 146
Ansuya, 125–26
anuloma, 137; defined, 207
Arjun, 101
Arya Samaj, 111
aspara, 4, 67, 122, 140, 172; defined, 207
audiences, 64, 65, 66, 72, 75, 91, 153–54; and nonverbal messages, 79; rural, 165, 166, 193; and singer, 78, 79
Aughar yogis, 115, 116–17
aukha, 6, 37, 185–87, 193; defined, 207
authority, 5
Ayodhya, 32

Badan Singh, 60
Baguri forest, 48
baigi, 35; defined, 207
Bakhtin, Mikhail, 5, 91
bali, 45, 109; defined, 207
Banaras, 21, 43, 133
Bangamgarh, 44
Bangle Sellers, 46, 49, 141, 160–63. *See also* glass bangles
The Banishment of Manjha (*Manjha Ka Nikala*), 9–12
Banjaras, 35, 166, 167–68, 193
Banvaris, 12, 88, 143, 163
Banyas (Merchants), 165, 168
barahmasi, 72, 74, 75; defined, 207
barat, 42, 89; defined, 207
Basmati, 164
Basukdev, 182, 184, 187; in The Battle of Chandrapal, 55; in The Battle of Kajariban, 54; in The Battle of Patal Lok, 18–21; daughter of, 20, 26–27, 128, 167, 171, 176; in Nal's Time of Distress, 35
Batana, 159
The Battle of Bhamartal (*Bhamartal Ki Larai*), 37–40, 137–39, 147–53
The Battle of Chandrapal (*Chandrapal Ki Larai*), 55
The Battle of Kajariban (*Kajariban Ki Larai*), 53–54
The Battle of Kampilagarh (*Kampilagarh Ki Larai*), 22–23
"The Battle of Kishanlal" (Ram Swarup Kachi), 98
The Battle of Lakhiyaban (*Lakhiyaban Ki Larai*), 40–43
The Battle of Patal Lok (*Patal Lok Ki Larai*), 18–21
Battle of Phul Bagh (*Phul Bag Ki Larai*), 40
Battle of Phul Singh Panjabi. *See* Battle of Phul Singh (*Phul Sinh Ki Larai*)
Battle of Phul Singh (*Phul Sinh Ki Larai*), 23–26, 44, 61, 180–81; goddess and, 99, 105–108, 113–18; performance of, 75–77; renamed as Panjab Battle, 63; sexuality in, 128, 129–32. *See also* Phul Singh Panjabi
The Battle of Shantiban (*Santiban Ki Larai*), 12–15
The Battle with Vir Singh (*Vir Singh Ki Larai*), 43–44, 133

Bavariya, 36–37, 188–90, 192
Behmata, 85, 105, 136, 143, 164, 185, 193; in The Battle of Bhamartal, 138; in Battle of Phul Bagh, 40; in Battle of Phul Singh, 106; in Motini's Marriage, 15–18, 83–90
Bengal, 6, 46–47, 56, 106, 114, 126–27, 167
bhabhi, 73; defined, 207
Bhagavad Gita, 8, 101; defined, 207
Bhagavati, 98, 106
bhagyavan, 177; defined, 207
Bhairavi, 108
Bhairo, 109
bhairon, 89, 99, 106; defined, 207
bhajan, 80; defined, 207
bhakti, 95–119, 181, 193, 194; defined, 207; and Matolsingh, 82
Bhamartal, 37–40, 137–39, 147–53, 183, 187
Bhamartal Ki Larai (The Battle of Bhamartal), 37–40, 137–39, 147–53
Bhangi, 167; defined, 207
Bharamal, 49–53, 53–54; described, 197
Bharatpur, 59, 61
Bhat, 166
bhent, 109, 110; defined, 207
Bhils, 53, 138, 139, 153, 166, 168–69, 171; in The Battle of Lakhiyaban, 40–43; described, 197
Bhim, Raja, 176, 190–91; described, 197; in Dumenti's Marriage, 26–31, 176–78; in Dumenti's Second Svayambar, 36, 37; in Nal's Time of Distress, 35
Bhim Sen, 137
Bhoja, King, 57, 214n31
Bhumasur, 28, 41, 85, 122, 173, 218n8; in Motini's Marriage, 15–18, 83–90
bij mantra, 148, 190; defined, 207
bindi, 134–35; defined, 207
Biram, Raja, 35
Bloch, Maurice, 78
blood sacrifice, 109
body, 5, 6, 105, 143, 153–54, 156, 158–60, 163, 171
boundaries, 133, 140, 141, 160; and caste, 142–43
Brahma, 125
Brahman Pandit, 9–12; described, 197
Brahmans, 102, 103, 145, 165, 166–67, 217n20
Braj, 3, 4, 59, 61, 64; bhakti traditions of, 95–119
Braj Kala Kendra, 56, 217n20
Brajesvari Devi, 105
bravery, 180–82, 183
Brhadasva, 192
Briggs, George Weston, 112
Brindavan, 108
British, 3, 60, 61, 111
Buddhism, 107
Budh Singh, Raja, 4, 136, 137, 140, 180, 183, 184, 190; in The Battle of Bhamartal, 37–40, 137–39, 149; in The Battle of Chandrapal, 55; in The Battle of Kajariban, 53–54; in The Battle of Lakhiyaban, 42; in Battle of Phul Bagh, 40; described, 198; in Maru's Marriage Fulfilled, 52; in The Pond of Magaghi, 55
Bulandshahr, 60
Butler, Judith, 153

cal, 85–86
Carrin, Marine, 140
cassettes, 61–64, 69, 72, 97, 187, 205; and Ram Swarup Dhimar, 62, 69
caste culture, 142, 165
caste hierarchies, 171
caste identities, 7, 141, 143, 144, 153–54, 163, 170, 171
caste status, 3, 7, 165
caste stereotypes, 4, 7, 142, 165, 166, 169
castes, 3–4, 92, 130, 135, 142–70, 171; mixing of, 6, 185, 186, 187; political orientation of, 144; women and, 141, 163
Chamars, 61
Chandi, 44–48, 106, 108–10, 160; described, 197
Chando, 23–26, 113–18, 181, 219n4; described, 197
Chandrakala, 44–48; described, 197
Chandrapal, 55
Chandrapal, Raja, 44–48; described, 198
Chandrapal Ki Larai (The Battle of Chandrapal), 55
chant, 78–79, 85
chaos, 6, 133
chap, 72, 75
chapbooks, 4, 63, 65, 79, 143
character development, 77
Chatani, 159
Chaudhuri, Nirud, 154
chetvani, 76, 78
Chhatris, 148, 165, 166
Chitra Reka, 115
Chote Lal, 82, 87–90
Chudaman, 40–43, 49, 51; described, 197
Chugal, 48
Churaman, 60
cikara, 62, 65, 70, 71, 72, 79, 80, 82, 83; defined, 207

Cilappatikaram, 140
cimta (steel tongs), 69, 71, 72, 83
circumambulation, 88, 154
clothing, 6, 7, 128, 154, *155, 157,* 160, 163, 171, 178, 188
Coburn, Thomas, 100
context, 91
Crooke, William, 146, 164–65
cultural themes, 5
cultural values, 154
curses, 193
cymbals, 82

Dakshinpur, 12, 14, 19, 20, 21, 105, 136, 163, 164
Damayanti, 4, 178, 184, 192. *See also* Dumenti
danava, 218n8
dancing girls, 39, 128–30, *131,* 149, 158
Dank, 35; defined, 207
danu, 218n8; defined, 208
darsan, 96; defined, 208
Dasharath, Raja, 32, 56, 57–58, 121
daughters and mothers, 135–40
demons, 40–43, 48, 53, 107, 118, 138, 139, 171, 172, 174, 218n8
Deothan, 42
desire and sexuality, 128–34
deva defined, 208
Devi Mahatmya, 100, 101, 107; defined, 208
Devi-Bhagavata Purana, 101; defined, 208
Devnarayan, 56, 146; defined, 208
dharam bhai, 20, 35; defined, 208
Dharamraj, 9–12, 173; described, 197
dharamsala defined, 208
dharma, 12, 101, 108, 126, 127, 145, 186; defined, 208
Dhimars, 218n2
Dhola (epic): cultural history of, 56–59; defined, 208; historical context of, 59–61
dhola (melody), 70–77
Dhola (son), 4, 5, *51,* 67, 106, 108–10, 111, 126, 136, 142, 153, 184; in Battle of Bhamartal, 138; in The Battle of Chandrapal, 55; in The Battle of Kajariban, 53–54; in The Battle of Lakhiyaban, 42, 43; in Battle of Phul Bagh, 40; in The Battle with Vir Singh, 44, 133; and Bhils, 169; described, 197; and gardens, 167; marriage and, 137; in The Marriage of Kishan Lal, 45–48, 160, 163; in The Marriage of Rewa, 49; in Maru's Marriage Fulfilled, 50–53; and Motini, 123; in The Pond of Magaghi, 54–55
dholak, 69, 71, 72, 83; defined, 208
Dhola-Maru, 58, 215n3; defined, 208
Dholpur, 60
Dhuj, 67
dhuni, 85–86
dice, 57, 122, 137, 151, 164, 183–85. *See also* gambling
Dig, 60
dipak mantra, 33
dipak rag, 149; defined, 208
disorder, 6, 185–87
doha, 72–75, 78, 79; defined, 208
Doniger, Wendy, 176
donors, 39, 66, 72, 149
Draupadi, 125, 184
dress. *See* clothing
drum (dholak), 69, 71, 72, 83
Dubois, Abbe, 144
Dum, 166
Dumaiti, 4
Dumenti, 3, 4, 6, *34,* 103, 120–41, 168, 172, 182, 186–92, 218n7; and Banjaras, 168, 193; in The Battle of Bhamartal, 37–38, 138–39, 147–53; in The Battle of Chandrapal, 55; in The Battle of Lakhiyaban, 42, 43; in The Battle of Patal Lok, 18–21; in Battle of Phul Bagh, 40; in The Battle with Vir Singh, 43–44, 133; described, 197; in Dumenti's Marriage, 26–31; and gardens, 167; marriage and, 137, 140, 172, 176; in Maru's Marriage Fulfilled, 49–53; as mother, 135, 136; in Nal's Bad Times, 73–75; in Nal's Time of Distress, 31–35, 185; in other renditions, 57; in The Pond of Magaghi, 54–55
Dumenti Ka Byah (Dumenti's Marriage), 26–31, 176–78
Dumenti Ka Dusra Svayambar (Dumenti's Second Svayambar), 35–37
Dumenti's Marriage (*Dumenti Ka Byah*), 26–31, 176–78
Dumenti's Second Svayambar (*Dumenti Ka Dusra Svayambar*), 35–37
Dumont, Louis, 144
Durga, 4, 6, 100–105, 118–19, 124, 141, 194, 216n13; in Banishment of Manjha, 9–12; in The Battle of Bhamartal, 139, 149, 151; in The Battle of Chandrapal, 55; in The Battle of Kajariban, 53; in The Battle of Lakhiyaban, 41–42; in The Battle of Patal Lok, 19; in Battle of Phul Singh, 25, 26, 99; in The Battle of Shantiban, 13, 15; in The Battle with Vir Singh, 44; described, 197; in Dumenti's Marriage, 28; and Kali, 6, 103, 105–12, 117; in The Marriage of Kishan Lal, 45,

Durga (*continued*)
46; in Maru's Marriage Fulfilled, 52; in Motini's Marriage, 16, 17, 18; and Nal, 98–99, 127, 136, 153, 182, 183, 187; in Nal's Time of Distress, 35; power of, 3, 96, 141

Entwhistle, Alan, 102
Erndl, Kathleen M., 108
Etah, 60

Farmers, 142
fate, 3, 6, 143, 171, 172, 174, 178, 185, 186, 192; and humanity, 192–95
female obedience, 125, 126
feminine, 95–96, 182. *See also* women
festivals, goddess, 102–103
film songs, 63, 70, 72, 215n3
folk drama, 71
folk song genres, 71–79, 85
folk songs, 63, 65, 70, 215n3
folk tales, 118, 128
folk traditions, 127, 137
food, 24–25, 38, 90–91, 129, 145, 148, 160, 186, 188; and sex, 128
forests, 167–68, 169, 171
Fox, Richard, 179
framing devices, 96, 98

Gahadwalas, 102
Gajadhar Singh, 80, 82, 86, 103, 106, 216n17
Gajadharsinh Varma, 99, 143–44
gali, 18; defined, 208
gambling, 16, 39–40, 122, 152, 153, 190. *See also* dice
Gangadhar, 166, 167
Gardeners (Malis), 32, 46, 47, 49, 166, 167
gardens, 32, 167, 169
gauna, 50, 54; defined, 208
gender, 92
gender identities, 143, 153
Gendwati, 45–48, 126, 127; described, 197
genealogy, 165
genres. *See* folk song genres
geography, 5, 6, 105, 142, 143
glass bangles, 134–35, 161. *See also* Bangle Sellers
goddess, 95–119, *97;* devotion to, 6; invoking of, 96–100; and Nath yogis, 112–18; in North Indian religious traditions, 100–105; power of, 95–96, 99, 100, 103–104, 122; role of, 96; and singer, 96–97
goddess worship, 103, 110
gods, male, 98
Gold, Ann, 127, 128, 180
Gopi Chand, 112, 118, 141
Gopi Chand, 127
Gorakhnath, 112, 117, 118
Goswamis, 108
Gramsci, Antonio, 4
Guga, 112, 118
Gujars, 59, 135
Gukharu forest, 48
gunas, 107–108
Gurgaon, 60
gurus, 112, 117, 118; and Ram Swarup Dhimar, 65, 66, 67

Hadamba, 218n3
hair, 134, 158
Hall, Stuart, 194
Hanuman, 98, 99, 104, 216n13
Hari Singh, 56–57
Harishchand, 57, 67
Hariyal, 52, 53–54; described, 197
Harlan, Lindsey, 111, 135, 169, 179, 180
Harman, 82, 87–90
harmonium, 62, 65, 70, 72, 79, 80, 83
Haroun and the Sea of Stories (Rushdie), 56
Hathras, 60
hierarchies, 4–5, 92, 154, 166, 171
Hiltebeitel, Alf, 56
Hinduism, 3, 8, 92, 100, 102, 106, 117, 125, 146, 172
"Hindustan ki kasam," 63
Hinglaj, 12, 99, 105, 106, 112, 117
human sacrifice, 6, 45, 84, 86, 96, 110
humanity, 171, 191; and fate, 192–95; Raja Nal's, 3, 5, 7, 145, 172–76, 178
humor, 72, 78, 79, 90, 91, 216n10, 220n8

Ibbetson, Denzil, 117, 154, 166
identities, 5, 7, 56, 60, 136, 153, 160, 192; caste, 7, 141, 143, 144, 153–54, 163, 170, 171; and gender, 143; human, 188; Motini's, 140; Nal's, 5, 144, 145, 146, 153, 163, 164, 171, 172, 181–82, 183, 184, 194; Rajput, 61; of women, 140
ijjat, 190; defined, 208
immorality, 127
immortality, 5, 7
Inden, Ronald, 144
Indra, 4, 6, 103, 122, 140, 147, 167, 176, 190–91, 218n3; in Banishment of Manjha, 9–12; in The Battle of Patal Lok, 19; described, 197; dice and, 184; in Dumenti's Marriage, 26–31, 177–78; in Dumenti's Second Svay-

ambar, 36, 37; marriage and, 137; in Maru's Marriage Fulfilled, 52, 53; in Motini's Marriage, 16, 17, 18; in Nal's Time of Distress, 31, 185, 186; and Narad, 172; and Shanidev, 57
instruments, 72, 83; on cassettes, 62, 63

Jahan, Shah, II, 60
Jalandhar, 112, 117, 128; in Battle of Phul Singh, 23–26, 99, 113–18; described, 197; sexuality and, 133
jaldariya, 18; defined, 208
Jamvai Mata, 110–11
jati, 135, 143, 145; defined, 208. *See also* castes
jatiya, 61; defined, 208
Jats, 4, 23, 59–60, 61, 66, 111, 118, *155,* 181, 185, 193; bhakti and, 194; clothing and, 154; defined, 208; female, 141; and Rajputs, 103
Jay, 67
jhikri, 80
jhulna, 85–86
Jodhpur, 61
Jogis, 102
juri, 15; defined, 208

Kabutri, 154
kaca, 148; defined, 208
Kachis, 216n10
Kachua Dev, 12–15; described, 197
Kahars defined, 208
Kaikeyi, 121
Kailash, 63
Kajari forest, 12, 52
Kajariban, 53–54
Kajariban Ki Larai (The Battle of Kajariban), 53–54
Kali, 6, 96, 116, 117, 118, 184; in Battle of Phul Singh, 23–26; described, 197; and Durga, 6, 103, 105–12, 117
Kalua, 106
Kamalada, Rani, 177
kamin, 151; defined, 208
Kamla, Rani, 26–31; described, 198
Kampilagarh, 22–23, 24, 99, 124, 159
Kampilagarh Ki Larai (The Battle of Kampilagarh), 22–23
kandakavya literature, 58
Kangrevali Devi, 105
kanya, 122; defined, 208
kanyadan, 42, 87, 88, 122, 137; defined, 208
kar, 174, 192; defined, 209
Karampal, Raja, 46
Karimpur, 211n1
karma, 174, 192
Kashipur, 35, 36, 187, 188
Kasmati, 164
kaula, 99; defined, 209
Kedar, Raja, 111
Keshav, Raja, 53
Keshvani, 53
Ketu, 31
Khacherudas, 173
khappar, 99, 105; defined, 209
khyal, 58; defined, 209
kings, 4, 6, 60, 61, 171, 186
Kinsley, David, 101, 108
Kisanlal Ka Byah (The Marriage of Kishan Lal), 44–48, 105, 108–10, 160–63, 182
Kishanlal, 98, 108–10, 126, 142, 160–63, 182; described, 197; and gardens, 167; in The Marriage of Kishan Lal, 44–48, 105, 108–10, 160–63, 182; and Motini, 122–23
Kishavgarh, 53
Kishnabhang, 46
Kishori, 61
Kolff, Dirk, 146
kos, 36, 190, 191; defined, 209
Krishna, 47, 96, 98–102, 194, 218n1
Kshatriyas, 153, 160, 166, 185; food and, 25, 160; gambling and, 16, 39, 184; Raja Nal as, 16, 38, 148, 156, 158, 164, 171, 172, 181, 184; rituals, 19; varna, 145, 148, 165. *See also* Rajputs
kuldevi, 110–11; defined, 209
Kusalalabh, 58
Kush, 56, 111

Lachhiman Seth, 168, 184; in Banishment of Manjha, 9–12; in The Battle of Shantiban, 13, 14; described, 197
lahadari, 72, 74, 75
Lakha Banjara, 31–35, 132; described, 197
Lakhiyaban, 26, 40–43, 48, 99, 107, 153, 168
Lakhiyaban Ki Larai (The Battle of Lakhiyaban), 40–43
Lakshman, 63, 82, 118, 180, 194
Lakshmi, 108, 135, 191
landscape, 169
Langas, 215n7
language, 62, 78
langur, 12, 99, 216n13; defined, 209
Lanka, 104
Laturi Lal, 63
Lav, 56
Laws of Manu, 125

Leatherworkers, 61
Levi-Strauss, Claude, 56
Lewis, Oscar, 193
life index, 20, 35, 56
lineage, 146–47; of Jamvai Mata, 111; Raja Nal's, 67, 176
linguistics, 77, 78
literacy, 165

Madadev, 125
Madari, 4
madman, Raja Nal as, 7, 143, 188–92
Magaghi Tal (The Pond of Magaghi), 54–55
magic, 117, 126–27, 135, 181; Bengal and, 56, 106, 126; Kali's, 96, 107; Motini's, 106, 107, 119, 122–24, 126, 127–28, 160; sex and, 113; women's control of, 6
magicians, 47, 126–27, 167
Mahabharata, 4, 7, 57, 58, 101, 106, 125, 176, 192; defined, 209; dice in, 183–84
Mahakali, 106–107
mahavidyas, 108; defined, 209
Mahendranagar, 55
Mahipal, 67
Mahisa, 100–101
Mainpuri, 60
Mal, Raja, 49; described, 198
male gods, 98
malhar, 33, 71, 85–86, 182; defined, 209
Malins, 47
Malis (Gardeners), 166, 167
Malwa, 49
Man Singh, Maharaja, 111
manas, 172; defined, 209
Manavati, 118
Mangiyars, 215n7
Mangtu Lal, 61, 95; described, 199
Manihars (Bangle Sellers), 46, 49, 141, 160–63; defined, 209
Manjha, Rani, 56, 104, 120, 121, 123, 144, 172–73, 185; in The Banishment of Manjha, 9–12; in The Battle of Kampilagarh, 22–23; in The Battle of Patal Lok, 19, 20; in Battle of Phul Singh, 75–77; in The Battle of Shantiban, 12–15; and Brahmans, 166; committing sati, 116; described, 198; in The Marriage of Kishan Lal, 46; and Merchants, 163–64, 168; as mother, 136; and Motini, 17, 165; in The Story of Nal, 21–22; and Sweepers, 167; and women's role, 135
Manjha Ka Nikala (The Banishment of Manjha), 9–12
Manjulal Lal Kachi, 216n10; described, 199
Mansukh Gujar, 63, 78, 123, 124, 126, 165, 186, 188; as Acrobat, 154, 156; in The Battle of Chandrapal, 55; in The Battle of Lakhiyaban, 43; in The Battle of Patal Lok, 18–21; in Battle of Phul Singh, 23–26, 113–18, 156, 158–60, 181; in Dumenti's Marriage, 28–30, 176–78; and gardens, 167; in The Marriage of Kishan Lal, 45–48, 110, 182; in The Marriage of Rewa, 49; in Maru's Marriage Fulfilled, 52; in Nal's Bad Times, 73–75; in Nal's Time of Distress, 32
Manu, 125
Manuel, Peter, 63
Maratha, 107
marital status, 134–35
Markandeya Purana, 57, 108; defined, 209
marriage, 7, 15, 63, 125, 136, 154, 176, 184, 193, 220n3; and Brahmans, 166; and caste, 142, 143; Chandrakala's, 44–48; Chandrapal's, 55; Dhola's, 42, 49, 123; Dumenti's, 26–31, 35–37, 103, 185, 192; hypergamous, 136, 140, 213n18; hypogamous, 140; and Indra, 137; Kishanlal's, 44–48; Motini's, 15–18, 83–90, 135, 136, 140, 143, 175, 176; Nal's, 15–18, 25–31, 35–37, 105, 122, 136; Rewa's, 49; singing *Dhola* and, 80
marriage alliances, 136–40, 146
The Marriage of Kishan Lal (*Kisanlal Ka Byah*), 44–48, 105, 108–10, 160–63, 182. *See also* Kishanlal
The Marriage of Rewa (*Rewa Ka Byah*), 49
Marriott, McKim, 144
Maru, 4, *51,* 106, 111, 153, 184; in The Battle of Bhamartal, 138; in The Battle of Chandrapal, 55; in The Battle of Kajariban, 54; in Battle of Phul Bagh, 40; as daughter, 136; described, 197; and gardens, 167; marriage of, 137, 140; in The Marriage of Rewa, 49; in The Pond of Magaghi, 54–55
Maru Ka Gauna (Marus' Marriage Fulfilled), 49–53
Marus' Marriage Fulfilled (*Maru Ka Gauna*), 49–53
Marwar, 4, 42, 43, 49–50, 51, 54, 61, 149
Mata Din Garariya described, 199
Mathura, 59, 60, 102, 103
Matolsingh Gujar, 65, 79–91, *81,* 98, 104, 135, 173; compared to Ram Swarup Dhimar, 83, 85, 91; described, 199; on fate, 192–93; and Motini, 123; sexuality and, 130
McGregor, Ronald Stuart, 58
Meerut, 60
men, 6, 128, 130, 132, 159

Merchants, 7, 13, 105, 128, 132, 142, 168; marriage and, 15; Nal and, 7, 146, 163–65; rituals, 19
Mewar, 107, 185
Mirabai, 218n1
monetary contributions, 72, 149
Moore, Barrington, 3–4
morality, 127, 145
mortality, 3, 5, 7, 171
mothers: and daughters, 135–40; goddess as, 100, 104–105, 111
Motini, 3, 98, 118–19, 120–41, 164, 165, 171, 190, 194; as Acrobat, 140, 153–60; as aspara, 4, 67; as Bangle Seller, 49, 160–63; in The Battle of Bhamartal, 139, 152; in The Battle of Kajariban, 53–54; in The Battle of Kampilagarh, 22; in The Battle of Lakhiyaban, 41–42; in The Battle of Patal Lok, 18–21; in Battle of Phul Singh, 23–26, 75–77, 99, 106, 113–18, 156, 158–60, 180–82; in The Battle with Vir Singh, 44; and Bhils, 169; and Brahmans, 166–67; curse of, 6, 184, 188–89, 193, 195; as dancing girl, 129–30, 158; as daughter, 136; in Dumenti's Marriage, 28, 29; and Durga, 101; and humanity of Raja Nal, 172–76, 178; magic of, 107, 160; marriage of, 4, 56, 140, 143, 176; in The Marriage of Kishan Lal, 46, 47–48, 110, 160–63, 183; in The Marriage of Rewa, 49; in Maru's Marriage Fulfilled, 52; in Motini's Marriage, 15–18, 83–90, 135; in Nal's Time of Distress, 185, 186; in The Story of Nal, 21–22; and yogis, 117, 118, 125
Motini Ka Byah (Motini's Marriage), 15–18, 83–90, 135
Motini's Marriage (*Motini Ka Byah*), 15–18, 83–90, 135
Mughals, 59–60, 185
Mulla, 166
Mundnagar, 50
music, 63, 83, 86, 91, 138. *See also* songs
Muslims, 169, 214n33

Nagarkot, 4
Naisadhacarita, 57; defined, 209
Nal, Raja, illustrations of, *34, 41*
Nal Banvari, 12, 88, 163
Nal Chhatravedi, 12, 164
Nal Ka Aukha (Nal's Time of Distress), 31–35, 185–88
Nal Katha, 167
Nal Ki Katha (The Story of Nal), 21–22
Nal Puran, 21; defined, 209
Nal Purana, 29, 213n5
Nala, 4, 5, 178, 183, 184, 188, 192
Nalacaritamrit arthat Dhola Maru, 96
Nalopakhyana, 4, 57, 176, 183–84, 188; defined, 209
Nal's Bad Times, 73–75
Nal's Time of Distress (*Nal Ka Aukha*), 31–35, 185–88
Nalwa, Vanit, 56–57
names, 158
Nandy, Ashis, 95
Nanhe Lal Kachi, 216n10; described, 199
Narad, 123, 163–64, 187, 188, 190, 193; in Banishment of Manjha, 9–12; in The Battle of Patal Lok, 19; described, 197; in Dumenti's Marriage, 30, 31, 177–78; in Dumenti's Second Svayambar, 36, 37; and Indra, 172; and Manjha, 173
Narayan, Kirin, 117
Narvar, 4, 7, 14–15, 60, 121, 167, 185, 186; in The Battle of Kajariban, 54; in The Battle of Kampilagarh, 22; in The Battle of Lakhiyaban, 43; in The Battle of Patal Lok, 19; in Battle of Phul Singh, 23–24; in Dumenti's Marriage, 27–30; in The Marriage of Kishan Lal, 45–46; in Maru's Marriage Fulfilled, 50; in Nal's Time of Distress, 31–32; in The Pond of Magaghi, 54
Narvargarh, 14, 19, 21, 55
Narwar, 60, 212n6
Nath yogis, 6, 61, 106, 212n3; and the goddess, 112–18; and Motini, 122; power of, 112–13
Nats, 24, 159, 191; defined, 209
nature and nurture, 144
nautanki, 71; defined, 209
Navar (Narwar), 212n6
nihalde, 71, 76, 77; defined, 209
Nilgagan, 9–12, 173; described, 197
nirbij, 220n8; defined, 209

Ocean of the Streams of Stories, 56
Oil Pressers, 7, 42, 57, 136, 142–70, 184; in The Battle of Bhamartal, 37–40, 137–39, 183; in The Battle of Chandrapal, 55; in Battle of Phul Singh, 115; female, 141; in The Marriage of Kishan Lal, 44–48, 108–10; Nal and, 146–53, 171; women, 120, 126
omens, 22, 43, 76, 109, 121, 134–36, 161, 180
oral performances, 65, 96, 98
oral traditions, 4, 56, 57, 121, 126, 128
order, 4, 6, 7, 106, 108, 118, 121, 133, 183, 186

Pabuji (epic), 56, 146
Pabuji (god) defined, 209
Padam Singh, 175
Padmani, 212n6
pagri, 137, 178; defined, 209
pakka, 148; defined, 209
Pandavas, 106, 125, 183–84
Pandits, 20, 21, 22, 43, 136, 167
Panjab Battle, 63
pap, 127, 174; defined, 209
Paramkuti, 113–14
Paras Ram, 158
Pareba, 49–53; described, 197
Pasu, 158
Patal Lok, 18–21, 28, 176, 184
Patal Lok Ki Larai (The Battle of Patal Lok), 18–21
pativrat, 6, 121, 134, 135, 136; defined, 209; Dumenti as, 31, 125, 132; Manjha as, 10, 13; Motini as, 122, 125–27, 132, 140
Pavan, 49–53, *51;* described, 197
performance styles, 58, 65, 82–83, 91–92
performances, 65–92
personhood, 144, 145, 194
Phoola Mali, 32
Phul Bag Ki Larai (Battle of Phul Bagh), 40
Phul Bagh, 40
Phul Singh Panjabi, 100, 123, 127, 129–32, 146, 153, 156, 165, 185; in The Battle of Kampilagarh, 22–23; described, 197. *See also* Battle of Phul Singh (*Phul Sinh Ki Larai*)
Phul Sinh Ki Larai. See Battle of Phul Singh (*Phul Sinh Ki Larai*)
Pingul, 4
poetry, 77, 78, 86
The Pond of Magaghi (*Magaghi Tal*), 54–55
Potters, 45, 46, 47, 66, 142
power, 6, 92, 135, 137, 172; Durga's, 3, 96, 141; goddess, 95–96, 99, 100, 103–104, 122; magic and, 127; Motini's, 126, 176; Nal's, 183; of Nath yogis, 112–13; religious, 121; of Shanidev, 147; of Vir Singh, 133; of women, 3, 5, 6–7, 95–96, 120–21, 127, 128, 140–41; of yogis, 118, 127
Prahlad, 135
prakriti, 95; defined, 209
Pratham, Raja, 56, 67, 104, 116, 121, 135, 164, 173, 185; in Banishment of Manjha, 9–12; in The Battle of Kampilagarh, 22–23; in The Battle of Patal Lok, 19, 20; in Battle of Phul Singh, 75–77, 123; in The Battle of Shantiban, 12–15; and Brahmans, 166, 167; curses on, 10, 193; described, 198; in The Marriage of Kishan Lal, 46; morality and, 112; in Motini's Marriage, 17; Nath yogis and, 112; in The Story of Nal, 21–22
printed versions, 80, 82, 98, 99; compared to sung versions, 83–92
Pritviraja rasau, 136; defined, 209
prose, 85
puja, 121, 193; defined, 209
punya, 174; defined, 209
Puranas, 218n8
purdah, 13, 120, 128, 129, 130, *132,* 134
Pushkar Sultan, 40–43, 185; described, 197

Qanungo, K. R., 61

racism, 219n4
Radha, 102, 103, 108
Raghu, 37–40, 149, 152, 153, 158; described, 197
Raghubar Kachi, 168; described, 199
Raghunandan, 37–40, 55, 149, 158
Raghuvansi, 12
Raheja, Gloria, 169
Rahu, 31
raja, 60; defined, 210
"Raja Nal's Second Marriage," 63
rajas, 107–108; defined, 210
Rajasthan, 59
Rajju, 73
Rajputs, 6, 59–60, 92, 96, 110–11, 130; clothing and, 154; disorder and, 185–86; identities of, 61; and Jats, 103; and marriage alliances, 137; Nal and, 153, 172, 179–83; order and, 183; ranking systems of, 146; women, 140; yogis and, 117. *See also* Kshatriyas
Ram, 12, 32, 57, 99, 118; bhakti and, 96, 194; compared to Raj Nal, 63, 180; and Durga, 101, 104; in sumeri, 98; women and, 121
Ram Swarup Dhanuk described, 200
Ram Swarup Dhimar, 65, 66–79, *68, 70,* 86, 105, 216n17; and Banjaras, 168; cassettes and, 62, 69; compared to Matolsingh, 83, 85, 91; described, 199; on distress, 187; Dumenti's Marriage and, 176–78; on fate, 194; female sexuality and, 134; and Harishchand, 57; and Motini, 122, 175–76; and Nal's Time of Distress, 185; on Oil Pressers, 147; and Phul Singh, 106; and sumeri, 97–98; on women, 135; on yogis, 117
Ram Swarup Kachi, 97, 98; described, 199
Rama, 111
Ramayana, 32, 56, 98, 111, 121, 125–26, 180; defined, 210

Rambha, 122
Ramchandra, 104
Rang Mahal, 14–15, 120, 171
Ranjit Singh, Raja, 56–57
ras, 130; defined, 210
rasiyaa, 63
Ratibhang, 46
Ravan, 32, 98
respectability, 92
Rewa, 49, 50, 54–55, 167; described, 198
Rewa Ka Byah (The Marriage of Rewa), 49
rituals, 142, 165, 193
Rohe, Mark, 104
Rohtak, 60
rural areas, 4, 5, 8, 91–92, 102, 142, 171
Rushdie, Salman, 56

sacred thread ceremony, 13, 39, 104, 135, 165
sacrifice, 6, 56, 111; animal, 103, 110, 111; blood, 109; human, 6, 45, 96, 110
Sakta, 102
sakti, 95, 96; defined, 210
sakti pithas, 102; defined, 210
Samudsikul, 27, 28, 29, 30, 35, 37, 137, 177, 220n8
Sankal Island, 48
Santiban Ki Larai (The Battle of Shantiban), 12–15
Sarasvati, 108
Sarbhang, 46
Saroja, Queen, 138–39
sarpanse, 16; defined, 210. *See also* gambling
Sarvati, 124, 126, 127, 128, 131, 133, 134; in The Battle of Kampilagarh, 22–23; in Battle of Phul Singh, 23–24, 25, 26, 113–18; described, 198
sat, 173; defined, 210
sati, 116, 121, 140, 174, 186
sati devi: defined, 210; Manjha as, 10
satiya, 40, 138; defined, 210
sattva, 108
Sawai Jai Singh, 60
Schomer, Karine, 179
self-sacrifice, 110
Seths (Merchants), 164–65
sexuality, 7, 126; on cassettes, 63; and desire, 128–34; forests and, 168; of gurus, 118; Motini's, 128, 140
Shaiva, 102
Shaivism, 101, 112
Shaivites, 6, 61
Shani, 29
Shanichar, 148
Shanidev, 125, 126, 147, 148, 167, 168, 184, 187, 188, 195; in The Battle of Bhamartal, 38; described, 198; in Dumenti's Second Svayambar, 37; and Indra, 57; in Nal's Time of Distress, 31–35, 185
Shankar Lal, Pandit, 64, 125, 187, 193; described, 199
Shantiban, 11, 12–15, 21
Sharda, 45
Shesh Nag, 18, 20, 53
Shila Mata, 111
Shiva, 6, 47, 53, 54, 101, 112, 193
Shivaji, 107
Shudras, 145, 148, 171
Shukra, 31–35, 38, 148, 184, 187; described, 198
Shulman, David, 176, 188
Silota, 159
sin, 174, 193
sindur, 135; defined, 210
Singh River, 50
Sisodiyas, 185–86
Sita, 32, 101, 104
Siya Nagar, 20, 28, 32, 45, 55, 110
Smith, Dorothy E., 145
social interactions, 3
social order, 4, 5, 105, 140, 143, 146, 165; and chaos, 6; forests and, 168; views of, 145
social space, 6, 7
social status, 92, 171
Somasur, 15–18, 24, 156, 218n8
Somnath, 214n31
songs, 71–79, 83, 85, 149; for donors, 39, 72, 149; film, 63, 69, 72, 215n3; folk, 63, 65, 69, 215n3; women's, 100, 143. *See also* music
space, 171; and caste, 169; social, 6, 7
speech, 75, 78–79
spousification, 101
Sriharsa, 57
Stallybrass, Peter, 5
steel tongs (cimta), 69, 71, 72, 83
The Story of Nal (*Nal Ki Katha*), 21–22
sugarcane, 41–43, 139, 153, 168
sumeri, 95, 96, 97, 98, 107; defined, 210
Suraj Mal, 60–61
Surajbhati, 46
Suryaji, 185
svang, 71; defined, 210
svayambar, 103, 137, 172, 184. *See also* Dumenti's Second Svayambar (*Dumenti Ka Dusra Svayambar*)

Sweepers, 135, 145, 166, 167; in Banishment of Manjha, 9–12; described, 198; in The Story of Nal, 21–22; women, 121
swords, 6, 107
synthesizer, 63

Tailors, 69, 73
tamas, 107–108
Tambs-Lyche, Harald, 140
Tantric, 102, 106, 108, 112–13, 117
Tara, 107
Taro, 49–53; described, 198
Telin, 37–40
Telis, 146; defined, 210. *See also* Oil Pressers
Thakurs, 60, 66, 151, 152, 153
thor, 85–86
Tikam, Raja, 35–37, 172, 187, 188–91; described, 198
Tilan, 73
time, 192–95
Tod, James, 61, 146, 179
toe rings, 134–35
transmigration, 192
truth, 5
Types of Indic Oral Tale, 57

untouchables, 145

Vaishnava, 102, 118
Vaishnavism, 101, 102, 103, 180
Vaishnavites, 6, 111, 194
Vaishno Devi, 103, 109, 117
Vaishyas, 145, 165, 168, 171
varna, 145, 165
varta, 72, 73–75, 75–77, 85–86; defined, 210
Vasuki, 55
Vaudeville, Charlotte, 58, 102, 103
Ved Singh, Raja, 49–53; described, 198
vegetarianism, 103, 105, 109, 110, 111, 165, 194
venues, 65–66
vikhau, 6, 185–87
Vikramaditya, 57
violin, 63
Vipati, 12, 163
vir, 26, 106, 113–14, 116, 128
Vir Singh, Raja, 43–44, 125, 128, 134, 136; described, 198; sexuality and, 133
Vir Singh Ki Larai (The Battle with Vir Singh), 43–44, 133
Viran, Raja, 182
Virmati, 49–53; described, 198
Vishnu, 6, 101, 125
Vityagarh, 52
vrat, 121, 193; defined, 210

Warriors, 15, 16, 142, 144, 164. *See also* Kshatriyas
Water Carriers, 24, 218n2
weddings, 90. *See also* marriage
Wheelock, Wade T., 78
White, Allon, 5
Williams, Richard, 58
Wilson, Elizabeth, 160
women, 120–41, 182; and caste, 141, 163; desire and, 128–34; and glass bangles, 134–35, 161; and gurus, 118; high-caste, 126, 147, 158; identities and, 140; lower-caste, 120–21, 127, 128, 130, 141, 159; and magic, 6, 127; Mali, 167; model of, 101; nature of, 134–40; in performances, 67; powers of, 3, 5, 6–7, 95–96, 120–21, 127, 128, 140–41; roles of, 4, 118–19, 141; sexuality and, 128–34; songs, 100, 143; and yogis, 118
worship, 111, 166

Yama, 143
yogis, 6, 42, 61, 96, 106, 112; Aughar, 116–17; in Bengal, 126; and Motini, 124–25; negative view of, 117; power of, 118, 127; and Rajputs, 117; role of, 116, 118; and women, 118. *See also* Nath yogis

Zeigler, Norman, 137, 179, 185

SUSAN SNOW WADLEY is Ford Maxwell Professor of South Asian Studies and Anthropology and Director of the South Asia Center at Syracuse University. She is author of *Struggling with Destiny in Karimpur, 1925–1984;* co-editor (with Lawrence A. Babb) of *Media and the Transformation of Religion in South Asia;* and co-author of a revised and expanded edition of William and Charlotte Wiser's classic *Behind Mud Walls.*